WITHDRAWN

HARVARD LIBRARY

WITHDRAWN

What Motivates Cultural Progressives?

What Motivates Cultural Progressives?
Understanding Opposition to the Political and Christian Right

George Yancey
and
David A. Williamson

BAYLOR UNIVERSITY PRESS

© 2012 by Baylor University Press
Waco, Texas 76798-7363

All Rights Reserved. No part of this publication may be reproduced, stored in a retrieval system, or transmitted, in any form or by any means, electronic, mechanical, photocopying, recording or otherwise, without the prior permission in writing of Baylor University Press.

Cover Design by *the*BookDesigners

Library of Congress Cataloging-in-Publication Data

Yancey, George A., 1962–
 What motivates cultural progressives? : understanding opposition to the political and Christian right / by George Yancey, David A. Williamson.
 279 p. cm.
 Includes bibliographical references and index.
 ISBN 978-1-60258-463-1 (hardcover : alk. paper)
 1. Right and left (Political science)—United States. 2. Progressivism (United States politics) 3. United States—Social conditions--21st century. 4. United States—Politics and government—2009- I. Williamson, David A., 1955– II. Title.
 JK1726.Y36 2012
 320.51'30973--dc23
                    2012003679

Printed in the United States of America on acid-free paper with a minimum of 30% pcw recycled content.

Contents

1 The Culture War in the United States 1
2 Dynamics of Social Movements and Cultural Progressives 29
3 Developing a Typology of Cultural Progressive Activists 47
4 Political Concerns and Cultural Progressive Activists 77
5 General Opposition to Religion in Cultural Progressive Activists 111
6 Cultural Progressive Activists and Critics of Christianity 139
7 The Framing of Cultural Progressive Activism 171
8 Cultural Progressives in the Continuing Culture War 205

Appendix 221
Notes 247
Works Cited 255
Index 271

CHAPTER 1

The Culture War in the United States

In 1992 during the Republican National Convention, Patrick Buchanan delivered what has become known as his culture war speech. In the speech, he expressed the idea of a clear demarcation between those with "traditional" values and individuals without them. Buchanan envisioned the Republican Party as the holder of the traditional values and thus in need of retaining power to maintain those values in our large culture. In doing so, he portrayed those supporting traditional values as heroes and portrayed those challenging traditional values as villains. This speech sparked a firestorm of controversy surrounding Buchanan and the Republican Party that allowed him to make such an appeal. Those that Buchanan identified as linked to the "failed liberalism of the 1960s and 1970s" did not waste any time defending themselves and their ideas. They argued that this speech marked Republicans as an intolerant party that is unwilling to take into consideration the views of others (Burack, 2003; A. B. Cohen, 2002; Dew et al., 2010; Ellison & Levin, 1998; Ferriss, 2002; Kinsley, 1994; Larson et al., 1992; Larson, Sweyers, & McCullough, 1998; Levin & Vanderpool, 1992; Vennochi, 2003).

But to be fair to Buchanan, his approach to a culture war was not an original idea. Indeed, J. Hunter (1991) may deserve credit for the idea that there is a culture war between cultural conservatives and cultural progressives in the United States. He builds on the work of Wuthnow (1988), who argues that the old denominational divisions are losing importance in explaining the religious perspectives of Americans. Hunter contends that the old religious arguments between denominations are losing their saliency in the United States and are being replaced by arguments between those who have a culturally conservative perspective and those with a culturally progressive one. Cultural conservatives can be defined as individuals who rely on a historical interpretation of their religion to define morality. Morality is generally seen as a set of absolutes that emerge from this traditional interpretation. Cultural progressives can be defined as individuals with a modern or postmodern understanding of morality that minimizes traditional religious explanations. Morality is conceived of as being determined by what the individual decides is best for himself or herself. Thus, arguments within denominations between cultural conservatives and cultural progressives are a better predictor of the actions and attitudes of religious individuals than of the denomination, or in some cases even of the religion, to which they belong.

Hunter's argument has not been accepted by all scholars. Fiorina (2005) argues that Hunter is accurate as it concerns disagreements among the elites but that there is a strong level of consensus among the general population. Furthermore, Demerath (2005) contends that any potential cultural war present in the United States pales in comparison to other societies where such cultural conflict is more pronounced, such as Northern Ireland, Guatemala, Israel, and India. Others have pointed out that these cultural differences still have vital influences on the attitudes and perspectives of nonelites (Abramowitz & Saunders, 2005; Knuckey, 2005), although perhaps not to the degree envisioned by Hunter. However, it is clear that Hunter has identified an important ideological conflict motivating a significant number of individuals to take political and social action. Understanding how this conflict continues to shape our society is critical if we are to comprehend the direction our culture may take in the near and distant future.

To gain the best perspective on how this culture conflict plays itself out, it is valuable to explore the perspectives of both the cultural conservatives and cultural progressives who are active in this conflict. In academia, most of the attention on the culture war concerns an assessment of culturally conservative activists (McConkey, 2001; Moen, 1992; Wilcox, 1992) or an examination of the conflict in general (Carroll & Marler, 1995; Dillon, 1996; Green, Guth, Smidt, & Kellstedt, 1996; Jensen, 2006; Zimmerman, 2002). Research that focuses extensively on the actions and attitudes of cultural progressive activists is missing. This is problematic since a phenomenon such as the culture war cannot be fully understood unless both "combatants" of that war are examined. Cultural progressive activists are of particular interest since, as we will soon show, much of their justification is built on the idea that they have a rational basis for understanding cultural questions as opposed to the supernaturalism of their conservative opponents. They tend to characterize their opponents as irrational and assert a desire for reason instead of religion in the construction of social order. It is not clear whether this emphasis on rationality has enabled them to develop a social movement relatively free of the irrational mechanisms that tend to shape social movements.

The goal of this book is to explore the perspectives and ideas found among cultural progressive activists in the cultural war. We use theories developed within social movement theory as a framework for understanding why certain ideas are likely to develop within a movement that serves cultural progressives. We believe that such ideas are to be expected in a social movement that has arisen to challenge cultural conservatives. However we will also show that these very ideas challenge the notion put forth by these cultural progressive activists that their actions are based upon a pure notion of rationality. Rather, their core ideas emerge from the same social-psychological needs and dynamics as those that develop in all social movements.

The Early History of the Church/State Debate

Assertions that religion should have limited influence in society may have begun with the development of science. Boas (1958) described a time before the advent of science as a period in which societies attempted to understand forces beyond their control through magical beliefs. Before the development of scientific inquiry, humans used the application of supernatural beliefs as an important way to understand our physical and social reality. Thus, the use of otherworldly religious beliefs allowed humans to answer questions about physical processes that they did not understand. These beliefs also informed humans about the nature of humanity and the type of moral values that would benefit us. Thus, the development of scientific inquiry quickly became a competitor with religious beliefs as the legitimator of knowledge. The dominant religious institutions of that day reacted with attempts to oppress scientific knowledge, such as the excommunication of Galileo. In response to such dangers, scientists and freethinkers helped to develop what would be known as the Enlightenment movement. This social movement pushed for the freedom of scientists to engage in inquiry without interference of religions institutions.

From this point on there was a conflict between those influenced by the Enlightenment movement who desired to reduce or even eliminate the influence of those with traditional religious faith and the traditional religious establishment. Auguste Comte (1896), founder of sociology, was one of the first scholars who envisioned the replacement of religion as the major justification for morality with legitimation based in science. Other advocates within the Enlightenment movement supported rationality over religious justification as the way to shape our society. Ian Barbour (1997) points out that these Enlightenment thinkers envisioned humans as basically good but corrupted by dysfunctional societal influences. They perceived science and reason as the way to produce a secular utopia that would allow humans to develop their full potential. Secularization was seen as the proper path by which a society could be created that would produce more human fulfillment. Humanity was conceptualized as perfectible if our societies were based upon science and reason instead of religion and faith. Modern Europe today reflects many of these expectations, as any cultural war between secularized and traditional Christian Europeans was long ago won by the secular Europeans.

However, recent scholars have questioned the perspective of a historical conflict between science and the church. Principe (2003) argues that conflict between science and religion is a modern, not a historical, phenomenon. Stark (2004) contends that the development of science did not occur separately from religion. Both researchers argue that the Galileo conflict with the church over his teaching of Copernicanism was more the result of interpersonal conflict with Pope Urban VIII than a conflict between the principles of science and religion. According to this argument, it is possible that there were only a few Enlightenment thinkers who perceived religion as a barrier to science but that generally religion did not work to inhibit the development of the scientific enterprise. If these critics are correct, then a perception of historical religion/science conflict may animate the modern division between scientists and individuals in faith communities more than actual resistance of religion against science.

It is against the backdrop of actual, or perceived, historical conflict between religion and science that we can contextualize the modern battle to limit the influence of religion in the United States. Many of the advocates for such a limitation envision justifying it through an ideology based upon the separation of church and state. They do not necessarily seek to eliminate religion but rather to keep the influence of religion limited to within church walls. As such, they look to Thomas Jefferson as a role model, with his famous letter to the Danbury Baptist Association, which coined the phrase "a wall of separation between church and State." The Treaty of Tripoli also became a document that weighed in on this debate as that treaty explicitly stated that the United States was not founded on Christian religion. These early precursors established the premise that the U.S. government was to be free of overt Christian or religious influences. For cultural progressives, this meant that the government could be used to promote a rational approach to rule, rather than rule by religious tradition.

The modern concerns over the relationship between church and state in the United States bear a great deal of similarity to concerns enunciated by many of the Enlightenment thinkers about traditional religion in Europe. The progressives in both contexts of this debate argue that reason and rationality must supersede religion. They envision a society in which traditional religion has very little influence, especially as individuals begin to grow away from their irrational faith. In this society individuals would utilize rational choices instead of supernaturalistic faith to guide them. As noted before, in Europe the battle about religious influence is over, at least as it concerns Christian faith.[1] In the United States, the combatants are still fairly evenly matched, and thus the struggle to replace the influences of traditional religious faith with rationality continues.

The Development of the Modern Culture War

The conflict described in the preceding section provides us with the context necessary to comprehend our modern culture war. In some ways this modern culture war can be understood in light of the fundamentalist/social gospel argument that raged in Christian circles in the late 19th and early 20th centuries. This argument pitted Christians who emphasized personal evangelism and traditional morality against those who emphasized the need for social change and taking care of the poor. The former group justified its stances with traditional sources of authority. For this group, the Bible, and other traditional religious sources, represented an external foundation for knowledge on how to live out one's life. They tended to dismiss morality determined by an individual's desire as unreliable since humans are vulnerable to subjective decision making. Since their interpretation of these sources indicated a need for traditional morality and proselytizing, they tended to focus upon these individualistic virtues instead of challenging the larger societal order. On the other hand, more progressive Christians emphasized what they acknowledged as the "social gospel." This led them to critique the social and economic inequities in the larger societies. Furthermore, they were not able to dismiss their personal experiences in the way traditional Christians had been able to do so with a focus on external verification of reality. Instead, experience and science became their dominant tools of legitimization for the types of social actions and attitudes they adopted. The role of humans to create their own morality was emphasized over the application of external, overarching moral traditions.

In time the character of both sides of this conflict begin to change. Among the traditionalists, there was a retreat from engagement with the social world (Noll, 1994; Ringenberg, 1984). They sought to protect themselves from what they perceived as the "ungodly" cultural influences of the larger society. This led them to send their children to religious schools and to limit their interaction outside of their religious community, unless they were seeking to proselytize for new members. A social identity of being identified as a fundamentalist developed through the sharing of the Fundamentals, a series of writings between 1910 and 1915 that defined the basic beliefs of these traditionalists. This identity transcended denomination but also established social boundaries by which these newly named "fundamentalists" could exclude those who did not share their traditional beliefs (Lienesch, 2007).

Among religious progressives, acknowledgment of religious influence became less relevant to their perspectives and organizations. For example, many of the educational institutions established by religious progressives deemphasized the place of religion since these organizations were to be places of open-minded learning (Marsden, 1996). In time, these organizations became more secular in nature and the pluralism that developed on these campuses once justified through religious ideology was now legitimized by nonreligious reasons. Thus, the campuses established by progressive religious traditions became nearly as secular as nonreligious educational institutions. In similar ways, religious progressives supported politically and culturally progressive reforms for nonreligious reasons at least as much as for religious justifications. They became an important part of social reform movements but were not a central legitimating force within these movements. The actions and activism of religious progressives became nearly indistinguishable from those of their secular allies. Furthermore, their attempts to bring about the "kingdom of God" were quite similar to the attempts to replace traditional justification for societal change with justification based on the ideas of reason and science.

Because the religious traditionalists had retreated from political and social engagement, the conflict between these two groups was reduced down to ignoring each other. However, in the 1950s this began to change. Carl F. Henry wrote about the need for Christian traditionalists to become more engaged in the larger society. He supplied the intellectual undergirding that enabled some traditionalists to rethink the separatist mentality that had developed within their communities. The basic argument that was pushed forth was that there are no separate sacred and profane spheres in our larger society. All of our society and culture is to be shaped according to the designs of God. Henry was not advocating a radical takeover of the government or a theocracy, but he did contend that Christians had to work to influence the larger society and not merely stay in their own communities.

In the other camp, we saw an emergence of new left movements in the 1960s. These movements gained great visibility and challenged the taken-for-granted racial, sexual, and religious assumptions of the larger society. The image of the United States as a benevolent nation was debunked, and demands for a new society built on egalitarian, individualistic values rather than the traditional hierarchical values supported by cultural conservatives grew. Alternative lifestyles and religious practices became popular within many of these progressive subcultures. Furthermore, traditional religion was labeled as racist, sexist, oppressive, and hierarchical. Some of the advocates of the new left movements adopted a Marxian approach in which they desired to see a withering away of traditional religion so that its ability to influence the larger culture would be negated.

The viability of the new left movements coupled with an emerging desire of Christian traditionalists to become engaged with the larger society led inevitably to conflict between the two groups. Traditional Christians found themselves horrified by the activism and what they perceived as overt flaunting of traditional values. They also became concerned over Supreme Court cases that supported abortion and that removed prayer from schools, perceiving these cases as signs that the culture was deteriorating. They become a major part of a backlash that developed against the new left movements in the late 1970s and 1980s. This backlash helped to establish a Reagan administration that placed some brakes on the progressive movement of the larger culture. But while the 1980s represented some movement in American politics toward conservative economic and foreign policy, cultural progressive positions such as support of evolution and acceptance of homosexuality continued to become more popular (Freeman & Houston, 2009; Hicks & Lee, 2006; Revenson, 1989). Thus, although Buchanan's speech was intended to energize what he hoped would be mainstream cultural conservative activists, it is plausible that it helped to consolidate cultural progressives who had been growing in number and influence over the past few decades.

At this point of our history, the previous battles over denominational prestige began to wane and be replaced by the culture battles we see today. In the 19th and 20th centuries, much of the cultural ire was focused against non-Protestant groups such as Catholics, Jews, and Mormons. Fears of a governmental takeover by one or all of these groups has historically been common among nativist Protestant groups (Jeansonne, 1996; Mattingly, 2006; Rackleff, 1972; Schalatter, 2006; Yorgason & Chen, 2008). However, these fears became less relevant with the advent of the new left movements, and many traditional Protestants began to fear progressives more than non-Protestant traditionalists. In fact, traditional Protestants began to perceive non-Protestants who shared their traditional values as allies instead of as enemies. They were especially open to linking with Catholics on issues such as abortion. Christian Protestants and Catholics dwarfed members of other traditional religious perspectives in number, but in time the contributions of traditional Jews, Mormons, Muslims, and others became appreciated.[2] While denominational and faith differences may remain important in theological arguments among members of traditional faiths, those differences appear to have little impact concerning social and political issues.

This culture conflict has not dissipated since Buchannan's 1992 speech and the onset of Hunter's work. The abortion issue has not gone away and in fact remains as controversial as ever. The issue of same-sex marriage has now become a new hot topic that splits Americans on cultural grounds. Scientific innovations, such as stem cell research, also provide the possibility of cultural conflict. Some have argued that President Bush was able to utilize conservative cultural concerns to win the presidency after eight years of President Clinton and again in 2004 (Abramowitz & Saunders, 2005; E. Cohen, 2001; Mulligan, 2008; C. Smith, 2002). President Obama may have been able to neutralize this advantage by the time he made his run during the 2008 campaign, but the culture conflict is not limited to presidential battles. These battles are also fought over local issues such as the types of books libraries should carry, the textbooks that are used in elementary and secondary schools, pornography, obscenity laws, and domestic partnership laws. Whether these battles engage only the elites in both camps or represent a wide-scale conflict within our society, there still are fights energizing media coverage and helping to shape important political dynamics within the United States.

Who Are Cultural Progressives and Cultural Conservatives Today?

Given the dynamics discussed in the previous sections, we are now in a position to consider what sorts of individuals are likely to be part of either the cultural progressive or cultural conservative social movement. We have moved away from a terminology of traditionalists and secularists to one of cultural conservatives and cultural progressives. While the social origin of cultural conservatives is based in traditional religion, there still are nonreligious individuals who endorse traditional values. Likewise, some cultural progressives have religious beliefs, and *secularist* is not an accurate term for all of them. The terms *cultural conservatives* and *cultural progressives* encompass all who fall into their general ideas about traditional or scientific bases of social order regardless of religious, or even political, beliefs on noncultural issues. How individuals envision the use of religion in their lives and society is an important factor for determining to which of these groups they are more sympathetic.

It is here that we should carefully enunciate how we are defining what we call cultural progressives. Basically, these are individuals who oppose the imposition of traditional cultural understandings promulgated by the Christian right. The reasons why they oppose those traditions may be varied. They may oppose them because of a generalized progressive political outlook, because they possess a general mistrust of religion, and/or because of their antipathy toward Christianity. In our book we explore all of these reasons for the opposition to the Christian right. However, we contend that just as adherence to a desire to promote traditional cultural values that are rooted in Christianity unites cultural conservative activists who may have different Christian theological or even religious beliefs, opposition to the imposition of these values can unite cultural progressive activists who have a variety of motivations for such opposition. In this book we seek to understand those who are part of this opposition.

We have previously defined cultural conservatives as individuals who seek to support historically traditional ideas about morality and social order. Their ideals are based within religious traditions, and they emphasize the importance of otherworldly faith. We have also previously defined cultural progressives as individuals who downplay historical traditions in the establishment of morality and social order. Their ideals are based upon the belief that human rationality and choice is the best way to construct social order. Whether individuals accept cultural conservatism or cultural progressivism is likely tied to the social and/or demographic milieu of individuals within these groups and how they may pursue their social interests. Certain groups are more likely to be served by either cultural conservatism or cultural progressivism, and it is in the social interests of members in such groups to adopt one philosophy or the other.

Cultural conservatives have acquired a base for their movement within the traditional religious churches/synagogues many of them attend. Only after being reawakened by the new left movements did prominent cultural conservative organizations emerge that were not directly rooted within a particular Christian denomination. However, cultural progressive activists have a longer history of nonreligious organizations as a base for their activism. The founding of the American Civil Liberties Union (ACLU) may have been the first national organization to focus at least some of its attention on challenging the imposition of traditional morality. The ACLU was formed in 1920 with the intent to fight for the civil rights of those who were not in the mainstream of society. Among those they fought for were cultural progressive groups such as homosexuals and social radicals. Their methodology has been based on legal intervention, and the ACLU today continues to advocate for the right of individuals to be free of interference from traditional morality. While they are not always fighting against cultural conservative activists, it is fair to assert that when cultural issues come up they are more likely to side with the cultural progressive viewpoint. This is at least partially due to the perception that cultural progressives are more likely to be rejected by the mainstream of society and thus are more likely to need legal protection.

In 1948 another organization formed to promote the aims of cultural progressives. The name of this organization was Protestants and Other Americans United For the Separation of Church and State. Eventually the name was shortened to Americans United for the Separation of Church and State and ultimately to Americans United (AU). The formation of AU was in response to the larger fear in society generated toward a possible Catholic takeover of the United States. At first AU focused on educating the public and building up its membership to become a more potent political force. Over time, however, it too became an organization that widely used legal action to limit the influence of cultural conservatives. The general focus of AU has been to stop religion from interfering with governmental functions or having religion unduly gain from government resources. Thus, they have been very active in opposing school vouchers, faith-based government programs, the teaching of intelligent design, and politicking by religious leaders from their churches. However, they have also been strong advocates for issues not automatically tied to church and state separation such as abortion, same-sex marriage, and stem cell research. Thus, they support most of the issues linked to cultural progressiveness.

In 1980 Norman Lear, a powerful television producer, left television to form People for the American Way (PFAW). We note this organization not merely because it is a progressive political organization but also because Lear formed this organization in response to what he feared was the growing influence of radical religious Christians. He openly lamented the increasing number of Christian radio stations that espoused the type of cultural conservatism he opposed. He envisioned PFAW as a way to neutralize this influence. So while PFAW has been an important part of the general progressive political movement, it has also placed a great deal of its attention on countering what it perceives as the powerful influence of the Christian right. This organization has been very active in setting up opposition to judges whom they believe will further the interests of cultural conservatives.

Finally, several culturally progressive organizations have developed to directly challenge religious aspects of cultural conservative activism. Although these organizations focus on the dysfunctions of religious beliefs, they also endorse the general political and social position of cultural progressives such as stem cell research, same-sex marriage, and abortion. For example, in 1978 the Freedom From Religion Foundation (FFRF) was founded by Anne Nicol Gaylor. As a feminist, she believed that organized religion was at the heart of the opposition to women's rights (Erickson, 2007), and thus the early motivation for FFRF was political. However, today the group promotes the idea that religion is a powerfully negative influence in society. They have been active in using lawsuits to limit the influence of religion in the United States. In 1963 Madalyn Murray O'Hair formed the organization American Atheists. She had previously achieved fame with her court case against school prayer. Her organization sought to promote the civil rights of atheists and the separation of church and state. Like most other cultural progressive organizations, it used lawsuits to promote its cause as well as to promote public knowledge of issues important to atheists. Finally, in 2005 Jews On First was created. It is an organization that was formed to directly challenge the influence of Christians in the United States and to forestall a possible Christian theocracy.³

This is clearly not an exhaustive list of cultural progressive activist organizations, but it does include many such organizations. In this list we can see certain traits emerging from activism among cultural progressives. Clearly, seeking legal remedies is one of the preferred choices of such organizations. This denotes a group that has access to political and legal power. These organizations also engage in lobbying when issues of importance to them come before the government. These are the characteristics of activism by individuals with financial and educational resources. While some of these groups may engage in street protests, it is not the major way they get their message across. They likely have the attention of financial backers who can support their legal actions, which suggests that cultural progressive activists are likely to be well educated and to have relatively high socioeconomic status.⁴

However, cultural conservative activists are not without their own legal resources. While their legal activism has gotten a late start relative to that of cultural progressives, today we can clearly see the influences of cultural conservatives. In what may be a play on initials, in 1990 Pat Robertson started the American Center for Law and Justice (ACLJ). The stated purpose of the ACLJ is to protect the legal rights of prolife demonstrators and ensure the constitutional and free of speech rights of religious groups. In 1994 Christian leaders such as Bill Bright, D. J. Kennedy, and James Dobson helped to establish the Alliance Defense Fund (ADF). The major concern of the organization is the perceived loss of religious freedom due to the rulings of American courts. The organization has attempted to mount a legal defense to protect such freedom and is engaged in issues such as allowing Christian groups to use public facilities, the protection of prolife protestors, and Christian acknowledgment in public places. Much of the previous activism of cultural conservatives had been based on actions at the community level such as passing out election scorecards at local churches or activism within local election organizations. These two organizations do not represent all cultural conservative legal efforts, but they do indicate that cultural conservatives have been relatively late in becoming legally and even politically active on a larger scale.

Clearly, cultural conservative activists are more likely to have higher levels of overall traditional religiosity than cultural progressive activists. Such religiosity provides some, but not all, of the basis for cultural conservatism. However, they do not have the degree of legal activism as cultural progressive activists, suggesting that they have fewer legal resources than their counterparts. This may denote the reality that such groups have lower levels of education than cultural progressives and possibly less per capita financial resources. Such realities may help to determine the type of political fights into which cultural conservatives are drawn. Those fights may be more local in nature.

It is important to note potential demographic differences between the two groups. Research has indicated that nonwhites tend to have higher levels of religiosity (Chatters, Taylor, & Lincoln, 1999; De la Garza, DeSipio, Garcia, Garcia, & Falcon, 1992; Gallup & Lindsay, 2000) and to be more culturally conservative (Bolks, Evans, Polinard, & Wrinkle, 2000; Bonilla & Porter, 1990; Carter, Carter, & Dodge, 2009; Ohlander, Batalove, & Treas, 2004; T. Smith, 1998) than whites. This may suggest that cultural progressive activists have relatively few nonwhites among their membership. Women generally have higher levels of religiosity than men (Feltey & Poloma, 1991; Kosmin & Keysar, 2008) but are more culturally progressive (Hertel & Russell, 2007; Kite & Whitley, 2003; Loftus, 2001; Patel & Johns, 2009). It is not completely clear whether there is a sex difference between the two groups. One would also expect a regional effect, as southerners have higher religiosity (Gunnoe & Moore, 2002; Hempel & Bartkowski, 2008; L. L. Hunt & Hunt, 2001) and are more culturally conservative (Carter & Borch, 2005; Knuckey, 2006; Loftus, 2001) than nonsoutherners.

Accordingly, cultural progressive activists are likely to be nonreligious whites. In many ways, they may be akin to secularized Europeans. Research indicates that most white Europeans have little need for traditional religions (Berger, David, & Fokas, 2008; Halman & Draulans, 2006) and may even see it as a hindrance to cultural and individual growth. If this is reflective of the ideas of cultural progressives in the United States, then the relatively high religiosity in the United States may be seen as a threat to cultural progressive activists. They are likely drawn to the appeals of rationality noted in a previous section and thus see traditional religion, and its constraints on individual liberties, as an impediment to achieving that rationality. In their mind-set traditional religions serve to victimize them, and thus they struggle to limit, or even eliminate, its influence.

Such attitudes would explain why cultural progressive activists seek to challenge cultural conservative activists on given political concerns (e.g., abortion, homosexuality) since conflict in those issues represents a way to limit the influence of individuals within irrational religious traditions. In fact, it is highly plausible that many of the political positions supported by individuals in these organizations are not supported purely on their own merit but rather so that the individuals in these organizations can better challenge the potential dominance of individuals with traditional religious beliefs. For example, there is no inherent reason why individuals who are atheists are overwhelmingly prochoice. The argument over abortion has been framed as one in which a woman's choice for her body is juxtaposed against a baby's right to live.[5] An ethic that prioritizes the life of the baby over a woman's choice does not have to be rooted in supernaturalist belief. Humanist ethicists can make a case that life and its potential is one of the highest, if not the highest, priorities in society since there is nothing awaiting us after death. But in practical political terms, siding with prolifers can provide those from a traditional religious background with an unwanted political and social victory, and thus cultural progressive activists may find an affinity with prochoicers instead of prolifers. There clearly are rational reasons why cultural progressive activists may favor a prochoice position, but we would be remiss not to observe that the value of defeating their cultural opponents may be more important to cultural progressives than the actual specifics of the political issues for which they fight. In this way, we can talk about a true war between the cultures as we explore the perspective of cultural progressive elites.

Methodology

To accomplish our assessment of the perspectives of cultural progressive activists, we must hear what they have to say in their own words. To achieve this task, we present two different sources of original data—each designed to allow cultural progressives to express their concerns, hopes, and desires. We first analyze the primary literature that we have collected from organizations dedicated to opposing either the religious or Christian right.[6] We subscribed to the newsletter of three of the organizations and received it either electronically or in hard copy. In addition to these publications, we also have investigated the websites of various organizations. This content analysis is key to seeing how the leaders of these organizations want to represent themselves to the larger society. As such, this printed and electronic material as well as the websites provides valuable information about the vision cultural progressive organizations have for our society.

Second, we conducted an online survey of members of several of these organizations. Two of these organizations fall in line with the general political organizations we first discussed in our previous section, and one of the organizations was clearly more antireligious in its intent. Several other smaller organizations were included in the sample with a varying degree of emphasis on religious or political conservatism. The survey recorded the general attitude of the members toward the Christian right and the type of society these members desire to see. The questionnaire also assessed the religious nature of the social networks of the members of those organizations to see if some of their perspectives developed from their interactions with members of traditional faiths or even from a lack of interaction with such individuals.[7] Many of the questions, which are listed in the appendix under A.1, were presented in an open-ended format, allowing for the respondents to express their opinions in as complete a manner as possible. This approach differs from a general strategy of surveys and face-to-face interviews. However, given that we do not have the resources to conduct a large probability survey, our method still allows us to gather rich qualitative information from a large number of respondents. We sacrifice some degree of quantitative accuracy, but even here the power of our quantitative results is such that we are comfortable making some assertions about some social and demographic characteristics of cultural progressive activists. Short of being able to finance a large-scale survey followed up with selected face-to-face interviews, our methodology provides the best opportunity to collect quantitative and qualitative information on cultural progressives.

A note on our strategy of including quotes from our respondents and citations from the primary literature is in order. Reading through the responses and literature has provided us with a good understanding of the perspectives of cultural progressive activists. Our sample is highly educated, and some of them were quite articulate in their responses. Other respondents made brief contributions that carried on the spirit of the perspectives we have found in our work but were not as insightful as other responses. We tried to make each point using four to six of the most articulate quotes or citations. Occasionally we used slightly more when presenting a perspective that was more pervasive in our sample. However, the reader can generally assume that we usually could have added many more quotes or citations, although some not quite as articulate as those presented, to most of the points we illustrate with our quotes. We did our best to provide an accurate representation of the attitudes displayed by our respondents. Any honest reading of the responses would lead a reader to the general themes, or those very similar to them, we articulate in our work. We did not look for outliers but sought to illustrate attitudes that were fairly common among cultural progressive activists. Of course the activists in our sample are not monolithic, and there are differing ideas among them. We point out such differences when they are evident.

The extensive use of such quotes and citations brings about another possible issue regarding our methodology. This material portrays a certain point of view about society, politics, and religion. It is easy for readers to believe that we, as the authors of the book, are using the ideas of the respondents in our sample to represent our own ideas on these matters. We seek to neither endorse nor refute the point of view of our respondents. Our job is to analyze this perspective and understand how it may shape the social movement of cultural progressives. We allow the respondents to speak for themselves, as this is the fairest way to allow those on the progressive side to enunciate their own perspective. We believe that comprehending this culture war is important for understanding the social conflict in the United States, and this work helps us to comprehend one side of that war. However, both authors have generally remained on the sidelines of this war. We use the quotes and citations to provide insight into the cultural war but not to represent us or to allow us to engage in that war.[8]

Our efforts focus on the elites in cultural progressive movements or individuals who are relatively active in promoting the aims of cultural progressives. One can question whether most cultural progressives are engaged in widespread disagreement about cultural values. In other words, this work may not be generalizable to individuals who hold cultural progressive beliefs but are not engaged in activism to further those beliefs. Indeed, work on Christian political activists may tell us a little about the general values of Christians, but it is not the best way to understand Christians as an entire category. Likewise, our research provides us with some insight into the general values of cultural progressives, but it does not necessarily provide us with a comprehensive understanding of all cultural progressives, particularly those who are not politically active. Furthermore, our focus is on the role of cultural progressive activists in the larger cultural war, and these individuals generally define themselves as opponents of the Christian right. By definition, individuals who responded to our questionnaire did so because they were part of an organization that is focused on opposing the Christian or religious right and can be conceived of as leaders of the movement to oppose religious traditionalists on cultural and/or political issues. Thus, we gathered attitudes from the leaders of the cultural progressive social movement, and it is difficult to challenge our findings based on their inaccuracy in capturing the intentions of cultural progressives who are actively fighting the cultural war.

Possible Criticisms

We contend that the methodology laid out in the previous section is sufficient for investigations into the nature and attitudes of cultural progressive activists. However, we suspect that some of our readers may question this contention and the premise of our work. Some individuals, especially those who are cultural progressive activists, may argue that what we present is not an accurate reflection of their perspectives. Of course all generalizations have to be carefully made. In a relatively large subgroup such as cultural progressive activists, there are likely important in-group differences. We will attempt to capture these different factions with our discussion in chapter 3, but some individuals will not be neatly described by our typology. However, this is always the case when researching a large population. Some generalizations will not fit; however, this does not mean that these generalizations do a bad job describing the tendencies of a given population. If they describe most or a major minority of the people in that population, then we consider those generalizations useful. We contend that the typology that will be discussed in chapter 3 accomplishes such a task.

Second, some may challenge whether there is an identifiable social movement among cultural progressive activists. Cultural progressive activists do not have institutions such as churches to create the community that cultural conservative activists enjoy. As such, there is a temptation to see cultural progressive activists as a decentralized group of individuals who may share some concerns but have little to do with each other. While this is true, we think that such a perspective underestimates the way modern forms of community are created. Research on the use of social media and other online tools indicates that new communities can emerge with individuals who live in different areas of the country and even the world (Bimber, 1998; Hampton & Wellman, 2003; Jones, 1998; Ling & Stald, 2010; Rheingold, 1993; Wellman, Hasse, Witte, & Hampton, 2001). Individuals do not have to be in close proximity to each other to share ideology, culture, perspectives, and concerns with each other or even to get to know one another. The organizations outlined earlier in this chapter can facilitate the bringing together of like-minded individuals just as much as churches by using modern technology to develop their own subculture. The use of certain catchphrases by several of the respondents in their answers (e.g., "they are neither Christian nor right") indicates that these individuals have communicated with each other enough to create their own lexicon of common meanings. The community of the cultural progressive activists may not be the same as the community of the cultural conservative activists, but that community meets the needs of those cultural progressive activists nonetheless.

Third, there may be concerns about the inflammatory language of some of the respondents. Some may argue that we are attempting to make cultural progressive activists look bad by including these comments. We could have eliminated the most inflammatory of the comments, but doing so would have distracted from the character of many of the respondents and provided the reader with an inaccurate perception of our results. Accuracy is more important than maintaining sanitized images of cultural progressive activists. In this book, we make no moral judgment of the comments of the respondents, although we do assess the accuracy of some of the claims. It is up to the reader to decide if the values and morality exhibited by the respondents are beneficial or detrimental to society. Our refusal to provide moral judgment of the respondents' comments should not be read as acceptance but rather as our attempt to allow cultural progressive activists to express themselves in their own words.

Finally, there are concerns that consistently tend to be enunciated when research like this is presented. For example, some can look at our data and have a different interpretation of the values that we claim are exhibited in the quotes we present. This is fair; however, we highly doubt that any alternative interpretation of these data would vary greatly from the values we have enunciated. Any differences are more likely matters of semantics than of substance. Furthermore, some may claim that there is nothing new to learn from our work. They may argue that it is clear that cultural conservative activists and cultural progressive activists hate each other and thus this book adds nothing new to our current knowledge.

But while the anger of cultural conservative activists is well documented (Crawford, 1980; Durham, 2000; Frank, 2004; Stein, 2001), this book is the first attempt to do concentrated analysis of cultural progressive activists and thus is the first one to document the animosity they feel toward cultural conservatives. Combined with our enunciation of the cognitive framework and values that cultural progressive activists exhibit, this research effort clearly adds to our current knowledge on the social conflict between cultural conservative activists and cultural progressive activists. In addition, some may accuse us of broadly stereotyping cultural progressive activists with the claims we make in this book. We do no such thing. Anyone who conducts social research understands that generalizations are not absolute. They merely indicate that members of certain groups have a higher likelihood of possessing certain qualities. Thus, our claim of the importance of political progressive philosophy of cultural progressive activists does not mean that every single one of them is highly motivated by a political progressive philosophy. In fact there were a couple of individuals who indicated that they were Republicans. But clearly the weight of the data indicates that our respondents were more likely to be driven by politically progressive ideology than the average individual, making such a generalization reasonable.

Outline of Book

In the second chapter we introduce theories concerning the development of social movements. In particular we use the theory of emergent norms as a way to understand why social movements develop. Nearly all social groups form a commonly held sense of injustice. The group has a disadvantage that is considered an injustice, and this perception is shared within the group. It is not necessarily the most economically deprived groups that merge into social movements, as there is a need for resources to facilitate the communication of these grievances to like-minded individuals. This communication allows the group to develop a collective identity that helps the group to maintain commitment and loyalty among its members. This precedes the need of the group to set goals, attract like-minded individuals, and develop tactics that sustain group unity. We predict that sustenance of the group will become more important than maintaining rational outcomes for cultural progressives as they are subject to the same social forces as are members of other social movements.

In the third chapter we explain our methodology in more detail and look at who is attracted to cultural progressive movements with a demographic exploration of our sample. The data from our survey indicate that individuals active in these cultural progressive movements are more likely to be highly educated, male, and white and to have a relatively high socioeconomic status (SES) compared to other individuals. These are not individuals normally thought of as being deprived in the United States. But cultural progressive activists are also likely to have a less religious and more progressive ideology that is threatened by the increased prominence of Christian conservatives. Factor analysis is used to develop a typology of who is active in these social movements and explore what motivates individuals within each type. We use three major reasons for why individuals may oppose the religious right (political concerns, concerns about religion in general, antipathy toward Christianity) to find seven smaller subgroups among the respondents. In this chapter we briefly describe the subgroups.

In the fourth chapter we look at the groups of cultural progressive activists motivated by political concerns. The three subgroups that fall under this category are *political activist*, *sexual progressive*, and *feminist*. Political activists demonstrate general support for progressive politics and oppose the Christian right because it is a faction that supports conservative political action. They are a highly educated group that perceives members of the Christian right as being uneducated. Sexual progressives tend to be focused on sexuality issues such as abortion and homosexuality. They perceive the Christian right as a political threat to their sexual freedom and have incentives to protect that freedom. Members of the feminist subgroup focus on battling the promotion of patriarchy by the Christian right. They have a fear that the Christian right will roll back some of the rights women have gained over the past several decades. At the end of this chapter, we explore some of the primary literature read by cultural progressives and examine how some themes from these groups are supported by this literature.

In the fifth chapter we look at groups of cultural progressive activists motivated by a general animosity toward religion. The two subgroups that fall under this category are *religion is poison* and *religion has been corrupted*. Those in the religion is poison group dismiss religion as having a dangerous influence in our society. These respondents argue that religion robs people of their ability to engage in critical thinking. Individuals in the religion has been corrupted group are concerned about how religion is practiced in modern society. They are worried about the tendency of members of the Christian right to interfere in the lives of others. Once again, we look at how the themes developed within these groups are supported in the primary literature these respondents read.

In the sixth chapter we look at groups of cultural progressive activists motivated by a specific antipathy toward Christians. We term such individuals *critics of Christianity*. The two subgroups that fall under this category are *Christianity as unevolved* and *Christians as political oppressors*. Respondents defined as members of the *Christianity as unevolved* subgroup perceive Christianity as a social movement retarding societal progress. They are particularly aggrieved by the propensity of Christians to have a detrimental effect on education and societal experimentation. Respondents in the Christians as political oppressors group are concerned about oppressive political elements they perceive to be tied to contemporary Christianity. They are especially concerned with what they see as the judgmentalism and intolerance in how Christianity is practiced by members of the Christian right. As in chapters 4 and 5, in chapter 6 we look at how the themes developed within these groups are present in the primary literature of cultural progressives. But we also discuss common themes within all seven groups. To be specific, these common themes are (1) a fear of mixing religion and politics, (2) the importance of rationality, (3) a desire to limit the influence of religion in society, and (4) the value of progressive politics over conservative politics. While there are distinctions between respondents in these groups, they tend to share similar concerns.

In the seventh chapter we return to the social movement literature as we look at the basic emergent norms of cultural progressive activists that come from the common themes enunciated in chapter 6. Those norms are the expectation that religion within conservative political activism is wrong and harmful to society, the appreciation of rationality as the way to solve social and political problems in society, the idea that traditional religion is dysfunctional to society and its potential impact must be limited, and the value of progressive political ideology. From these norms, diagnostic, prognostic, and motivational collective action frames can be surmised. The perceived intrusion of religion into society and the perception of persecution by the Christian right are diagnosed as problems created by cultural conservatives. Solutions are framed as the taking of political and legal action to stop the Christian right. Interpersonal contact as a solution is downplayed by most except for a few respondents. Finally, fear of an imposed theocracy and/or the gaining of disproportionate power of the Christian right creates the motivating frame of cultural progressive activists. These emergent norms and collective action frames are linked to a collective identity of cultural progressive activists. This identity is dominated by the values of irreligiosity, rationality, and progressive political action.

In the eighth chapter we summarize our basic conclusions. The values of irreligiosity, rationality, and progressive political action reinforce each other to create a collective identity that serves the social interest of cultural progressive activists. But the nature of a social movement is not dependent on the stated attempts of the members of a movement to remain rational, but rather it is subject to the social forces that persuade those within successful social movements to promote beliefs not always grounded in reality. Such beliefs serve to meet the needs and interests of individuals from a given subculture. The promotion of those beliefs allows the movement to compel commitment and recruit new members. Cultural progressive activists use the creation of an image of the Christian right villain to recruit individuals who perceive certain types of injustices, and this helps them to perpetuate their social movement. Since such tactics serve cultural progressive activists well, this movement's opposition to the Christian right will remain relevant for the foreseeable future. Because needs are met by this social movement for certain progressive subcultures, just as the needs of certain cultural conservative subcultures are met by Christian right movements, there is little reason to believe that either side will surrender in the culture war for some time to come. The culture war is here to stay. We conclude the book by suggesting possible directions for future research in the exploration of the culture war and the role cultural progressives play in that war.

Conclusion

The actual political power of cultural progressive activists is in dispute. Our work does not shed much light on that argument. However, the societal influence of cultural progressive activists is significant. We have already noted that cultural progressives are likely to have a relatively high level of economic and educational resources. At the very least we know that they have ample legal resources, as seen in the various organizations that file lawsuits on behalf of their causes. Furthermore, the origin of antireligious activism within the sciences also suggests that this is a social movement that has scientific allies. Indeed, a previous book by one of us (Yancey, 2011) suggests that biases in academia favor cultural progressives over cultural conservatives. It can also be argued that individuals in the media and arts are more supportive of cultural progressive concerns since cutting-edge art and ideas are more likely to come from cultural progressives than cultural conservatives. Perhaps this is why political progressives and the irreligious are overrepresented in the art and media communities (Guveli, Need, & De Graaf, 2006; Lichter, Rothman, & Lichter, 1986; Sutter, 2001). Given all of these factors, we are comfortable making the argument that cultural progressive activists have a real, although undetermined, amount of social, legal, and political power in our society, and understanding how they may use it is a task that should not be taken lightly.

The emergence of cultural progressive activism occurred as a result of the argument between those advocating reason against those advocating a traditional moral and religious order. As such, individuals involved with cultural progressive groups are theoretically likely to utilize rationality in ordering their lives and possibly the social movement that emerges to replace the traditional religious order. If cultural progressive activists value rationality and reason, then they may be eager to exhibit such qualities in the larger movements that they are a part of. However, it is also quite plausible that individuals who support culturally progressive causes are susceptible to the same social forces that influence other individuals as well. They may be just as likely to engage in unsubstantiated stereotyping and to become victim to unreasonable fears as other social actors. A study of cultural progressive activists may lead us to an examination of the full potential of humans to create a rational society and rational social movement.

In the next chapter we begin exploring the possibility that cultural progressive activists are able to create social movements rooted in rationality. Our examination of social movement theory provides possible predictions of what we may find as we examine the literature and thoughts of cultural progressive activists. Then in the later chapters we will determine the degree to which our predictions prove to be reality.

CHAPTER 2

Dynamics of Social Movements and Cultural Progressives

Efforts to deal with the Christian right are efforts encased in a cultural progressive social movement. These efforts do not represent a series of individuals attempting to stop the Christian right on their own. Rather, individuals interact with like-minded people who desire to accomplish the same goals. Social movements are the way such individuals are able to link themselves together to accomplish their stated goals. It is within these social movements that social-psychological dynamics impact these individuals as they are influenced by other members within the movement. Even a movement based on the idea of a rational approach to society is not likely to escape such sociopsychological dynamics.

An ample amount of work has been done on the dynamics of social movements (Benford & Hunt, 1992; Diani & McAdam, 2003; Ferree & Miller, 2007; Gamson, 1992; S. Hunt & Benford, 2004; Melucci, 1989; Morris & Mueller, 1992; Swidler, 1995; Taylor & Whittier, 1995). Research into collective behavior has generated several usable theories to help scholars understand how social movements impact the actions and perceptions of individuals who become involved in them (Ferree & Miller, 2007; Gamson, 1992; Snow & Benford, 1992; Taylor & Whittier, 1995; Turner & Killian, 1987).

This research has also enabled us to have a better understanding of why such movements have developed and how this origin influences the eventual trajectory of these movements. Understanding these theories will provide us with insight as to what may be occurring within the social movements of cultural progressives.

This chapter introduces theories concerning the development of social movements. Theories of emergent norms and collective action frames have surpassed resource mobilization theory to explain the development of social movements, and as such we use those theories to speculate about the development of social movements. Hobsbawm (1959) argued that modern challenges are built more on rationality and utilitarianism rather than primitive rituals. But we contend that modern activism is just as rational, or irrational, as previous challenges to dominant culture as these movements are subject to the same social-psychological forces that generally impact social movements. Thus, modern theories of social movements challenge the notion that cultural progressive activists have built social movements purely centered in rational choices, but rather it is to the social advantage of cultural progressive activists to portray their movement as based on rationality. We suspect that although there is logic behind the social and political positions taken by cultural progressive activists, irrational forces identified in social movement theories also play an important role in how they conceptualize issues. In the following chapters we provide evidence that supports our speculation.

Resource Mobilization Theory

The earliest theories surrounding the development of social movements were built upon resource mobilization. Resource mobilization is the idea that social movements are successful when those movements are able to take control of sufficient economic and social resources and to use them wisely (Turner & Killian, 1987). This theory helps to balance out the assumptions that the success of social movements depends on the intensity of the movement's grassroots activism as it explores the type of formal and informal organizations that are effective. Groups that have the advantage of accumulating resources will be the groups that are able to achieve their aims through social movements. Theories developing out of a resource mobilization perspective have tended to investigate how certain social groups are able to gather resources and how they use those resources to achieve their goals. Thus, the basic premise of the resource mobilization theory is that the dominant movements possessing resources are able to maintain an advantageous status quo.

For example, a city may decide that there needs to be a new garbage dump. The dump can be placed on either the east or west side of the city. Each side of the city may develop a social movement to prevent the dump from being built in that area of the city. Both social movements will attempt to take advantage of the resources that are available. But if the west side social movement possesses greater wealth and its members have more social prestige and power than those in the east side social movement, then it has greater resources and thus the dump is likely to be built in the east. This example shows how resource mobilization theory predicts the outcome in the clash of social movements. Social movements with sufficient resources persist as they are able to accomplish their goals and thus justify their existence to the members of the movement.

However, this approach fails to fully account for what brings together individuals to support a given social movement. The resource mobilization theory suggests that these individuals come together to take advantage of the resources available to the movement. However, such a utilitarian approach tends to minimize the emotional investment individuals make toward their social movements. Individuals in a social movement may have a powerful desire to accomplish certain social reforms that is so strong that they can overcome a social movement with more "resources." Their belief system and psychological investment in the movement can provide a solidarity that is a resource in and of itself. Yet the resource mobilization theory generally fails to appreciate social-psychological dynamics that develop within social movements. For this reason, contemporary social movement theories of emergent norms, collective action frames, and collective identity have developed to explore the constructivist nature of social movements.

Emergent Norms and Collective Action Frames

Rather than a largely utilitarian approach to social movements, there is great insight in exploring the socially constructed nature of social movements. There is temptation to use a materialist approach to resource mobilization theory. But why individuals decide to mobilize is not always tied to economic or cultural resources. If individuals do not perceive that they have a problem, then mobilization is not likely to occur and a social movement will not develop. Economic deprivation is not enough for a social movement to develop, as the members of the groups suffering from that deprivation must perceive themselves as deprived before they possess motivation to act. For example, the contemporary rural poor do not have a robust social movement fighting for their rights. However, in the early part of the 20th century, African Americans, who in many ways did not have more social resources than the rural poor have today, did mobilize and develop a powerful social movement that led to the civil rights movement. The difference between these two groups is not disparity of resources, but rather African Americans were able to socially construct their economic deprivation in ways that escape the rural poor.

Why were African Americans able to generate such a social construction? Theories of relative deprivation suggest that subcultures that feel deprived are likely to mobilize and become social movements. Their perception of deprivation matters more than if they actually are deprived. The emotion that comes from the perception of deprivation is the effective motivator for those in the movements and helps these movements to sustain themselves. African Americans may have been in a better position to compare themselves to the whites and develop an understanding that they were unfairly deprived. However, the rural poor lack such a reference group if they are relatively isolated from wealthier individuals. As such, it is not necessarily the most deprived groups or individuals who form social movements but those who have developed a sense of loss who are more likely to mobilize. Therefore, social movements do not automatically correlate with the level of inequality in a society but with the level of social discontentment.

This enables us to begin to look at a major constructionist approach to social movements, which are the ideas surrounding emergent norms (Turner & Killian, 1987). Without these emergent norms, organized collective action is not possible. These norms help a group to define itself as deprived and in need of redress. They also provide a guide for groups and allow them to construct goals and actions for achieving these goals. Nearly all social groups develop a sense of injustice. But it is when the members of the group can share the perception of injustice with the other members of the group that a unity within the group can develop. A sense of intolerability of, and solutions to, the current situation is soon perceived by the members of the group. Social definitions of the intolerable position and what to do about this position are soon accepted by members of the group as their own perception, and not a perception that has been imposed on them by the group.

Since individuals are brought together with similar grievances, they soon develop tangible goals they want to achieve through the use of this movement. Movement norms merge into a movement ideology that offers simplifying perspectives for understanding complex social realities and issues. This ideology is soon used to approach others not yet in the movement but open to perceiving the same type of grievances that originally helped to form the movement. Those who are convinced may leave their former concerns to concentrate on ending the new injustices that have been brought to their attention. Thus, commitment to the movement may come from the process of conversion, esprit de corps, participation rewards, personal identification with the movement, and breaking ties with conventional life. As friendship patterns change, the norms continue to reinforce the movement's ideology among its members and intensive interaction fosters social control of group members. A communication system also must develop, and it too is embedded in the group's identity. Intellectuals often play an important role in articulating the injustice. Successful groups often have the resources to recruit such intellectuals or other cultural resources that allow them to easily communicate their concerns. The ability to foster communication reinforces their perception of injustice regardless of the degree of actual injustice they suffer.

Just as the perception of injustice, more than actual injustice, is important to set up the norms to establish a group, the perceived reality of the group members, rather than their actual reality, is more important to develop the ideology necessary to maintain the social movement and to keep the members of the movement hopeful in obtaining their desired goals. Specific values arise out of such an ideology, and these values help to dictate the perceptions of the members in the group. The values of the group members help to identify the problem to be dealt with, provide an explanation for how to fix a problem, and help to sustain attention/activity (Turner & Killian, 1987). These values also help to set up who can be included in the group and who is excluded. Some of those who are excluded are stereotyped as the villains who are a major source of the problem or the injustice the social movement attempts to address. Turner and Killian (1987) point out that the development of villains or conspiracy theories is important for four key reasons: it (1) protects groups members from looking at their own inadequacies, (2) helps to simplify a complex situation, (3) helps to justify the way a social movement socializes others, and (4) reinforces the moral character of the members of the movement by establishing the movement as a struggle of good and evil. As such, social movements have a powerful tendency to create out-group members who can be the scapegoats for all that is wrong in their social reality. The perception of villains is due to the social needs met by emergent norms more than the actual problems created by these out-group members.

Emergent norms are important factors in the creation of social movements formed to deal with a perceived injustice. Once established, these norms can take on a life of their own, regardless of any attempt to rationally understand the social reality the members of the group face. These norms develop to meet the needs and preconceived ideologies of the movement members rather than to be an accurate representation of the social world surrounding the social movement. In this way, it is likely that members in social movements have a difficult time developing accurate assessments of social reality but rather develop assessments based on addressing the injustices perceived by members of the group. A humorous example of this is found in a statement by the former professional basketball player Latrell Sprewell, who, when offered a three-year, $21 million contract, refused it and stated that he needed more money because "I have a family to feed." His statement was made in 2004, just five years after a lockout labor dispute, and clearly Sprewell was drawing off of the ideology of owners victimizing players, but he did so with a statement that clearly was out of proportion to economic reality.

Another way of understanding this propensity can be seen in the development of ideas surrounding collective action frames. Although emergent norms may best explain how the original ideologies of social movements develop, collective action frames may best explore how social movements are able to maintain that ideology over time. Thus, there is tremendous value in looking at theories of collective action frames to understand how members in social movements maintain their perceptions of social reality.

Taylor and Whittier (1995) argue that collective action frame theory builds and extends theories of emergent norms. This theory, developed through the writing of Snow and Benford (1988, 1992) and Benford and Hunt (1992), contends that we cannot take for granted that events will be interpreted through a lens favorable to a social movement. To ensure such advantageous interpretation, a social movement has to attach meaning to certain events that can trigger and support the desire for social action. "Framing" is what Snow and Benford (1988) call the attachment of meaning to certain events and circumstances so that action is furthered within a social movement. Today, some claim that political individuals attempt to put a "spin" on events to make themselves look good and their opponents look bad. This is very similar to the concept of framing.

Framing can be broken down into three basic tasks. First, there is the need to interpret the event or situation as a problem. This is called diagnostic framing, as the meanings attached in this process are used to diagnose the source of the injustice that the social movement faces. A cultural progressive movement may diagnose the problem creating the injustice as the undue influence that individuals with traditional religious beliefs have in our society. Second, the social movement has to prescribe a possible solution to these problems. This is known as prognostic framing. It is used in social movements to provide the solution that the members of their groups seek. A cultural progressive movement may decide that the solution is to use political activism to reduce the power and influence of individuals with traditional religious beliefs. Finally, there has to be a way to move the members of the group into taking action. Motivational framing is the meanings social groups use to provide a rationale for engaging in corrective action. These frames enable the social movement to maintain its ideology and its will to advocate for social change. Cultural progressives may develop arguments about the threat of traditional religious beliefs in an effort to motivate other cultural progressives to work with them to reduce the ability of individuals with those traditional beliefs of taking over society.

Whether the frames are successful in persuading individuals depends on whether the meanings attached to these frames are perceived as true by members of the social movement. Some individuals may be convinced of the veracity of these frames through logical arguments, but often what is more convincing is whether individuals experience the reality claimed in the frames in their everyday life. Not many African Americans can accurately cite the income differentials between whites and blacks in the United States, but their everyday experiences with racism help to explain their willingness to support civil rights social movements. Thus, frames have to develop the proper level of extension if they are going to maximize their potential to garner support for their social movement. If members of movements overreach in their conclusions about social reality through the meaning attached to their frames, they may lose the support of individuals who do not experience such conclusions. For example, claims that African Americans are still slaves are not likely to be widely supported since that is not the experience of most blacks today, although there are radical African American activists who use slavery as a metaphor for contemporary racism. Likewise, frames that are not expansive enough also fail to attract a sufficient number of supporters in a social movement. A social movement to correct injustice for African American engineers is not likely to get much support if it cannot be tied to a broader civil rights movement since there are few blacks who experience the unique problems engineers may have. Thus, frames must be set up so that their claims motivate a comparatively high percentage of individuals positioned to become supportive of this movement.

However, once the frames are set up, it becomes difficult for them to be altered. Groups that join social movements rely upon the frames set up by the early groups in the protest movement to diagnose their injustice situation, prescribe a solution, and motivate individuals to take action. Groups that are formed at later stages in the movement are generally limited to the previous frames that have been set up. Thus, the initial framing of a social movement has a significant effect on how the movement will eventually develop. It becomes very difficult to alter the frames of the movement once there is initial momentum created by the original collective frames.

Snow and Benford (1992) argue that frames help to explain the cyclical nature of social movements; when the culture climate changes so as to no longer sustain the understanding of the frames, social movements connected to them decline, and we see a decline in the cycle of protest. The most certain way for a collective action frame to change is for the social movement connected to it to deteriorate. As such, these frames retain tremendous power to shape social movements as long as the movements persist. But when these frames are no longer seen as relevant, then new frames have to be developed that can begin a new cycle of protest movements. For example, as social movements built upon white supremacy began to lose legitimacy, the framing of racial issues as whites having innate advantages over people of color disappeared. However, scholars of race and ethnicity point out that new movements emerged to protect the interest of whites and to protest efforts to correct racial inequalities, built upon new frames on color blindness and reverse discrimination (Balibar, 2007; Bonilla-Silva, 2003; Carr, 1997; Marx, 2006).

Emergent norms and collective action frames are important conceptual mechanisms that help to explain how the initial values that originally shape social movements tend to remain relatively unchanged over time. The stability of these values occurs in part because of the sociopsychological needs that these social movements meet. The notion of a collective identity represents how social movements are more than political activism, but they are also mechanisms to meet the psychological desires of the movement's members. Understanding the concept of a collective identity helps us to comprehend important sociopsychological dynamics that are formed within social movements.

Collective Identity

Social-psychological theories suggest that people who engage in social movements do so for the same reasons that people engage in social actions in general. They do so to meet important social needs that may not be easily met elsewhere. Because of the payoff they receive from the group, individuals develop a loyalty to the group. When the identity and the goals of the group are threatened, individuals in the group also feel threatened. Individuals not only make a rational decision based on their interests but also consider the interests of the group (Gamson, 1992). A collective identity develops whereby a person infuses at least part of his or her identity with membership within the social movement. This collective identity serves the social movement well as it helps to produce commitment to the group through solidarity with the other members of the group (Gamson, 1992; S. Hunt & Benford, 2004). The development of a collective identity also helps a movement to survive the loss of the original members (Melucci, 1995). New members take on the values and perspectives of the departing members, and thus the group is able to continue without the original members. Thus, while collective identity meets some of the felt social and psychological needs of the members of the group, it also serves the group by maintaining loyalty among its members.

Collective identity creates social relations that embed individuals into the movement and change the way the individuals in the movement perceive reality. In this way, a collective identity also helps to meet the need individuals have for social relations. Theories of homophily (Hatfield & Rapson, 1992; Kandel, 1978; McCroskey, McCroskey, & Richmond, 2005; McPherson, Smith-Lovin, & Cook, 2001; Roth, 2004) suggest that individuals tend to develop friendships with those from similar backgrounds. For example, it is well established that individuals tend to develop friendships with those of the same race (Fetto, 2000; Hallinan & Williams, 1989; Moody, 2001), perhaps because they are more likely to have similar social experiences. Generally, ideology is not conceptualized as a category by which we may measure the social diversity of one's friendship patterns. However, collective identity allows individuals with similar perceptions of society and their place in society to develop relationships with each other. Such relationships may do more than reduce the degree of loneliness that individuals may experience. They may also enable these individuals to perceive themselves as part of a movement greater than their own lives and provide a similar understanding of purpose to be shared with other members in the social movement. Such experiences clearly meet important social needs for group members as they address the desire to belong to a social entity greater than themselves and make having a collective identity a critical part of a successful social movement.

Collective identity theory suggests that the development of a collective identity is the most salient task of social movements that want to promote major social changes (Melucci, 1989). S. Hunt and Benford (2004) point out that collective identity is a widely utilized concept in the understanding of social movements. They contend that in almost all modern treatment of research into social movements, there is some category of collective identity, whether it is seen as a peripheral or central concern. Collective identity has developed such importance in research on social movements possibly due to its ability to replace the Marxian concept of class consciousness as a mechanism to create social change or even social revolt. Class consciousness is generally limited to notions of class struggle, which are not always relevant in social movements. But with collective identity scholars have a way in which individuals may become linked together for a common cause regardless of whether they are driven by the desire for economic justice or not.

For example, environmentalists are driven not by a desire to protect their own class position but rather from a collective identity that their movement has been formed to save the planet from environmental disaster. Such a collective identity allows the individuals in the movement to perceive themselves as part of a cause that is larger than their own self-interest and helps to motivate them to make sacrifices for this social movement.

Collective identity is a vital mechanism used to promote social change. It binds people together to take some kind of action that will promote that social change. Since this concept is not locked into rank materialism as the motivating factor for social change, as is the case for class consciousness, it can be used to conceptualize the uniting of groups that can change the status quo based upon factors such as race, sex, sexual preference, ethnicity, and so on (Melucci, 1995). The new radical movements of the 1960s, which have also been called the new social movements, became possible even though the members of the movements were largely made up of middle-class individuals. Economic deprivation is not necessary to motivate the impulse toward social change.

But collective identity also reinforces the in-group mentality of the group's members. Those who do not share in the group's collective identity can easily be dismissed. In this sense the collective identity feeds into the ongoing intergroup conflict that may already be present in a society. Taylor and Whittier (1992) point out that there are three important analytical tools that can be used to understand collective identity. First is the boundary that allows group members to set themselves apart from out-group members. Such boundaries are important because part of the way in-group members define themselves is by who is not in the group as well as who is allowed to identify with the group. Second is the consciousness that helps a group to define its own interest, and generally that interest is defined in opposition to the dominant society. This consciousness is often perceived as having an oppositional attitude toward the larger society. Third is the negotiation a group enters into in an attempt to change the social definitions and symbolic meanings in a given society. This negotiation often results in changes in the lifestyles of the members of the group so that they can fully experience the implications of their collective identity. These tools indicate that social movements utilize their collective identity to provoke social changes and to enter into conflict with groups and organizations that defend the status quo. Collective identity often goes hand in hand with political activism and conflict.

All social movements produce culture. They also seek to shape the discourse to fit with this new culture and frames. Contemporary theorists see culture itself as a form of power (Swidler, 1995), and all social movements are doing is creating new identities and ideologies by which to shape that culture. Collective identities place members of the social movement within a culture and help determine which side of the cultural conflict the members of that movement will be on. The collective identity has to be understood in the context of the larger culture and the other social groups that are part of that culture. Collective identities cannot be understood in isolation from other aspects of the larger culture, as the perceived place individuals with a given collective identity have in that culture is a vital aspect of that collective identity. Cultural conflict is not merely a peripheral aspect of collective identity, but this conflict is a central characteristic that helps to shape collective identity.

The symbolic nature of collective identity also feeds into the intergroup conflict inherited within society. Individuals make a significant investment in the development and maintenance of the collective identity within their group. That identity symbolizes their perception about their social position. If social movements are built upon the notion that individuals are challenging the injustice in a society, then this identity will symbolize an individual who is confronting an unjust status quo. Thus, contemporary social movements often are represented as symbolic challenges to the dominant society. Conflict can be understood as having great symbolic importance as well as utilitarian consequences. Symbolic expressions that threaten the collective identity of the movement have to be confronted since that identity plays such an important role in the shaping of the movement (Melucci, 1989). Actions of those in a social movement are not gauged only on their practical effectiveness but also on how they support the collective identity developed within the movement. Many actions may be symbolic in nature and yet hold a high degree of value to those inside the movement. Outsiders to the movement may not understand why certain symbolic actions are important to the movement's insiders, but those in the movement understand the value of protecting their collective identity through such action.

A practical example from one of the groups that we visited may help to illustrate this point. The group had brought in an advisor to help encourage more productive social activism among the members of the group. One of the individuals attending the event asked about passing out scorecards as a way to indicate which members of Congress were most in line with the values of the group. The advisor told the members of the group that it was technically legal for them to do so as a 501(c)(3) organization, but they did not want to do it. When the individuals pressed the advisor for an answer, the advisor stated that the organization had come to the conclusion that many conservative churches had used such scorecards as ways of promoting politics from the pulpit. Since they were also a nonprofit group, they did not want to imitate what they thought the churches were doing wrong. So although it was legal to have some sort of political scorecards, the leaders of the organizations did not allow the affiliates of the organization to use them. We can see here that the use of scorecards is a symbolic way in which the members of the group can differentiate themselves from the religious organizations they oppose. This symbolic differentiation helps the members of the group to maintain a distinctive collective identity from the dominant religious groups they envision as the source of the injustice they must face. Symbolic gestures have real social meaning and serve a vital function in helping a group to identify itself.

Cultural Progressives and Social Movement Theory

None of the processes discussed in the preceding sections happen in a vacuum. They occur in the context of the society in which they are located. In the first chapter we discussed part of the history of the social conflict between cultural conservatives and cultural progressives. That conflict clearly shapes the type of social movements likely to develop among cultural progressives. For example, the out-group members for cultural progressive activists are cultural conservatives. Cultural conservative activists are also likely to be part of the problem perceived by cultural progressive activists and can serve the role of the villain in helping them to understand social reality. Interaction with cultural conservatives shapes the reality perceived by cultural progressive activists, and this perception, at least as much as an unbiased, accurate accounting of objective reality, helps to determine the direction of social movements led by cultural progressives.

Social movements are also shaped by the institutions they confront (Swidler, 1995). The way these institutions attempt to combat these movements helps to determine the type of tactics the movements use. If cultural progressive activists perceive themselves as individuals who face injustice at the hands of cultural conservatives, then they will develop tactics and perceptions that aid them in overcoming such injustice. To understand cultural progressive activists, we have to comprehend their perception of cultural conservatives. As noted in the opening chapter, part of the cultural conflict that has developed in the United States is legitimated by the idea of promoting rationality instead of supporting ideas based on religion or tradition. The logical conclusion from such legitimization is that individuals who have developed culturally conservative ideas have irrational perceptions that are inferior to the ideas developed by cultural progressives. Cultural conservatives are seen as the villains who are responsible for the irrational state of our society. Their inferior ideas are seen as the primary source of the problems cultural progressives attempt to address. Such an assertion justifies efforts of cultural progressives to limit the influence of ideas emerging from cultural conservatives. Rational debate may not be seen as plausible given the perceived irrationality of cultural conservatives.

However, such an assertion would run counter to the notions of rationality that stipulate that all ideas must be tested before being discarded. The implication of the preceding paragraph is that the cultural positions of conservatives have already been tested or that they do not need testing since they are clearly irrational. The empirical work in later chapters will provide some insight as to whether cultural progressive activists possess ideas about cultural conservatives that have been sufficiently tested and logically rejected. A full vetting of the accuracy of the perceptions of cultural progressive activists about cultural conservatives is beyond the scope of this book. But we will see that there are sociopsychological, as well as logical, reasons why certain perceptions of cultural conservatives have been developed. We should not be surprised about such sociopsychological effects since it is very difficult, if not impossible, to maintain a rational perspective within a social movement. The sociopsychological dynamics discussed in this chapter indicate that individuals in social movements have social needs that have to be met. These dynamics indicate that the righteousness of the cause of the social movement has to be defended at all costs. These dynamics indicate the importance of finding villains on whom to blame societal problems. Even a movement that prides itself on its rationality is unlikely to completely maintain that rationality when confronted with all of the various social and psychological needs that have to be met in social movements.

It is our contention that a social movement based on a rational objective assessment of social reality is simply not plausible given the sociopsychological aspects previous scholars have suggested are part of social movements. Cultural progressive activists articulate a rational approach to social reality as a counter to the nonscientific and nonrational approaches of traditional religions. Doing so provides them with legitimation as they push forth a social and political agenda that serves their members. They have tremendous incentive to exhibit such rationality in their social movement so that they can justify their approach to social order and their challenge to religious and political conservatism. They do have logical reasons for accepting their perspectives, but, we contend, contrary to their own claims, that rationality is not the only reason they have adopted those positions.

Previous work on social movements in the culture war has concentrated upon cultural conservative activists (Gilgoff, 2008;

Knuckey, 2005; McConkey, 2001; Moen, 1992; Wilcox & Larson, 2006). Some of this work has suggested that these activists are often irrational in their perspectives (Almond, Appleby, & Sivan, 2003; Hedges, 2007; Morone, 2004). We do not dispute that assertion. But we do not accept the implication that it is the particular social conservative philosophy that creates this irrationality. Rather, it is the need for social conservative activists to meet the important social and philosophical concerns of their members that buttresses the illogical conclusions that some social conservatives have developed. Likewise, the philosophy and values of social progressive activists are also driven by the need to meet the needs and concerns of the individuals who are drawn into this social movement. Likewise, there are common concepts and understandings among social progressive activists that can be conceived as illogical, despite the fact that this is a social movement built upon the notion of being "rational." In this way our work acts as a reminder of the powerful forces that shape the development of social movements and a needed corrective to the image that only the social conservatives manufacture illogicality in their social movements.

Conclusion

Social movements cannot be based only on rationality. These movements meet important social and psychological needs that are not in the realm of rationality. Even social movements by groups that envision rationality and reason as highly valuable are influenced by the obligation to meet these needs. They must develop norms that do more than assess the objective reality of members of the group, but rather, these norms must motivate members of the movement to engage with the larger society. These social movements have created frames to compel commitment to the movement. One of the most valuable ways to create this type of commitment is the development of these frames in such a way as to envision enemies lurking to victimize the individuals in the movement. There must be a collective identity based on the need to galvanize the members of the movement to protect each other, not based on the actual social positions of the members in the movement. These aspects must occur if a social movement is to be successful, and thus the success of a social movement begun by cultural progressives may naturally move it away from the type of objective assessment that the originators of the movement envisioned.

To assess the degree to which cultural progressive activists are replicating the dynamics discussed earlier in this chapter, we want to explore what they have to say in their own words. We want to hear how they describe their current social position and their assessment of cultural conservatives. It is important not only to document what members of culturally progressive movements are stating but also to read the literature generated by these movements and to gather the messages that organizations that support the social and political goals of cultural progressives provide to their members. In this way, we not only gain insight into the perceptions of cultural progressive activists but also can determine what part of their perspectives comes from the organizations that buttress this social movement.

Answering these questions requires an empirical examination of cultural progressive activists. In the following chapter, we begin this assessment by looking at the results of our content analysis of the primary material and the results of our open-ended online survey. This assessment allows us to determine the degree to which the sociological dynamics we have already documented are a reality for individuals in social movements led by cultural progressive activists.

CHAPTER 3

Developing a Typology of Cultural Progressive Activists

Social movement theories suggest that individuals with certain ideologies are more likely to be drawn from certain sectors of our society. If these theories are accurate, then cultural progressive activists should be more likely to come from certain demographic and social groups. Since we are exploring individuals who conceptualize themselves as fighting the Christian right, we may be in a position to predict what these groups may be. For example, one would obviously expect individuals fighting the Christian right to have relatively low levels of traditional religiosity. Individuals who do not subscribe to traditional notions of faith are highly likely to develop a contrasting understanding of social reality to that of members of the Christian right. This can create the potential for social conflict as members of each subculture attempt to promote its understanding to the general society.

Beyond religious preference, it is also likely that individuals who resist the Christian right are highly educated. Research has indicated that education is negatively correlated with traditional religiosity (Gallup & Lindsay, 2000; Glaeser & Sacerdote, 2008). This negative relationship may be due to the contrasting values promoted by highly educated individuals in comparison to the highly religious.

The highly religious may prefer the status quo, while education promotes tolerance for nonconformity (Ohlander et al., 2004). Thus, even highly educated individuals who are highly religious may use their religion to promote a nonconformist attitude to social life than their lower educated contemporaries. Furthermore, highly religious, white Christians are more likely to be politically conservative than other whites. Yet the highly educated are more likely to be politically progressive relative to other individuals. Politics may become another arena where conflict between the religious right and the highly educated becomes commonplace.

Concerning race, it is unclear what type of prediction to make. On the one hand, whites are generally less likely than blacks and Hispanics to see religion as important (Gallup & Lindsay, 2000; L. L. Hunt & Hunt, 2001). This indicates that whites are more likely to be overrepresented within groups that resist the religious nature of the Christian right. On the other hand, it has been suggested that whites are overrepresented among the Christian right (Green, 1995; Rozell & Wilcox, 1995). Therefore, whites may be underrepresented in groups that oppose the Christian right. Thus, we have contradictory information as to the role race may play in shaping the subculture of those who oppose the Christian right. We may be similarly ambivalent about predicting possible sex effects. We have already seen that women generally have higher levels of religiosity than men. However, the Christian right has been characterized as patriarchal (Joyce, 2009; A. Smith, 2006; Snyder, 2007) and may be less attractive to women than to men. However, there is no empirical evidence that this is the case. Finally, research has suggested that older individuals are more likely to be highly religious (Gallup & Lindsay, 2000; Kosmin & Keysar, 2008). However, it is not clear whether they are more likely to be members of the Christian right. Thus, age is also a variable that is difficult to predict.

Religiosity has also been correlated to larger family size (Christiano, 2000; Preston & Sten, 2008). Furthermore, members of the Christian right have often touted what they call "family values," which may encourage them to have larger families than other Christians. Individuals who are not in the traditional role of raising children may be more likely to resent the imposition of values that reward pronatalism. Indeed, there have been some social movements discouraging larger families in an effort to better take care of the environment (Dowbiggin, 2008; Hartmann, 2009; White et al., 2008). Given this potential propensity, we predict that individuals who oppose the Christian right will be less likely to have children than other individuals.

Finally, income may also be a factor for encouraging individuals to combat the Christian right. Research has suggested that higher levels of income may lead to more progressive social values including support of abortion and homosexuality (Ellison, Echevarria, & Smith, 2005; T. Smith, 1994). Those with higher SES have more social options and thus may be more willing to resist any limitations on their sexual behavior. If this is the case, then it is plausible that individuals with higher SES will be more likely to be members of groups that resist the Christian right.

Finding Opponents of the Christian Right

To gain knowledge about individuals involved in social organizations that oppose the Christian right, we devised a survey to send to them. In doing so, we sought to locate individuals who actively worked to oppose the agenda and aims of the Christian right. Since we did not know the size of such a group, there was no guarantee that a national probability survey would find enough individuals to gain meaningful data. Thus, we decided to locate and work with several organizations that had as one of their primary missions to resist the Christian (or in some cases the religious) right. Members of such organizations were supporting institutions that have made one of their primary causes the limitation of the influence of the religious right. Thus, membership in such organizations by definition indicates an individual's willingness to resist the religious right.[1]

For the sake of privacy, the names of the organizations remain confidential. However, two of the organizations possess a national scope, while a third is located in a southern state. Although this organization has members located outside of the state, the vast majority of the members reside within that state, and its presence skews any attempts at assessing the regional distribution of individuals who resist the Christian right. We understand that a major weakness of our technique is that we cannot claim a probability sample, but what we do claim is that we have obtained a sufficiently large sample that we can reasonably locate patterns among cultural progressives and identify different types of cultural progressives. Furthermore, we utilize a methodological technique—open-ended questionnaires—that allows us to assess the perspectives of a large number of respondents and thus make good use of the large sample we were able to collect. A fourth source of respondents was a contact within a small organization. The contact spread the survey to members of other smaller organizations and thus provided us with further respondents for our survey. When we finished with our data collection, we had gathered results from 3,577 respondents. One final bias should be noted. The organization from which we obtained the greatest number of responses has as its major purpose the resistance of religion in general. We anticipate that this organization likely artificially increases the number of atheists and agnostics in our sample. Thus, when we discuss the religious preferences of the respondents, we do so with and without the respondents from this particular group.

To conduct the research, we used the online tool SurveyMonkey. We sent the link to the survey to the leaders of the organizations. Those leaders then sent the link out to their members. We kept the link open for the smaller organizations as long as plausible. One organization contributed slightly more than half of all respondents and did so with the link out for only two days. We shut down the link from that organization to limit its influence on the general results. However, the number of respondents was slowing up after just two days, and we likely would not have gotten a great deal more respondents if we had kept the link open.

The survey used can be seen in the appendix table A.1. The survey is a combination of closed- and open-ended questions. This allowed us to conduct both quantitative and qualitative analysis of the results from our respondents. Questions about the demographics and social characteristics of the respondents allow us to explore if, and how, these individuals differ from the larger society. Open-ended questions were coded and then analyzed. The technical information of how the results were coded is in the appendix, but from the analysis of these codes we can explore the different reasons why individuals choose to resist the religious right.

Finally, we also explored the primary literature generated by the three major organizations and the website of a fourth organization. We gained access to both their web and paper newsletters and thoroughly read through a selected sample of them. This gave us background knowledge of the type of information the members of these organizations receive on a regular basis. In this way, we were able to understand the ways these organizations influence the social understandings of their members.

Demographics of Cultural Progressive Activists

In table 3.1 we indicate the basic demographic and social characteristics of our sample of cultural progressive activists. We can instantly see that this is a group that is highly male, white, educated, older, and non-monotheistic. Furthermore, it is a group that does not have a lot of children and tends to have relatively high levels of income. Our first observation is that, except for age, the percentage of respondents with children, and religious orientation, all of these demographic and social data indicate that individuals who resist the religious right have majority group status. Males, whites, the highly educated, and those who have high incomes possess a dominant, and not marginalized, position in our society. It is only on issues of religion that members of these groups can claim any sort of marginalized status.

The percentage of whites in our sample is stunning. Our sample suggests that only 1 of every 14 members of these organizations is nonwhite. Yet according to census data, in 2010 almost 1 of every 4 individuals was nonwhite.[2] Given the fact that one of the major sources of these respondents is located in a state in the South that has a relatively low percentage of whites, we have even more evidence that whites are the dominant race in resisting the Christian right. We can only speculate about such a finding. There is evidence

TABLE 3.1
Demographic Characteristics of the Sample

Percentage male	64.1
Percentage over 65	25.9
Percentage over 55	52.5
Percentage white	93.7
Average number of children under 18 at home	0.326
Percentage having children under 18 at home	18.3
Percentage bachelor's degree or above	79.6
Percentage master's degree or above	43.5
Percentage doctorate	16.7
Percentage making over $75,000	52.6
Percentage non-monotheistic[a]	88.4
Percentage non-monotheistic[b]	71.4

a. Measures of monotheism include all those who state themselves as Christian, Jewish, or Muslim.
b. Eliminates overt atheist group from sample.

that among some nonwhite groups religiosity is not linked to conservative political orientation (Battle, 2006; A. B. Cohen, Malka, Hill, Hill, & Sundie, 2009; Emerson & Smith, 2000). Irreligious individuals of color may perceive religion to be less of a threat to a progressive political ideology than do irreligious whites. Perhaps this lack of a threat makes such organizations less attractive for politically progressive and/or irreligious people of color.

The fact that the percentage of men is so high is especially surprising since there is evidence that men are less likely to respond to surveys than are women (Dey, 1997; Sax, Gilmartin, & Bryant, 2003; Sax, Gilmartin, Lee, & Hagedorn, 2008; Ward, Bruce, Holt, D'Este, & Sladden, 1998). If this pattern holds for cultural progressive activists, then it may be the case that there is an even greater sex disparity than seen in this survey. Furthermore, women are more likely to take part in voluntary organizations than men (Bureau of Labor

Statistics, 2010). Yet it is men who dominate these cultural progressive organizations. This may not only reflect the fact that men are more likely to be irreligious than women but also show that men are more likely to engage in activism due to their irreligiosity than women. The percentages of women in these organizations are so low that it is hard to believe that organizations that make up the Christian right have lower percentages of women among their members. Although groups that make up the Christian right may be patriarchal, it is unlikely that they do a worse job attracting women than organizations that resist the Christian right. If one is to contend that patriarchy is a driving force behind Christian right social movements, then it is unwise to use the sex composition of the Christian right as an indication of that argument. The sex ratio of cultural progressive activists is so badly skewed toward males that a similar argument can be made about them.

This is also clearly a sample that is older than the general population. According to census data, in 2010 only 13 percent of all individuals in the United States are over 65.[3] More than a quarter of this sample (25.9 percent) is over that age. Furthermore, more than half of the sample is over the age of 55. It is plausible that older individuals have more time to become involved in voluntary organizations and this accounts for their membership in these groups. It is also plausible that, as we will see later, this is a more educated group and it takes time to accumulate such education levels. It is unclear whether this age discrepancy is due to a cohort effect, and thus as these individuals die off the groups will grow smaller, or a true age effect in that cultural progressives become more active as they grow older.

Individuals raising children may have a different perspective on the viability of religion than others. Such individuals may desire to use religion to help them to socialize their children. Given the age of this group, there is little surprise that this is a group that has relatively small number of children under the age of 18 at home. Only 18.3 percent of the respondents have children under the age of 18 at home, but 34.2 percent of the general population have children under the age of 18 living at home.[4] When we look at only respondents who are under 65, we still find that only 23.9 percent of the respondents have children under 18 living at home. Thus, this difference is not merely due to an age effect. This is a group that is less likely to be influenced by the concerns of raising children than is the general public.

This is an incredibly highly educated group. Census data indicate that only 24.4 percent of all individuals older than 25 have a bachelor's degree. In this sample, 43.5 percent of all individuals have a master's degree. Nearly four of five respondents have a bachelor's degree. Given this higher level of education, it is not surprising that this is a group with a higher than normal SES. According to census data, the median household income in 2010 was $50,046.[5] But over half (52.6 percent) of these respondents make more than $75,000 a year. The way the income question was set up does not allow us to compare the mean income of the respondents to the mean income in the United States, but given the type of high income outliers included in the SES data, measures of median income are generally better anyway. Predictions about the higher education and higher SES of the cultural left are confirmed, and we have no basis for disputing the rationale for the overrepresentations of the highly educated and wealthy in this sample.

Since our sample is not a probability sample, some caution is necessary when generalizing about the demographic and social makeup of this sample. However, other studies substantiate these trends among groups that tend to be cultural progressives. For example, one would expect those who are not religiously devout to be the sort of cultural progressives who are active in resisting the Christian right. We have previously noted research indicating that religiosity is negatively correlated with being white, educated, and male (Chatters et al., 1999; Gallup & Lindsay, 2000; Gunnoe & Moore, 2002; Johnson, 1997; Kosmin & Keysar, 2008; Yancey, 2002). Furthermore, the Christian right social movement is famous for its opposition to abortion and homosexuality; however, support for these political positions is correlated to being highly educated and wealthy (Bolks et al., 2000; Herek & Capitanio, 1996; Legge, 1983; Loftus, 2001; Ohlander et al., 2004). Finally it should be noted that there is documentation that personal animosity toward fundamentalists is correlated with higher levels of education and being male (Bolce & De Maio, 2008; Yancey, 2010). The very qualities that define cultural progressives are also correlated with higher educational, financial, racial, and gender status. Given this type of external verification, it is not surprising that cultural progressive activists in our sample come from a relatively highly privileged group. What is surprising is the degree of majority group educational, economic, gender, and racial status our sample enjoys. While we cannot be certain that the members of these organizations enjoy this degree of social status advantage in our society, we are confident that social status advantage to some degree exists for cultural progressive activists relative to other members in the United States.

The degree of relative advantage the members of our sample have in comparison to others in the United States is noteworthy. Among those who are over 25, 31 percent of the respondents are white, are male, have at least a bachelor's degree, and make at least $75,000 a year. One can look at such individuals as majority group members in every conceivable way that we can measure majority group status. According to 2000 census data, the percentage of all Americans over 25 who were white, were male, had at least a bachelor's degree, and made at least $75,000 a year was 12.8 percent.[6] As a group, cultural progressive activists are more likely to enjoy privileges due to their social or demographic status than are other Americans. The fact that they enjoy these privileges does not necessarily mean that they do not have perceptions of injustice necessary to motivate a social group. In the following chapters we will observe that many of the respondents do conceive of themselves as victims despite the societal advantages connected to these demographic measures of cultural progressive activists. Despite their perceptions of victimization, the financial, educational, and social advantages that these activists have undoubtedly help them to marshal the resources necessary for them to promote the interests of social movements that serve social progressives.

Finally, as expected, individuals who resist the Christian right are less likely to adhere to traditional religiosity. Less than 12 percent of all respondents adhere to one of the major monotheistic religions of Christianity, Judaism, or Islam.[7] Since it is plausible that some of this 12 percent have more of a cultural identity other than the religious one implied in their designation of faith, this 12 percent should be seen as the ceiling of possible participation by those with a traditional religious identity. We also looked at the sample after removing the one organization that is dedicated to opposing religion itself. Without this group, the percentage of monotheistic participants rises to 28.6 percent. While this is more than double in comparison to the entire sample, it still indicates that almost three of four respondents do not possess traditional religiosity.

While these respondents tend to have a majority group status in race, gender, class, and education, they are nonconformist according to religious identity. It is plausible that this is a group that has grown comfortable with the majority group status they generally enjoy in nonreligious dimensions. Thus, they may experience an unusually high amount of frustration due to the rejection of their religious identity by the general public. This may lead to hostility toward the influence of traditional religion in general society. Efforts by members of the Christian right to influence the larger society can touch an emotional and psychological nerve among such individuals and provoke them to resist the Christian right. Such a group would clearly have economic and educational resources to engage in such a battle but, because of their religious status, can still claim victim status. Thus, part of the rationale for the existence of groups that oppose the Christian right can be seen in the demographic makeup of this group.

Developing a Typology of Who Resists the Christian Right

The respondents in this group all have one thing in common—they are members of an organized group that resists the Christian right. However, why individuals have taken the action of engaging in this opposition clearly varies among the different group members. To this end, it is valuable to distinguish the subgroups among cultural progressive activists as to why they desire to combat the Christian right. As we do this, we will be able to understand some of the complexities within this social movement and begin to see some of the emergent norms that unite these individuals. From those norms, eventually we will be able to discuss the type of collective identity that encourages members of cultural progressive organizations to marshal their resources and promote the movement's causes.

To understand the contrasting reasons why individuals have hostility toward the Christian right, it is helpful to understand how different individuals conceptualize the Christian right. Conceptually, there are three aspects of the Christian right that may draw attention from cultural progressive activists. Cultural progressive activists may oppose the Christian right for purely political purposes. The fact that the Christian right promotes conservative political issues may be the motivation for some cultural progressives to actively oppose this movement. Cultural progressive activists may also oppose the Christian right because of its religious nature. For some cultural progressive activists, religion itself is the problem and the manner in which members of the Christian right promote religion in general is seen as troublesome. Finally, some cultural progressive activists may resist the Christian right because it tends to promote the specific religion of Christianity. If the particular form of Christianity practiced by members of the Christian right is seen as especially dysfunctional, then some cultural progressives will have sufficient motivation to oppose the Christian right.

Our survey contained a series of open-ended questions that allow us to explore these three avenues of motivation for cultural progressive activists. We coded the answers to the surveys and then used factor analysis to determine the subgroups that emerged from this sample. The methodology of how we used this factor analysis is presented in the appendix. From this analysis, it became clear that three groups discussed above could be broken down into seven smaller general subgroups. Those who primarily oppose the Christian right for political reasons were divided into three groups: *political activists*, *sexual progressives*, and *feminists*. Those who indicated a general aversion to religion fell into two groups: *religion is poison* and *religion has been corrupted*. Those who specifically criticize

Christianity or who are critics of Christianity were divided into two groups: *Christianity as unevolved* and *Christians as political oppressors.*

In the balance of this chapter we briefly look at these seven groups, including some of the basic characteristics of each group and their rationale for opposing the Christian right. Once we have done that we will be in a position to look at each of these groups more deeply and use the qualitative data to better understand each group. We will see some of the distinctions between the groups and how each group also reflects a larger collective identity that drives cultural progressive activists.

There is value in gaining a sense of how prevalent each of these groups is in the sample. To this end, we coded the respondents using factor loadings to determine which subgroup a given respondent was most likely to fit into. The results of our efforts can be seen in table 3.2. This method produced not exact matching but more of a rough estimate of how best to place a given respondent. Let us be clear in asserting that we are fully aware that we do not have a true probability sample, and such a breakdown cannot automatically be generalized to the larger cultural left community. We also know that our methodology for placing respondents in a given category is not exact. However, this breakdown does provide us with some information about which subgroups respondents are most likely to be found in. We can see that there is roughly a 50–50 split in whether political or religious considerations drive the respondent to oppose the Christian right. We can also see that in our sample that the *political activist* and *Christians as political oppressors* motivations are the most powerful ones, while those of *religion has been corrupted* and *feminist* are the least powerful explanations. Ideally, future work will provide data that either confirm or refute the relative importance of these possible motivations among the cultural left.

A research caveat is in order here. Although we discuss these subgroups as being distinctive to each other, in reality there is a great deal of overlap among the different groups. It is quite common that elements of more than one subgroup are found in the same respondent. In fact, multiple motivations are much more likely than a single motivation to drive a respondent to oppose the Christian

Table 3.2
Percentage of Cultural Progressives in Each Subgroup

Subgroup	Percentage
Political activist	18.1
Sexual progressive	25.1
Feminist	3.1
Religion is poison	15.5
Religion has been corrupted	1.2
Christianity as unevolved	13.9
Christians as political oppressors	22.4
Total	**100.0**

right. However, to fully understand the forces behind each motivation, it is useful to explore each subgroup as if it were the only motivation in that given instance. Doing so produces clarity within that category and allows us to better understand the dynamics of why individuals adhere to the politics and activism of the cultural left. However, in reality it is better to conceptualize the motivations we describe as prevailing propensities that influence many and possibly most of the respondents rather than influences that impact members only in a given subgroup.

Groups with Political Concerns

Political Activist

Among the respondents, a sizable percentage indicated a concern about the political activity of the Christian right. Among these were those who exhibited concern about the political landscape in general. They indicated a concern that the members of the Christian right were creating a powerful political push toward conservatism. These individuals did not have a certain set of political issues that they were concerned about, but rather they indicated fear about the political movement of the country in general. Thus, we have termed this group *political activist* as their concerns are for the general political nature of the Christian right and they do not indicate an unusual amount of concern on single-issue topics.

Our sense of the political activists is that political ideology in general is the feature that dictates the desire of certain individuals to oppose the Christian right. They conceptualize a polarizing dichotomy where they separate the political world into conservatives and progressives. Since the Christian right is recognized as individuals within the conservative domain, they have to be seen as the enemy that is opposed. One of the questions from our online survey is, "Imagine that you choose who is going to be your neighbor. Please rate the desirability of having one of the following individuals as your neighbor—'A vocal Republican who is not a Christian' or 'A vocal Christian who is apolitical.'" The respondents' answers to this question indicated that those who fell into the *political activist* group are significantly more negative toward Republicans than Christians. These individuals are no more likely to be atheists or agnostic than other cultural progressive activists, and it may be the case that they perceive Christianity as a problem only to the extent that it promotes political conservatism. The following statement from a respondent in this category may be quite representative of this particular perspective.

> Just want to underscore that for me what matters is the politics. I would be just as disturbed by secular Ayn Randians if they were as powerful as rightwing Christians are. The Nazis were not religious, in fact, many were anti-religious. It's possible to be Christian and feminist, Christian and progressive. I don't believe in God, but if someone believes in liberal values, it doesn't bother me if they are religious. I don't understand it, but I don't understand many things about people. (female, 56–65, master's degree)

More examination into the demographic differences between those who tend to be *political activists* and other cultural progressive activists indicates other interesting insights into what may motivate such individuals. *Political activists* tend to be better educated than other cultural progressive activists. Yet they are also more likely to live in the South than other cultural progressive activists. This possibly indicates that such individuals find themselves surrounded by individuals they disagree with and their educational training provides them with tools of critical thinking they believe their southern neighbors lack. Some of the correlation data do indicate that these individuals have a propensity to complain about the disregard that the Christian right has for science, which would fly in the face of the values these individuals gained in their educational training. Their experience with the Christian right may shape them by providing a negative reference group. This possible explanation is reinforced by the fact that these individuals tend to have had more born-again Christians in their social networks than other cultural progressive activists. Their experiences with conservative Christians may provide them with the opportunity to develop a distain for such individuals' way of thinking.

Finally, it is also noteworthy that men are more likely to be *political activists* than women. However, women are significantly more likely to belong to the other political categories. Those categories tend to focus on a set of certain political issues rather than a critique of a general political philosophy. It may be the case that male cultural progressive activists are more likely to be drawn toward a general political ideology while female cultural progressive activists are more likely to be energized by specific political issues.

Sexual Progressive

The next subgroup category is that of the *sexual progressives*. These individuals oppose the Christian right on issues that center around a modern sexual lifestyle. Specifically, they are concerned with issues of abortion and homosexuality. Their opposition to the Christian right is because of the traditionalist stance that members of that group have on those key sexual issues.

It has been suggested that issues of abortion and homosexuality represent more than the actual medical procedure or sexual practices. Instead, they represent an alteration of the sexual norms of our society (M. Gross & Landers, 2008; Inglehart & Welzel, 2005; Lind, 2009). Abortion represents sexual freedom as it relieves women of the potential economic costs of pregnancy. Acceptance of homosexuality indicates a desire for a society where individuals are free to engage in sexual activity without condemnation. Social traditionalists tend to have a higher level of comfort with the traditional rules and regulations that have dominated sexuality in the past. Norms of heterosexuality and postponement of sexual activity until an individual intends on having children are connected to a traditional framework of sexuality. However, individuals with a modernist outlook likely accept nonconformist sexual norms and reject controls based on ideas of traditional sexuality. This may represent a larger modernist mentality of self-empowerment as opposed to a conservative notion of societal control over the individual. Previous work on the culture tends to focus on how religious conservatives conceptualize their legitimization of conventional sexuality and social norms (Burack, 2008; di Mauro & Joffe, 2009; Klemp, 2009; Wilcox & Larson, 2006). The *sexual progressives* in this sample indicate a need for us to also understand the perspectives of those who desire to challenge those traditional notions.

Unlike the *political activist*, the *sexual progressive* has maintained a good deal of social separation from the Christian right. They are less likely to have born-again individuals in their social networks when they were 15 and still are less likely to have such individuals in their social networks today than other cultural progressive activists. They are less likely to live in the South than other cultural progressive activists. They likely grew up with little or no religious belief and have taken steps, whether consciously or not, to limit their social interaction with individuals of faith. This may enable them to develop sexual morals that are not influenced by interaction with those with more traditional norms. This distance can also provide them with the social space that allows them to stereotype those with traditional sexual norms as out-group members.

The religious effects are also insightful for us to fully understand the attitudes of the sexual progressives. In the battle for conventional or modern sexual morality, religion can become either an important tool or an important hindrance to a given side. Much of traditional morality has been legitimated by conservative religious systems that hold with high esteem the sexual values of past societies. However, the challenge of modernism has convinced many individuals that they have the right, and even obligation, to make their own sexual choices. Part of the way religion shapes sexual values is through persuasion. However, we have a history of traditional sexual values being supported by legal sanctions. The fear that the Christian right will buttress a new movement toward such sanctions is the political motivation that *sexual progressives* use to legitimate their actions.

Females and older individuals are more likely to be *sexual progressives* than other cultural progressive activists. It may be the case that older individuals were socialized during the sexual revolution of the 1960s. One of the major cultural revisions that developed in that time was the notion of sexual freedom, and these individuals may envision themselves continuing on in that struggle. The members of the Christian right can be seen as the defenders of a traditional sexuality that such individuals sought to overthrow during the countercultural social revolution. Women may also be likely to perceive traditional sexuality as a burden relative to men in the sample. Some social thinkers have articulated how traditional sexual mores have been used to exploit women (Ryckman, Kaczor, & Thornton, 1992; Swim & Hyers, 2009; Viki & Abrams, 2002), and thus females may have a higher desire to protect modern sexual freedoms from the political challenges of the Christian right. If that is true, then it is not surprising that female activists are more likely to accept a *sexual progressive* mentality than are male activists.

Feminist

The final political category we found among the respondents was that of the *feminist*. These were individuals who used feminist ideology to motivate them in their struggle against the Christian right. They were highly likely to complain that one of the driving features that shaped their attitudes toward members of the Christian right was issues connected to gender. The rights of women are seen a paramount to such individuals. Since they conceptualize the Christian right as a group that is an imposing roadblock for women seeking to gain complete rights in our society, opposition to the Christian right can be legitimated by members of this subgroup.

Interestingly, abortion is not a driving force behind the individuals in this subgroup. Those who use abortion as a motivating factor in their opposition to the Christian right tend to belong in the *sexual progressives* group. This group is more specifically focused on the problems women face rather than merely the protection of reproductive rights. However, it is worth noting that concerns about homosexuality were also an important factor in shaping the opinions of such respondents, although they were not as important as gender issues in general. This indicates a possible linking of the concerns of women and homosexuals. It is plausible that individuals who appreciate the need to fight for equal rights based on sex also perceive it to be important to resist differential treatment because of sexual preference. In academia, there has been a good deal of work discussing issues of the intersectionality of race, class, gender, and sexual preference (Berg, 2010; Davis, 2008; McCall, 2005; Nash, 2008; Pyke, 2010; Shields, 2008). These individuals may rely upon such work to legitimate the merging of their concerns for women and for homosexuals.

Those who are *feminist* are more likely to have had social networks with more atheists when they were 15 and in their current social networks. However, they are no more likely to be atheists than other cultural progressive activists. We speculate that if *feminists* have an aversion to the patriarchal nature of Christians, then they may be more comfortable with atheists regardless of their own religious preference. Indeed, a great deal of research has indicated that Christian religiosity is correlated to sexist social and political attitudes (Glick, Lamerias, & Castro, 2002; R. M. Gross, 1996; Hayes, 1995; Martos & Hegy, 1998; Peek, Lowe, & Williams, 1991; S. D. Rose, 1987; Ruether, 1974), supporting the possible fears of *feminists*. It is not surprising that women are more likely to be in this subgroup than in other subgroups. Since women still have minority group status in our society, concerns about gender issues are more likely to resonate among female progressives than male progressives. Previous research (Boles, 2001; Gullett, 1995; Yancey, 1998) has substantiated the fact that even though male progressives are concerned with gender issues, their concern is significantly less than the concern exhibited by female progressives. Members of this subgroup are also younger than other cultural progressive activists. It is unclear whether this is due to younger progressive activists having a higher degree of concern for gender issues in general or if they are more concerned about sexism within a religious context.

Finally, there was some evidence that members of this subgroup were more likely to criticize the Christian right for their unwillingness to support science. On the surface, such a concern does not appear to be linked to the general fears about gender that members of this group tend to have. However, it is plausible that the scientific concerns exhibited by such individuals deal more with the social sciences as opposed to debates about evolution. The use of science and academia to conceptualize a more gender-equitable future may be behind such findings.

Of all these groups, only the *political activists* had substantially more antipathy toward Republicans than toward Christians. This can be seen in our question about whether the respondent prefers an apolitical Christian or an irreligious Republican. The intention of this question was to assess whether religious or political concerns are more important in the potential hostility a respondent has for the Christian right. For *political activists* the political leanings of the Christian right may trump all other concerns. However for *sexual progressives* and *feminists* religion may produce nonpolitical social changes that are just as undesirable as the political alterations the Christian right seeks to promote. As such, we did not find a significant relationship between preference for the apolitical Christian/irreligious Republican and belonging to either of the latter two subgroups.

Groups That Oppose Religion in General

Religion Is Poison

The first group of individuals approached these issues from the perspective that religion has a toxic influence on society. Since religion in general is seen as so toxic, these individuals oppose the efforts and intentions of the Christian right. They do not necessarily single out Christianity in particular but rather tend to see all religions as problematic for society. It is merely that in the United States the form religion is most likely to take to create a toxic influence is Christianity.

In light of this perspective, we have named this the *religion is poison* group. We conceptualized the idea of poison based on the recent popular book by Christopher Hitchens, *God Is Not Great: How Religion Poisons Everything*. It is the subtitle of poison that accurately captures the attitude of such respondents. Indeed, the idea of religion as a poison can be seen in some of the respondents' comments, regardless of whether or not they are part of this subgroup.

> [T]hey [the Christian right] would tend to fall into patterns such as . . . fear-based circular thinking that poisons virtually every aspect of human life. (male, 46–55, master's degree)

> They "poison" everything they touch. (male, 56–65, some college)

> Religion is the poison of the earth. (male, 26–35, bachelor's degree)

> I cannot say anything positive about them without risking that it be misconstrued as them having a good quality. Their religion poisons every aspect of their lives. (male, 26–35, master's degree)

In his book Hitchens does not limit his criticism to merely Christians. He produces examples of "poison" from a variety of different religions. As we can see from the comments of some of the respondents, his idea that religion is a poison has been adopted by some of the cultural left and legitimates their distrust of the Christian right.

Why do such individuals perceive religion as so poisonous? One of the reasons is because respondents in this subgroup are more likely to have had a negative encounter with a member of the Christian right than other respondents. They are not any more likely to have grown up among born-again individuals as a child, and thus they are not more likely to have interacted with conservative Christians at a young age. However, when they have interacted with conservative Christians, they are more likely to have had a negative experience relative to other cultural conservatives. Whether these negative experiences are due to actually being mistreated by Christians or whether they are due to a propensity on their part to interpret their encounters as negative is not quite clear. But their negative experiences are part of what drives their antipathy toward religion in general and Christianity specifically.

Perhaps related to these negative experiences is the fact that these individuals are more likely than the other respondents to have a current social network made up of atheists. If their negative experiences have influenced them to become less trustful of religious individuals, then they may place more trust upon individuals with no religious beliefs. Indeed, Hitchens argues that at the very least religious faith does not improve a person's character but instead likely worsens that person's morality. If these respondents are picking up their social cues from such writings, then naturally they would seek to avoid interaction with believers of all faiths.

Finally, it is also worth observing another feature that helps to explain why such respondents perceive religion as a phenomenon that "poisons" society. They are more likely than other cultural progressive activists to conceptualize individuals of the Christian right as being unintelligent relative to others in society. This higher propensity to attach an assessment of dumbness to members of the Christian right suggests that a key way they see religion as a poisoning influence is that it robs individuals of the ability to engage in critical thinking. One might assume that this group perceives education as the antidote to such a deficiency. However, members of this group actually have a lower level of education compared to the other respondents. Yet given the extremely high level of education of the entire sample, even this group likely possesses higher educational levels than the general population. It is possible that they are compensating for not being as highly educated as some of their peers by their emphasis on the stupidity of the Christian right, which may highlight for them the fact that they are still highly educated relative to their ideological opponents.

Religion Has Been Corrupted

The second major group that opposes religion in general is a group that we have called *religion has been corrupted*. There is some crossover with members of this subgroup and *critics of Christianity* as members of this group are more likely to single out Christianity for special condemnation than the *religion is poison* group. However, the larger influence within the members of this group is the notion that religion itself has become corrupted in modern times and Christianity is merely one form of that particular type of religious corruption. Unlike the general *critics of Christianity*, members of this group do not generally limit themselves merely to attacks upon Christian faith but rather perceive Christianity as merely an example of the larger corruption of religion. Those influenced by the *religion has been corrupted* motivation can be conceptualized as falling in between the *religion is poison* motivation and the motivations generated by *critics of Christianity*.

If religion has been corrupted, then it is possible that at one time religion had an acceptable form. Indeed, many of these respondents complain about how religion has become more intolerant and less loving. These respondents do not necessarily oppose religion in all of its forms. But they tend to reject the current manifestation of religion as a dysfunctional force in our larger society.

An interesting aspect of this subgroup is that they are more likely than other respondents to state that they previously lived in a neighborhood near the Christian right. Yet they are less likely than other respondents to currently live in the South. Since the Christian right is more prevalent in the South (Conger, 2009; Green & Guth, 1988; Lienesch, 1993), it can be speculated that a significant portion of these individuals likely left the South to get away from their Christian right neighborhoods and the larger influences of living in a community dominated by religious ideas. They may understand religion as corrupted since it is a judgmental force that inhibits their lifestyle choices.

It is of note that both of these motivations indicate more hostility toward religious traditionality more than toward political conservatism. Once again, the question concerning whether one desires an apolitical Christian or a nonbelieving Republican provides insight. In both subgroups the Republican was preferred over the Christian, suggesting that concern about religion, rather than politics, motivates such individuals to resist the Christian right. We do not argue that political concerns are irrelevant, as often political and religious concerns are intertwined. However, the individuals in these subgroups have made political differences secondary to their general aversion to religion.

Groups That Are Critics of Christianity

Christianity as Unevolved

Two groups emerged that indicated concerns that were specifically targeted at Christianity. While these members may not have much appreciation for religion in general, they particularly have animosity toward Christianity. The first group seems to operate based on the idea that Christianity is a problem because it inhibits progress or can be seen as a backward religious expression. Thus, advocates of this perspective come from the group we term *Christianity as unevolved*.

Respondents in this group tend to look at the Christian right as a backward group. The Christian right is seen as inhibiting the progress of humans. A key way that the Christian right can be seen as unevolved is through its promotion of conservative political and social policies. The advocacy of conservative Christians is seen as taking our society back to the "Dark Ages." Thus, there is an important political component to the idea of Christianity as a backward religion. Activists may not care as much about the regressive nature of Christianity if it is practiced in private, but since Christianity affects our political reality, it is something to be feared. This differs from some of the activists in the groups that oppose religion in general, as many of those individuals were upset with the fact that individuals were religious at all. It is not surprising that members of this group have more animosity toward an irreligious Republican neighbor relative to an apolitical Christian one since their concerns are tied to how Christianity retards political progressiveness rather than the existence of Christianity itself.

Interestingly, individuals within this subgroup also loaded relatively high on their perception that living in a neighborhood with those of the Christian right is not a big problem for them. In fact being a member of this subgroup was also significantly correlated with having a high number of "born-again" individuals in their current social network and living in the South. They are also more likely to label themselves Christians than other cultural progressive activists. Christians in this group likely perceive that it is not their own interpretation of Christianity that is a problem but rather the religion of conservative Christians who turn the faith into a regressive force. There is little evidence that these individuals have personal animosity toward members of the Christian right. Their concern appears more to be linked to the possibility of the Christian right promoting social changes that they perceive as regressive than to avoiding personal interaction with Christian Republicans. At the very least we have confidence that individuals in this subgroup do not flee areas where members of the Christian right are located such as conservative neighborhoods or the South and are willing to have them as friends.

One can speculate regarding a positive component to the motivations driving this subgroup. Members of this subgroup likely perceive a positive vision of a progressive society of tolerance and acceptance. Their personal acceptance of members of the Christian right can be seen as a feature of that tolerance. But it is the regressive elements of this group that such individuals resist and is the source of their motivation to oppose the Christian right.

Christians as Political Oppressors

The final subgroup we found was individuals who had an unusually high level of animosity toward Christians in general. They perceive Christianity as a proxy for Republicans and as a politically oppressive force. In many ways Christians can be the foot soldiers of the Republican Party and make it possible for Republicans to rob other groups of their rights. Motivation to oppose the Christian right can be seen as necessary to limit the political oppression in our general society. Thus, we name this subgroup *Christians as political oppressors*.

There is clearly an important political component within this subgroup as well as a powerful religious dimension. The members of this subgroup are more likely to perceive irreligious Republicans as worse neighbors than apolitical Christians. Furthermore, they also were more likely than other respondents to state that Republicans are bad individuals. Thus, the political system opposed by members in this subculture is supported by the Christian right. However, the focus is more upon religious than political aspects of the Christian right. We developed a measure that allows us to determine the animosity directed at Christian fundamentalists relative to other religious groups.[8] Individuals in this subgroup are more likely to have animosity toward Christian fundamentalists relative to other religious groups.[9] It is not religion in general but this particular representation of Christianity that buttresses the political oppression they worry about. This measure indicates that while political concerns are an important part of this group, the members of this group place the real blame for the problems inherent among the Christian right as linked to the religious nature of this social movement. Political issues are a problem only because Christianity has created an atmosphere in which bad political policies are easily accepted.

Interestingly, when asked about whether we need laws to deal with the Christian right, members of this subgroup were more likely than other cultural progressive activists to answer that they did not want such laws in order to promote free speech. This tendency may be tied to the fact that this is a group that is more likely to have some degree of belief in the supernatural. If they perceive themselves as practicing a higher form of spirituality than their religious opponents, then they may be more likely to support the ideals of religious tolerance. This is not to say that atheists and agnostics in the group do not value free speech. In fact, a main point of contention between Christian fundamentalists and religious progressives is the claim of truth exclusivity (Guth, 2007; Noll, 2001; B. G. Smith, 2010; C. Smith, Emerson, Gallagher, Kennedy, & Sikkink, 1998). Religious progressives tend to dismiss the notion that there is one true path, and thus it would be quite difficult for them to maintain their moral objections to fundamentalism if they are willing to politically silence them. The highly educated and wealthy progressive Christians who make up this subgroup may have a higher level of motivation than the other respondents in the sample to protect the free speech rights of the Christian right.

It is worth noting that the members of this group have higher levels of education and SES than do other respondents. Given the already high levels of education and SES in the general sample, this is a group that has elite educational and income status. Many of them may be highly educated and wealthy Christians embarrassed by the way their religion is implemented by Christian fundamentalists, who may have lower education and SES than the general population. In this way, some members of this subculture may be engaged in a war within their own religious tradition as much as in a war against or with the rest of the general culture. One need not be an atheist or agnostic to have a *critics of Christianity* perspective if one has antipathy toward certain conservative Christians, even if one is a Christian oneself. Since many in this group do not have religious leanings or education, there may be alternate ways in which nonbelief produces a *critic of Christianity* perspective. Previous research has indicated that significant hostility toward fundamental Christianity is present within the United States (Bolce & De Maio, 1999, 2008; Yancey, 2010) and may produce discrimination against fundamentalists in the highly educated world of academia (Gartner, 1986; Hodge, 2002; Ressler & Hodge, 2003; Yancey, 2011). The highly educated, whether they are religious or not, may have a natural animosity toward those with a fundamental Christian faith.

The question about whether an individual prefers an apolitical Christian neighbor to an irreligious Republican one indicated an interesting difference between the two *critics of Christianity* groups. Members of the *Christianity as unevolved* group tend to favor the latter, while members of *Christians as political oppressors* favor the former. This appears to be an important way to differentiate between the two groups. Both groups have animosity toward Christians, but those who tend to belong to the *Christianity as unevolved* group have anger toward how the practice of Christianity is used to limit progress in society, while those embarrassed by the political aspects of Christianity are linked to the *Christians as political oppressors* subgroup. This may be the defining feature that separates the two groups since there is a powerful correlation ($r = .885$) between the degree to which an individual belongs to the *Christianity as unevolved* group and the degree to which an individual belongs to the *Christians as political oppressors* group.

Like members of the previous *critics of Christianity* subgroup, the members of this group are more likely to label themselves as Christians relative to other respondents. Furthermore, individuals in both groups are also less likely to be atheists or agnostic than other respondents. However, the *Christians as political oppressors* group is also less likely to have atheists in their current social networks, and the *critics of Christianity* category seems particularity adept at attracting Christians who are concerned about the type of Christianity practiced by the Christian right. Conservative Christianity may produce its own worst critics. Hostility toward fundamentalists for *Christians as political oppressors* is not due to an aversion to religion in general, but rather it is due to the unique application of religion in fundamentalist Christianity. The political aspects inherent within critics of Christianity indicate that they likely tie that fundamentalist religious expression to political conservatism, which is a big determinant of their hostility.

Conclusion

The motivations of those who oppose the Christian right can vary greatly. By its very name, the Christian right can be conceptualized as both a religious and a political group. Thus, we broke down the motivations for opposing them into religious and political arenas. However, even with this breakdown there was, with some exceptions, a great deal of overlap between the two sources of motivation. That is, there are religious elements in the opposition of some of those whose opposition is largely politically motivated (especially among the *sexual progressives* and the *feminists*), and there are political elements among those who oppose the Christian right for largely religious reasons (especially those who fall into the *critics of Christianity* category). The Christian right may be understandably categorized as a group whereby religious conservatism and political conservatism tend to feed into each other. It may be an oversimplification to seek motivation that is either purely religious or purely political. However, the analyses conducted on these variables do indicate that religious or political dynamics can be the dominant source of the motivation of individuals to oppose the Christian right, even if there are other elements in that opposition that are not purely religious or political.

While there are distinctions between the motivations of cultural progressive activists, there are also important social ties that help to produce compliance among them. For example, the image of politically active conservative Christians helps shape the emergent norms that develop among our respondents regardless of the motivations that drive them. This allows cultural progressive activists to benefit from having a common enemy who is seen as the originator of the problems that they seek to deal with. It also allows cultural progressive activists to see themselves as victims—a useful collective action frame by which they can make demands upon society. This is a sample that is more white, educated, male, and wealthy than the general population, suggesting that in almost every way cultural progressive activists are a group that enjoys societal advantage. Yet their political and/or religious standing provides for them the claim of marginal status regardless of the societal advantages they already enjoy. Rejection of Christianity can clearly be seen as a minority position in a society where Christianity is clearly the most influential religious force. Even though the United States is now led by a politically progressive president, eight years of a Bush White House provided justification for political progressives to have perceived themselves as marginalized as well. Regardless of the exact source of their motivation, we can expect collective norms to have developed that will allow the members of the cultural left to legitimate their claims of victimization and the need to be protected from the excesses of the Christian right.

Much of the assessment of this chapter is speculation. Such speculation is unavoidable when dealing with quantitative methods. Quantitative methods are valuable for helping us to see generalizable trends but do not always inform us about the processes that are behind these trends. However, in the next three chapters we will put a qualitative face on these speculations. We will look more at what the respondents actually said in an effort to illustrate some of these speculations and to help us better understand how cultural progressive activists perceive society and their adversaries—the Christian right.

CHAPTER 4

*Political Concerns and
Cultural Progressive Activists*

In theory, there are two major reasons why individuals oppose the Christian right. First, they oppose the political agenda of the Christian right. Second, they oppose the religious nature of the Christian right. In reality, we found that many of our respondents combined both political and religious animosity in discussing their opposition to the Christian right. Disentangling political versus religiously motivated opposition is not always possible with some respondents. However, it is useful to break down the opposition into its most basic elements of political and religious motivations. This helps to simplify why opposition has developed and enables us to understand certain elements that motivate cultural progressive activists. In this chapter we explore the political motivations enunciated by the opponents of the Christian right. In the following two chapters we examine the religiously inspired reasons for this opposition.

Even though we present only one chapter on political reasons for some individuals opposing the Christian right, rather than two chapters as for religious reasons, this is not to imply that political opposition is less important than religious opposition. However, some individuals grounded their religious opposition in the fact that religion even exists, regardless of the conservative type of

Christianity practiced by members of the Christian right. None of our respondents argued that political activism should not be practiced at all, but those who were concerned politically were upset at the particular political goals of the Christian right. As such, there is need for only one chapter to explore the political motivation of respondents, while differing religious perspectives made it necessary for two chapters dealing with religious motivations.

In the first part of the chapter we discuss the process by which we determined the political categories.[1] Next we explore, one at a time, the *political activist*, *sexual progressive*, and *feminist* categories. Using answers to the questionnaire, we provide explicit examples of the major concepts that make up each of these groups. Then we look at some of the primary literature read by cultural progressive activists and indicate how the ideas that sustain these political motivations are motivated by formal in-group support. Finally, we summarize our discussion of the political motivations of cultural progressives before moving on to the next two chapters to discuss religious motivations.

Determining the Categories

As noted in the previous chapter, we coded the open-ended responses and created a series of dichotomous variables with our codes. Then we used factor analysis to determine the characteristics of the subgroups that emerged from the data.[2] This technique led to an important challenge as we analyzed the data. As we looked at each subgroup we limited ourselves to only the respondents who were included in a given subgroup. In other words, if a respondent's answers provided a higher score for *Christianity as unevolved* than for *political activist*, then we use that respondent's answers only when discussing the *Christianity as unevolved* subgroup. The problem with such an approach is that there is a great deal of overlap among the seven groups. Table 4.1 includes the correlations of the factor loadings of each subgroup and not the dichotomous indicators of whether an individual belonged in a subgroup. In this table we can clearly see that these factors are highly correlated. This is especially true as it concerns the variables within each grouping. For example, the variables relying on political concerns are all highly correlated, with the lowest correlations being between *political activist* and *sexual progressives* at .407. *Religion is poison* is correlated to *religion has been corrupted* at .165, which is relatively low but still significant. However, *Christianity as unevolved* and *Christians as political oppressors* are highly correlated at .885. Furthermore, we find some powerful correlations between the groupings. For example, *political activist* is correlated to *Christianity as unevolved* at .742, *religion has been corrupted* is correlated to *Christianity as unevolved* at .648, and *political activist* is correlated to *Christians as political oppressors* at .630. *Religion is poison* appears to be the only factor that is not highly correlated to other factors, but for the most part the factors are clearly connected to one another.

TABLE 4.1
Correlations of Different Groups of Cultural Progressives

	1	2	3	4	5	6	7
1. Political activist	—	.407[b]	.625[b]	−.002	.152[b]	.742[b]	.630[b]
2. Cultural warrior		—	.626[b]	−.076[b]	.018	.268[b]	.239[b]
3. Feminist			—	−.027	.080[a]	.436[b]	.367[b]
4. Religion is poison				—	.165[b]	.025	.007
5. Religion has been corrupted					—	.648[b]	.614[b]
6. Christianity is unevolved						—	.885[b]
7. Christians as political oppressors							—

[a] – Correlation is significant at the .05 level; [b] – Correlation is signficant at the .01 level.
N = 2,816.

Given this reality, we believe that the best explanation for the subgroups is that they represent certain focuses within cultural progressive activists but are not mutually exclusive. In fact, most respondents answered questions in such a way that they scored in multiple subgroups. A respondent in the *Christianity as unevolved* subgroup likely also thinks along the lines of those in the *political activist* subgroup, as the .742 correlation strongly suggests. For this reason, we believe it to be artificial to strictly limit ourselves to only those who were placed within a subgroup for our analysis, although using these subgroups to find representative respondents cannot be totally discounted. Therefore, as we present each subgroup we will attempt to limit ourselves to the comments of those within the categories we are discussing, although we understand that this will not always be feasible, and it is particularly difficult with some of the smaller categories. In those cases, we freely used the comments of all our respondents since we know many of these categories are correlated to each other and the difference between being in one of the categories instead of another is often due to a slightly higher score in the included category. These subgroups represent prevailing trends within the entire group, although some individuals may have few or none of the attributes of certain categories while others have a great deal of a category's characteristics. The only real exception to this is the *religion is poison* group, and we will limit, although do not eliminate, our use of individuals who are not in that group as we discuss the *religion is poison* group. We signal when we are using all respondents by stating whether we are looking at the respondents in general or are quoting only respondents of a particular subgroup in advance of the quotations.

Political Activist

The *political activists* have a very basic motivation for opposition to the Christian right. Their motivation is that members of the Christian right are on the wrong side of the conservative/progressive political debate. Respondents in this subgroup have a progressive political perspective and appear to have little patience for those with more conservative political perspectives.

They advocate foreign and domestic political actions based on mythology that seriously threatens happiness and global peace. (male, 56–65, doctorate)

[B]y putting all their money, influence on the Bush administration, they forgot about the poor. (female, 66–75, master's degree)

I also feel this group has been co-opted by power-seeking business and political interests as an easy target base for support. Generally I am tired of and frustrated by the "dumb-ing down" effect of their involvement in political and social discourse. (female, 26–35, bachelor's degree)

Their political agenda and social goals exceed their ability to understand the complexities of the modern world and they respond with dangerous programs and beliefs. (male, 56–65, some graduate training)

I've had recent debates with a good friend, a conservative Catholic, on topics such as abortion, national politics, decriminalization of marijuana. In all of these, her dogmatic beliefs severely skew her thinking. I find it highly annoying that she is so illogical in her reasoning. (female, 36–45, doctorate)

Publicly conservative moral and financial values (but frequently hypocritical or secretly corrupt), and eager to impose their will on everyone else. (male, 46–55, some graduate training)

As suggested by these quotes, individuals with this motivation have a hard time understanding how individuals can hold onto political ideas that differ from a progressive viewpoint. They learn to mistrust the judgment of individuals who support nonprogressive political perspectives. The degree of their mistrust is such that they are often hesitant to live in neighborhoods with individuals who promote conservative political perspectives or political perspectives that are generated by religious ideology. When we asked respondents in this category about their comfort regarding living in a neighborhood with many Christian right members, some of them pointed to the political changes that would occur in the neighborhood as a reason why such neighbors are undesirable.

They are [living in the neighborhood], it does [bother me]. Because I cannot depend upon them to vote or make choices that affect me based on logic. (male, 56–65, doctorate)

[T]hey would become a sounding board, "yes men," for each other, and without a critical mass of contrary voices around to rebut them, they'd elect officials and pass laws that were exclusive and contrary to freedom, religious and otherwise. Of course, even if there were enough other voices, I've already decided that I think the Christian Right doesn't listen to anyone that doesn't agree with them anyway, so there really is no debate with them, which is unfortunate. (male, 26–35, bachelor's degree)

It would bother me considerably, as it would undoubtedly affect the political climate of my community adversely. (female, 66–75, master's degree)

Because they would be trying to dictate what is being taught in our schools, what pharmacists may sell and to whom and they would support extremely conservative politicians. (male, 66–75, doctorate)

It [having Christian right living in the neighborhood] would bother me 100 percent—since I view them as untrustworthy and dangerous to political stability. (male, 66–75, some college)

[T]he local laws enacted would likely be hostile towards myself and invited visitors to my residence. In addition, I would be fearful of my property being vandalized if I were to be recognized as a non-Christian who is against their use of government to try to control my life. (male, 26–35, some graduate training)

It is clear that these respondents fear the political changes that having Christian right neighbors would bring to their lives. While not all respondents had such a fear of the Christian right at the local level, there was a common theme that the politics of the Christian right simply makes life worse for society. The Christian right is seen as a problem since it is a movement that helps to generate and sustain conservative political ideology. These cultural progressive activists are concerned about the manner in which the Christian right provides support for a conservative political philosophy. Several of them were quite specific as to how the Christian right aids conservative political positions. Members of this subgroup clearly perceived the Christian right as providing religious justification for political conservatism.

> Their theology has been hijacked by right-wing politicians for their right-wing political agenda. This interferes with having a valid theology, because Christian Right preachers and organizations abuse theological values in pursuit of their political agendas. I'm sorry they have sacrificed valid beliefs for simple-minded rigidity, and I'm sorry they have been co-opted or hijacked for war, guns, anti-woman positions, etc. (male, 56–65, master's degree)

> A group that depends on a literal interpretation of the bible to define their political positions. . . . Their religious and political beliefs end up hurting people and destroying ecological systems. (female, 56–65, some graduate training)

> . . . cites the validity of their Christian faith in defense of "conservative" political actions (defined as supporting federal/state/local governmental restriction on personal behavior considered "immoral" in their faith, including but certainly not limited to: homosexuality, seeking abortions, or public displays of non-christian faith or nonfaith). (male, 26–35, master's degree)

> A belief that a selfish, consumeristic form of free-market capitalism is the god-ordained way to live. This allows them to justify all types of self-serving behavior that harms the poor and needy in our country. (male, 36–45, bachelor's degree)

Respondents in the subgroup often perceive supporters of conservative political ideology as blinded to its potential effects. This is particularly the case as it pertains to their image of individuals with lower levels of education or SES. Such individuals are seen as supporting policies that keep them poor and uneducated. Supporters of the Christian right can be seen as victims of the results of political conservatism, even as they provide the human power necessary to impose that conservatism on the rest of the country. As such, several respondents from the entire sample contended that individuals who support conservative political perspectives often advance ideas that worked against their own personal interest.

> Their ignorance and willingness to act against their own interests will eventually doom them. (male, 46–55, master's degree)

> A hypocritical money-making political machine pushing an agenda of bigotry and intolerance on undereducated people, against their best interest. . . . An economically underprivileged woman who was still going to vote for Bush, obviously against her own best interest, simply because he opposed abortion. (female, 36–45, master's degree)

> The Republican Party uses religion (esp. Christianity) to control people and fool them into voting against their best interests. (male, 36–45, master's degree)

> They want to impose their irrational concepts (dogma, theology) on other people. They let their leaders, who I think may often be corrupt, lead the members against their own best interests. (male, 66–75, doctorate)

> My sister-in-law is (was) a very intelligent woman. Joining her boyfriend's fundie church at a low, scary point in her life has convinced her to stop thinking for herself and adopt opinions that are totally against her own self interest. (female, 56–65, bachelor's degree)

Since respondents who hold to a *political activist* perspective tend to be more highly educated than other individuals, they may have a tendency to perceive members of the Christian right as uninformed about the social and economic reality around them. This can lead them to developing a premise that membership in the Christian right promotes an ignorance of important political issues and leads individuals to reject the progressive political positions they tend to support.

Such a possibility fits right in with the tendency of *political activists* to complain about the hostility members of the Christian right have against science. The perception of the Christian right's animosity toward science is repeatedly exhibited by many respondents in this subgroup.

> They are anti-science, anti-reason, anti-evolution and often anti-common sense. They cling to outmoded beliefs in spite of all evidence, scientific or otherwise. (male, 46–55, doctorate)

> Yes. I perceive that the Christian Right is anti-intellectual, i.e., the Right is anti-science (evolution, stem cell research, environmental change, etc.), not accepting of differing philosophical views and intent on telling others how to live a meaningful life. Most important is using "the pulpit" to effect political change. (male, 66–75, master's degree)

> Destructive to democracy, poisonous to politics and an erosive process in education, science in general and particularly to the biological sciences. (male, 46–55, doctorate)

> Fostering attitudes of anti-intellectualism, a strong anti-science agenda, appealing to the lowest common denominator. (male, 26–35, bachelor's degree)

> I think it child abuse to insist that they be taught anti-science, and to rely on others' interpretations of scripture instead of thinking for themselves. (male, 36–45, some college)

Of course the study of science is a key value found among educators. Given the relatively high number of doctorates in the general sample, it is likely that many of them are educators. Furthermore, even those respondents who are not directly responsible for the education of students may place a high value on education as a way to understand society and politics. For this reason, the fact that many respondents were frightened by the influence of the Christian right in our educational system should be expected. But beyond education, we can also see that respondents desire to see science and scientific thinking as part of the political and/or public decisions made in our society. Their perception of the refusal of the Christian right to take science seriously has important ramifications for the political direction of our society. This can be an important reason why some activists are concerned about the lack of support of science that members of the Christian right often generates.

As stated earlier, education has been linked to political progressiveness. Whether education produces politically progressive attitudes or whether there is a self-selection effect whereby political progressives tend to seek more education than political conservatives is an argument for another day. However, the relationship between education and political progressiveness indicates a large subgroup in the United States that would perceive any diminution of education due to the efforts of the Christian right as problematic. It may not only be problematic for the obvious reasons of interfering with our education system but also be troublesome since it may rob educators of the power to promote politically progressive ideas. This potential is true regardless of whether education directly promotes politically progressive ideas or if it acts as a self-selection screen whereby political progressives make educational gains more rapidly than political conservatives, gaining a greater ability to use education to achieve higher status positions in society. The promotion of such ideas is not the intended purpose of the education system. But we have already established that for certain cultural progressive activists, politically progressive ideology is extremely important, and such a threat to education would also threaten the promotion of their political ideals.

While there is a generalized concern about a rightward political drift, individual issues do not dominate the perspectives of the *political activists*. Even the discussions of education and science can be seen as more general concerns than concerns about specific issues. Educational and scientific issues are linked to larger concerns about the overall political climate of the society. However, it was clear that for some individuals specific issues were more important than the overarching political climate. Indeed, it may be that for such individuals the overarching political climate is important insofar as it helps them to fight for certain political realities. The next two subgroups are excellent examples of this perspective.

Sexual Progressive

One of the biggest issues of contention between cultural progressive activists and cultural conservative activists is sexuality. Cultural progressive activists envision sexuality as being determined by individual choice. The role of society is to make the decision as easy for individuals as possible. Cultural conservative activists envision sexuality issues as individuals' desires being secondary to societal concerns. Traditional mores of procreative, instead of recreational, sex drive such norms. This leads to conflicting ideas in the cultural war. Those for whom issues of sexual lifestyle are important and who take a progressive position can emerge in the cultural war as a *sexual progressive*. Issues of abortion provide a freedom from the potential costs of childbearing, which allows for more sexual freedom. Issues of homosexuality are linked to notions of sexual experimentation and individualized sexuality. These concerns were often stated by the respondents, and those in this subgroup were especially worried about the effect the Christian right has on these issues. The ability of the Christian right to create political barriers to sexual freedom is the key motivation for respondents in the *sexual progressive* subgroup.

As stated in chapter 3, members of this subgroup are less likely than other cultural progressive activists to have members of the Christian right in their social networks. This lack of influence by members of the Christian right can lead to a propensity among the members of this subgroup to create excessively hostile images of their cultural opponents. For some respondents, the Christian right is seen as the opponent of all that is good in society. The respondents in the subgroup are even more explicit about their perception of the Christian right as an enemy than the other respondents. Note how freely these respondents use the term *enemy* to describe the Christian right.

> It is good to keep an eye on the enemy. (female, 46–55, bachelor's degree)

> Their desire to overtake the government and force their beliefs on others has motivated me to get involved and fight against their influence. (male, 36–45, master's degree)

> They are my enemy. (female, 36–45, bachelor's degree)

They are as much of a threat to American freedoms and ideals as any foreign enemy. They have infiltrated every facet of American society and politics from the grassroots level to the White House, more often than not in violation of our Constitution. (male, 66–75, bachelor's degree)

They are the enemy of all I believe in. They are the greatest threat to the country. (male, 56–65, doctorate)

They are THE MOST DANGEROUS ENEMY of America today. They threaten our founding principles, modern thought, and intellectual progress. They are Enemy #1 of all of humanity. They are worst {sic} than Al-Qaeda because they have captured the American Flag and the word "patriotism" to hide their destructive agenda. At least A-Q has honestly stated their intentions towards us. "When Fascism comes to America, it will wrapped in the Flag and carrying the Cross." The difference between them (the Bibleban) and the Taliban is only one of degree, not of kind. (male, 56–65, some graduate training; emphasis in original)

The enemy. I hate them. (female, 66–75, doctorate)

While other respondents can envision the Christian right as an enemy for a variety of reasons, the members of this subgroup tend to concentrate on the traditional sexual mores pushed by members of the Christian right. This conflict over sexuality combined with the relative isolation that members of this group have from individuals in the Christian right seems to have heightened the idea that the Christian right is an enemy needing to be vanquished.

It is clear why we have named this group *sexual progressives*. They take special care in protecting sexuality issues from undue influence by members of the Christian right. These sexuality issues are seen in the political issues of abortion and homosexuality. Previous work (Dillon, 1996; Mazur, 1997) has documented that these issues are central to the concerns of the Christian right as they threaten the traditional social order with which they have become comfortable. Some members of this group may have had abortions or engage in homosexuality. But we do not contend that the members of this subgroup are merely looking out for their personal sexual desires.

Rather, we argue that the promotion of abortion and homosexuality represents their desire to replace traditional social and sexual mores with ones shaped by a modernist or postmodernist perspective, regardless of whether they engage in modernist sexuality practices or not. Indeed, some respondents in the general sample indicated support for progressive sexuality political issues even though they stated that they themselves were not homosexuals or seeking abortions.

> Anti-gay yelling in church-2xs (I am not gay, but would not feel ashamed if I were) in group meetings. (female, 56–65, master's degree)

> While it hasn't affected me personally, I hope that a woman will continue to have abortion rights. (female, 56–65, some college)

> I would like to know why they discriminate against gays and want to deny them the rights that other Americans have. I'm not gay but I enjoy a marriage and don't understand how they can be denied the same rights that I have. (female, 46–55, high school diploma)

> I would hope that abortion would never be needed but no one should be able to tell another how to live, including lifestyles. (male, 56–65, some graduate training)

Furthermore, several respondents argued that members of the Christian right had the freedom not to engage in modern sexuality themselves but that they should not seek to stop others from doing so. The problem is not whether members of the Christian right want to participate in a more sexually open society but in providing religious individuals with the political power to impose their will on others. Rather than merely living out their own lives, the Christian right is seen as seeking to force others to live out conservative Christian values. As such, respondents in the general sample indicated a desire to promote reproductive and sexual freedom and believe that the right laws can accomplish this without interfering with the rights of those in the Christian right.

> Believe as you wish, but stay out of politics. I would never force a member of the Christian right to get an abortion, or force a fundamentalist church to marry gays if they didn't want to do so—so why do they want to try to force their beliefs on me by passing laws that reflect their religious views? (female, 56–65, master's degree)

> These laws actually would not affect the Christian Right as they can make a personal choice not to have abortions or marry a same-sex partner, and they can teach alternative creation theories at home. i.e. The availability of abortion, gay marriage, or evolution studies does not directly affect them. (male, 46–55, bachelor's degree)

> *Roe v. Wade* and the legality of same sex marriage do not impinge on the rights of the CR (no one is forcing them to have an abortion or marry a gay or lesbian). (female, 56–65, bachelor's degree)

These respondents exhibit sympathy for those who are affected by political issues of abortion and homosexuality. They attempt to empathize with such individuals. In theory, such individuals may support these sexuality issues out of such empathy rather than out of hostility toward political conservatives.

While individuals throughout the entire sample indicated a preference for modern notions of sexuality as opposed to traditional norms, individuals in the *sexual progressive* subgroup were more likely to bring up these issues than other cultural progressive activists. Furthermore, they indicated less confidence that the Christian right could be trusted to allow individuals to practice whatever form of individualized sexuality they desired. They envisioned the Christian right as a group that was angry at the emerging sexuality norms and desired to impose their outdated sexual norms because of that anger and hatred. Thus, respondents in the *sexual progressive* subgroup were also more likely than other respondents to attribute hatred as the motivation that Christians use to justify their political actions.

> They are just as much a group of zealous hate mongers and just as violent as the al queda {sic} who used the word of their god to

kill thousands on Americans on September 11th. (male, 36–45, bachelor's degree)

For a religion that is supposed to espouse love and acceptance as Jesus does in the New Testament they sure seem to hate a lot and wish whole groups of peoples to hell. (male, 46–55, master's degree)

Their faith, hope, and love are extremely misguided based upon what their faith dictates. Instead, their values turns into the opposite of what they aspire to. Their hope turns into fear, their faith turns into ignorance, and their love turns into hate. (male, 18–25, bachelor's degree)

The Christian Right are hate-mongers whose beliefs promote poverty, sickness and loss of empowerment for many while privileging the few who share these hate-mongering beliefs. (male, 26–35, master's degree)

I believe they are hateful, and want a society similar to Hitler's vision. (male, 56–65, doctorate)

The use of the concept of hate by these respondents engenders an emotional appeal in their opposition to the Christian right. There was generally a more emotionally suspicious attitude toward the Christian right among those in the *sexual progressive* group as opposed to the rest of the sample. They showed a significant concern that the Christian right will seek power to rob others of their political and sexual rights. They exhibited a powerful fear that if the Christian right got its way then individuals would not be able to practice modernist sexual norms. It was the interference of the Christian right that so many of them objected to. This fear of political interference produced within many respondents in this group a wariness of the violations of church and state that members of the Christian right seek to engage in.

[The Christian right's] desire to install a Christian government and to make belief in Christianity a litmus test for political acceptance. (male, 56–65, bachelor's degree)

> The lie about the US being a "Christian Nation" when the 1797 Congress clearly states it is not. . . . They do not care there are some eighty million members of other religions and over 25 million Atheists living in the US. (male, 66–75, some college)
>
> Pushing their religious doctrine into gov't building and public places and into schools. (female, 56–65, bachelor's degree)
>
> Using the Bible to push anti-choice legislation, compulsory prayer, public religious displays and destroying the wall of separation. (male, 56–65, some college)

Sexual progressive frames the tendency of Christians to oppose certain political issues as an expression of hatred and a desire to take over the society. Members of this subgroup see the possibility of a replacement of modern sexual norms with traditionalist norms driven by hatred and misguided political power that is propelled by religion. These respondents are concerned not just with looking for reproductive rights or sexual freedom for themselves but these issues represent larger arguments about social order and who is to establish that order. The social order proposed by the Christian right is seen as one of hated and intolerance, and thus these respondents want to limit the ability of those in the Christian right to establish social and sexual mores for the rest of society.

While abortion and homosexuality can both be considered important symbols in the battle over sexuality, the way they play out in that battle is similar but not identical. We noted different approaches toward these issues among the respondents. As it concerns abortion, respondents in the *sexual progressive* group envisioned a violent takeover by the Christian right. Abortion clinics often were used as symbols to illustrate that takeover. When asked about personal encounters with the Christian right, several respondents recounted stories about the battles they had with demonstrators at abortion clinics.

> Acting as an escort at an abortion clinic, I was faced by a mob of screaming people calling the woman trying to enter the clinic a murderer, showing her blown up pictures of aborted fetuses,

> screaming horrible things. It was all I could do not to scream back and punch someone. (female, 66–75, bachelor's degree)
>
> I worked clinic defense at the '92 Democratic Convention in NYC for a 10-day stretch and I was very fearful of the violence by the time it was over. (male, 46–55, bachelor's degree)
>
> Abortion clinic escort volunteer—weekly face to face confrontations. These experiences really lead me to despise this faction. (female, 46–55, doctorate)
>
> Abortion protestors protesting around abortion provider's facilities when I had a pregnancy termination. I was angry that they felt they knew what was better for me and my life than I. I didn't bother to debate them, just went on with my procedure but I did not appreciate the hassle. (female, 26–35, doctorate)

If such events are the first thing one thinks of when asked about encounters with the Christian right, then it is not surprising that hostility toward Christian right members is commonplace. In such encounters, the demonstrators are easily distilled into a common stereotype of angry Christians and can be dismissed.

When asked about possible laws to deal with the Christian right, a very small percentage (1.0 percent) offered the possibility of laws to protect abortion clinics. However, this question was designed to allow the respondents to come up with their own ideas without prompting. Thus, it is likely that a much higher percentage would happily support such laws if specifically asked. If that is true, then the following statements from those in the *sexual progressive* group in response to that question may indicate a valid representation of the attitudes many of them have about abortion clinics. As we can see, this is particularly relevant to females in this group.

> With respect to a woman's right to choose, we need to ensure that the law of land is upheld and that women are not harassed when they try to seek an abortion. (female, 46–55, master's degree)

> The exception would be Hate Crimes and laws. If they break those laws, I think they need to be punished severely. I'm thinking of that picketing at abortion clinics, at shootings at churches, at driving around with hate slogans on their cars. (female, 66–75, some graduate training)

> The only law we should be talking about is upholding the laws in the constitution that give women the right to privacy, and to protect women who go to clinics seeking medical help. There is no reason these protesters should be allowed to disrupt, harass and intimidate women seeking medical help. It is not protesting, it is domestic terrorism. If they were unable to protest it would help so much to take away the limelight they crave. I would love a law that would ban protesting around abortion and planned parenthood clinics. (female, 46–55, master's degree)

> Laws creating safe access to family planning clinics seem fair to me. (female, 26–35, master's degree)

> I do not wish for laws that tell people what to think and feel, but I do think some of their activities (e.g., preventing women from entering abortion clinics) should be given stricter laws. (female, 46–55, bachelor's degree)

Abortion clinics may have great symbolic value for those in the *sexual progressive* group as they represent social spaces that need protection. Thus, demonstrations against these clinics can strike at the very heart of some cultural progressive activists as they indicate that cultural progressives cannot be safe even within institutions they highly value. If this is the case, then there is little wonder why cultural progressive activists are particularly concerned about demonstrations against abortion clinics.

While abortion clinics represent institutions under attack from the Christian right, issues of homosexuality become more personalized for some cultural progressive activists. We did not ask the respondents to identify their sexual preference; however, many of them did so nonetheless.[3] Among those in the general sample who did, there was a powerful concern among them about the willingness of the Christian right to impinge on their rights.

> I would expect them to be hostile to me and/or harass me, if they knew I was gay and agnostic. (male, 56–65, doctorate)
>
> I am gay and feel the Christian Right, if successful politically, would remove my rights not only as a citizen, but as a human being. (male, 46–55, bachelor's degree)
>
> I . . . live in Texas where it is actually illegal for us to be married. My cousin, another born again, told me that she wished I wasn't gay, and my dad who is borderline born again didn't show up to our wedding. My partner and I have been together for 10 years and had the support and love of all these people until suddenly we raised "the issue." (male, 36–45, bachelor's degree)
>
> A preacher for the Church of Christ told me that I was going to hell if I continued in my homosexual behavior. . . . All people should have the same civil rights but the Christian right wants to incarcerate gay and lesbian people. (male, 66–75, master's degree)
>
> I'm gay for one. According to them I should be either in denial and get married or I should be penalized legally by having my personal freedoms taken away. (male, 56–65, some graduate training)

A common theme among many individuals was a desire for social distance from the Christian right. They perceived the Christian right as homophobes who did not care for them. Therefore, they did not care for the Christian right. This theme was advanced not simply by those who identified themselves as homosexuals. Several individuals in the *sexual progressive* group who did not indicate their sexual preference, or who indicated that they were not homosexual, also objected to the Christian right based on the idea that it is a social group that seeks to rob homosexuals of their rights.

> Let's start with denying equal rights under the law to gays. (If God hates fags, why does He keep making so many of them? And, no, I am not gay and I am married.) (male, 56–65, some graduate training)

> I am pro-choice and in favor of gay marriage, and I am furious that the religious right wants no one to enjoy these rights, simply because they are against them. (male, 46–55, bachelor's degree)
>
> I believe that laws should allow everyone the right to follow their beliefs as long as they don't infringe on anyone else's. For example, I don't understand how allowing gays to marry infringes on Christians' marriages. (male, 36–45, master's degree)
>
> Gay marriage is a great example. Their God doesn't approve of it, so they are against it. I feel sorry for them that they are under an obligation to accept a story book as a foundation for law. I'm also afraid of the political power they seem to have possession of, so much so that they can enforce their ideology. (male, 36–45, bachelor's degree)

These quotes may indicate a reason why those in the *sexual progressive* group have relatively few born-again Christians in their social networks. They perceive a homophobia from religious individuals that is personally distasteful to them. This homophobia is generally connected to conservative Protestants or those who see themselves as "born-again." Their desire may be for more than political separation, including also personal separation from those who would take away the rights of others. For them, the homophobia of the Christian right may be equated to the racism of the white supremacist and creates a distaste for personal contact.

The *sexual progressive* subgroup clearly conceptualizes encounters with the Christian right as battles and sees the Christian right as the aggressor. The Christian right is either seeking to invade the protected social spaces of cultural progressives, as with abortion clinics, or seeking to rob certain cultural progressives, such as homosexuals, of their rights. As such, the issues of abortion and homosexuality are similar in that they are conceptualized as evidence that members of the Christian right are invaders or, dare we say it, crusaders. However, abortion may be more about issues of the sanctity of public spaces, while homosexuality is about the rights of citizens. As we have noted, this aggressor status is not limited to political issues as the *sexual progressives* also maintain a social distance from the

Christian right. One potential reason is the distaste for some of the political issues espoused by the Christian right. However, we also noted another reason for this personal distance. The *sexual progressives* also are more likely than other respondents to object to the tendency of Christians to engage in proselytizing.

> I would be annoyed by any proselytizing by the vocal Christian. (male, over 75, doctorate)

> I also have a huge issue with the aggressive proselytizing (as in, trying to convert) and preaching (just attacking rather than trying to convert). (female, 36–45, some college)

> I encounter them regularly and they are entitled to their beliefs as long as they don't proselytize or try to impinge upon my rights. (female, 46–55, bachelor's degree)

> I don't care what others believe as long as they do not try to legislate their beliefs on me or try to proselytize me personally. (female, 66–75, some college)

> . . . sexually repressed, superstitious, proselytizing hypocrites. (male, 66–75, some graduate training)

These comments indicate that for the *sexual progressives* proselytizing is rude at best and perhaps should be illegal at worst. This proselytizing may not be limited to merely attempts to convert individuals to one's religion. Activity in opposition to abortion and same-sex marriage can be seen as attempts of the Christian right to impose their political will upon the general population. As such, proselytizing can be seen as attempts to impose their religious will on that population as well. Such proselytizing can be seen as efforts to influence others to reject modern sexuality norms and produce less support for the progressive sexuality supported by members of this subgroup. This may be why proselytizing may be more offensive to members of this subgroup than other cultural progressive activists. Having members of the Christian right in their subgroup may produce more opportunities for proselytizing and is more of an unpleasant reminder of the presence of traditional sexual norms.

It became clear how belonging to the *sexual progressive* subgroup plays an important factor in why individuals choose to oppose the Christian right. They resent the influence of the Christian right to shape our sexual mores as they envision inclusive sexual mores as better for society. The combination of political activism and traditional religious values is a potent force that threatens modern sexuality values. Just as some cultural conservatives may be "single-issue" candidates (e.g., abortion or homosexuality), some of these respondents may find their motivation located almost totally within their understanding of these sexuality issues.

Feminist

A final category that focuses upon political concerns is one we label *feminist*. According to table 3.3 it is the smallest of the political categories, and an examination of the interviews tends to confirm that this category is not as prominent as the other political categories. However, this does not mean that it is an unimportant category. We have already noted previous research suggesting that conservative Christians are more likely to have patriarchal attitudes than other individuals. The respondents in general seem knowledgeable about such research and perceive the Christian right as a group motivated by sexism and the disempowerment of women.

> They perpetuate archaic structures (sexism, racism, ethnic chauvinism, faith-based logics) of social divisiveness that undermine human unity necessary to correct contemporary problems. (female, 46–55, master's degree)

> I find them to be sexist, often working to undermine women's right to choose and working against LGBT rights. . . . I also feel that the power of the patriarchy, which is so apparent among the Christian Right, creates an environment where children and women often suffer abuse—all in the name of Christianity. (male, 36–45, some college)

> A culture of patriarchs and authority figures pervades the Christian Right. One bible study leader was dismissive of anything I said, publicly said men should lie to their wives about their

> pasts, and refused to give women any modicum of power in class. (male, 26–35, some graduate training)

> They seek to use the power of the state to enforce religious patriarchy, oppress women, reduce individual choice, deny science. (male, 56–65, doctorate)

However, understanding the research about religion and patriarchy by itself may not always be a sufficient motivator for respondents to oppose the Christian right. For some respondents, their own personal experiences may serve to encourage them to oppose the Christian right. They have personally seen examples that reinforce the connection between the Christian right and sexism. There are two ways in which this type of personal experience may have an effect. First, this reinforcement may occur because of what the respondents have actually suffered.

> When I was 16, I wanted to become a pastor. I was told by my pastor at the time that I could not pursue this goal because I was female and because it was wrong for women to preach or speak to a congregation of men. From then on, I built up a strong skepticism against organized Christianity. (female, 26–35, some graduate training)

> I was told, with finger pointed, that I had no right to call myself a Christian when I took issue with Paul's admonition about women submitting to their husbands. The issue was who makes decisions and I said we made decisions together and was told I was wrong. When I was told I had no right to be teaching Bible in a Methodist church because I did not believe in inerrancy, a stand the Methodists have never taken. (female, over 75, some graduate training)

> When my mother told me that anyone that has an abortion should be murdered just like their child was. I did nothing but try not to blurt out that I should be dead because I have had an abortion. (female, 26–35, bachelor's degree)

> As a teenager I asked a Catholic priest why I could not be an altar server and he indicated that I could not because I was female. I

immediately felt unwelcome and have felt that way ever since. (female, 26–35, master's degree)

Such experiences likely have a powerful effect on the respondents' perspectives. In all of these circumstances, the females felt victimized. It is natural that individuals want to distance themselves from those they fear will victimize them, and this helps to indicate how some females have feminist notions that lead them to mistrust the Christian right. But it is also possible that the respondents may have witnessed examples of sexism as it happened to other women. This is the second way that personal experiences are a powerful motivating factor for members in the *feminist* subgroup.

> The service was all scripture reading, seven or so with only two from the New Testament. All those quoted were admonitions to the bride to be obedient and subservient. I knew this woman and had worked with her for seven years. It bothered me to see such a person reducing herself to an extension of someone else. This same woman once explained to me that she believed the Earth to be only thousands of years old. And yet she worked in a technical capacity, writing software. That told me that the Christian Fundamentalists have a powerful ability to disassociate themselves from and ignore realities which might contradict even the slightest portion of their creed. I found this to be a self imposed delusion which scared me. (male, 36–45, bachelor's degree)

> Attending a fundamentalist wedding ceremony and causing the woman to submit and obey. (male, over 75, doctorate)

> On a couples retreat from the church, a man stated that his wife could not attain salvation on her own; she had to go through him! I know the Bible enough to "tear him a new one," and I think he was sorry he opened his mouth. (female, 66–75, some college)

> I was having a discussion with some women friends about feminism (I was/am pro) when a CR woman started screaming at me about how the Bible says that women must subjugate themselves to their husbands. Her anger surprised me at the time but looking back but not so much now. She probably felt that if she had to

be under somebody's thumb, then dammit so should every other woman! (female, 56–65, bachelor's degree)

In these situations the respondent was not personally victimized, but he or she had empathy for women who may be victimized. While this may not create the same type of personal motivation to remove oneself from the presence of the Christian right, it does frame that group as dangerous. Such a frame clearly provides motivation to join a group opposed to the Christian right.

Regardless of whether it is from experiences or research, there clearly is a small but important subgroup of cultural progressive activists who oppose the Christian right because of gender issues. Their concern that the Christian right promotes a societal vision that is disadvantageous for women is the major reason why they oppose this group and may help explain why they are cultural progressive activists. Opposing sexism as a reason for their opposition to the Christian right is quite clear in some of the answers they provided.

> I also dislike that they want to make laws to force others to behave in keeping with their religious values such as passing anti-women's rights legislation. (female, 56–65, some graduate training)

> Patriarchal, anti-feminist, Bible literalist, anti-progress, anti-government, anti-science, anti-reason. In short: nutjobs. (male, 26–35, some graduate training)

> Their attitudes toward women as subservient class, their stance on a woman's right to chose, their insane homophobia, their prejudice toward minorities, and the politicization of everything. (female, 46–55, master's degree)

> Besides the fact that the "sheep" of the Christian Right seem to think that their god would speak exclusively through males with wretched haircuts . . . on to another generalization . . . their support of anti-feminist, anti-gay, anti-environment. (female, 46–55, bachelor's degree)

Concern about homophobia also loaded highly with this subgroup. It is plausible that concern for women's rights is highly correlated with concern for the rights of homosexuals. The linking of sexism with homophobia has been discussed in other empirical literature (Black, Oles, & Moore, 1998; Ficarrotto, 1990; Kimmel, 1994; Pharr, 2000). Furthermore, cultural progressive activists may perceive both women and homosexuals as suffering from marginalization by religious individuals. Cultural progressive activists with a special concern for individuals marginalized by the Christian right can be drawn toward this subgroup.

Of all of the political groups, it was the *feminists* who loaded most highly on having a concern that the Christian right opposes science. We have already documented how some of these respondents had concerns about this potential opposition in the examination of *political activists*. However, the strength of its loading on *feminist* indicates an even stronger concern with this subgroup than among *political activists*. It is worth speculating why *feminists* have such a strong concern about a lack of science, especially since some feminists have argued that the application of science has been tainted by sexism (Harding, 2005; Hubbard, 1989; Keller, 1982; H. Rose, 1994). Despite these criticisms, science has also been used to establish more egalitarian gender roles instead of the traditional gender roles legitimated by religious tradition.[4] We speculate that those in the *feminist* subgroup perceive science as a way to break the hold traditional conservatives have on gender norms. This may particularly be the case with the social sciences that document the prevalence of sexism in society and that tend to support a feminist solution to it. Given this potential reality, *feminists* may have a powerful concern about the potential neglect and/or misuse of science by members of the Christian right who may delegitimate scientific work so that traditional gender norms will be preserved.

Finally, it is not surprising that women are more likely than men to be *feminists*. But the implications of this fact need to be considered. It may be the case that feminism is a popular way in which women become socialized into opposing the Christian right. Since women generally are more religious than men, they may have a greater hesitation to criticize religion than men. Thus, they may feel more comfortable attacking the political, as opposed to the religious, dimensions of the Christian right. Thus, a concern for gender roles, and the political issues connected to feminism, may be an important motivator for women who do join organizations that have as an expressed purpose to resist the Christian right.

The motivations for *feminists* are quite clear and indicate why this group is appealing to women. The Christian right is seen as a group that wants to take women back to a time in which they did not enjoy complete equality. The comments from members in this subgroup reinforce the presence of this fear.

> General anti-science, anti-woman agenda. . . . Policies should not be driven by the 2,000 year old beliefs of cattle-sacrificing primitives. (male, 26–35, some college)
>
> Cave-man ideas about women, gays, etc. (female, 56–65, doctorate)
>
> A certain sub-set of white protestants who want to return to the Dark Ages of ignorance; who want to abolish the Constitution and re-instate certain parts of the Old Testament as governmental rules (a Christian version of Sharia Law); who are opposed to evolution and biology and science and civilization; who want to revoke the right to vote from women and blacks and everybody else who is not just like them. (male, 66–75, some graduate training)

Therefore, to oppose the Christian right is to promote the rights of women. This motivation has an evident utilitarian value for the female respondents. However, even among the male respondents, there is likely a moral desire to promote equality over sexism. Casting the Christian right as a group that wants to "turn back the clock" on woman's rights is a potent legitimating force for cultural progressive activists.

Political Concerns and Primary Literature

In addition to the surveys sent out to the members of a variety of culturally progressive organizations, we also examined the primary literature of several of the organizations. Some of the organizations sent out messages electronically, while others used traditional newsletters. For the most part these transmissions focus on public issues relevant to the concerns of a given organization. Relatively little of the space was devoted to internal organizational matters. The length of time we examined a given type of communication depended on the frequency we received the newsletter or electronic transmission. At times we also visited the websites of these organizations to provide us with some background information on them.

The purpose of examining this literature is to explore the type of messages these organizations are sending to their members. As we read the answers to the surveys, it became clear to us that there were common sayings and values that likely emerged from an external source. For example, several respondents made some variation of the comment that the Christian right is neither "Christian nor right." We have a great deal of doubt that all these individuals thought of this comment on their own. What is more likely the case is that some speaker or writer included this saying in some form of communication, and now it has become part of the common ideology among those who oppose the Christian right. Likewise, values and ideas may become part of that common ideology. Exploring these documents will enable us to see what types of values and ideas are enunciated by the primary sources of information that a significant percentage of respondents likely rely upon to gain insight into the nature of their struggle.

One theme that comes out of the primary literature is the pressing need to politically confront the Christian right. The concern of many of the individuals is the use of religion to justify conservative politics. At times within the readings there was a clear attempt to link conservative political ideology to religious, and usually Christian, belief.

> In keeping with fundamentalist theology, activists seek to ban all abortions, deny civil rights protections for gays, fund religious schools and other ministries with tax dollars and teach the Bible and creationism in public schools.

> Over the years we've all seen how religious-right pressure groups wade into areas that would seem to have nothing to do with

promoting "traditional family values" (whatever that means to them) and other "culture war" issues. Case in point: a group called CRAVE—Christians Reviving America's Values—is calling on supporters to oppose the Obama administration on health care reform.

With such a linkage, it becomes clear that the Christian right is perceived in this literature as a problem because it is a movement that supports political conservatism. The readers of these documents are likely to have generally progressive political beliefs or at least are politically progressive on key issues. To this end, the opposition expressed in these documents falls on ears eager to support progressive political ideology. Calls about the need to engage in the culture war are common in the primary literature of cultural progressives.

> These setbacks mean we will have to redouble our efforts to fight the religious right on the state board. In fact the board's far-right members have already promised that the revisions of social studies curriculum standards—now underway—will be even more divisive than the recent battle over science!

> Religious Right forces regrouped under TV preacher Pat Robertson's Christian Coalition. This organization focused heavily on local politics, playing special attention to public school boards. Its supporters demanded an end to public education and the "Christianization" of politics. Through a series of in-depth reports and by working with the nation's media, [organization's name] exposed the radical agenda of the Christian Coalition.

> The Religious Right has targeted local school boards, local communities and local elections—and what it achieves there may have sweeping implications for us all. . . . Please stand with me to meet this growing religious threat to our American way of life.

> The culture wars may be fading across the rest of the country. But they're still causing casualties in Texas.

These messages are consistently put out to cultural progressive activists to remind them of their political enemy. Emergent norms develop that envision conservative politics as the source of the problems in the United States. The religious justification provided for political conservatism becomes a major reason why many respondents seek to limit the influence of the Christian right.

Within these norms are themes that are easily accepted by cultural progressive activists. Myths and traditions develop in reaction to these themes. For example, homosexuality and abortion emerge as important issues in the culture war. In many ways they develop an importance that may go beyond the actual value of the issues. In fact, one of the organizations produces an electronic newsletter five times a week, and it contains a section devoted almost exclusively to dealing with civil rights issues of homosexuals. This level of attention indicates that the cultural issue of homosexuality provides a central way by which supporters of this organization construct their identity. Remember that several respondents noted that they supported such civil rights even though they were heterosexual. The attention provided to such issues by these organizations suggests that such respondents can use this cultural issue to identify themselves as tolerant and even accepting of differences of sexual preference, unlike their Christian right counterparts. In fact, 61.3 percent of respondents made at least one assertion about the intolerance of the Christian right as a part of the problem of this group, and thus the homosexuality is more than merely another political issue but rather allows cultural progressives to create their identity.

If abortion is conceptualized as a right of women, then it too can be seen as a cultural issue that helps to shape the identity of cultural progressive activists. While none of the primary material we examined had a unique place for abortion, it still was a political issue that came up quite often. One of the common ways this issue was brought to the forefront was through the murder of Dr. George Tiller, who was known for performing late-term abortions. His name was mentioned several times in the primary sources.

> The patients are gone and so are the protesters. Once the site of daily anti-abortion picketing, the Kansas clinic run by murdered doctor George Tiller is busy only with workers shutting down the facility. But as an uneasy peace settles over Wichita, abortion rights supporters say the fatal gunshot that closed Tiller's clinic

is part of a wave of attacks threatening to and, in some cases, succeeding in stopping women's access to abortion.

While it is true that Dr. Tiller was killed by a bullet fired by a religious madman, it is also true that the inflammatory rhetoric that spews from the empty heads of religious zealots was just as much to blame for this heinous act.

The shooting death of abortion provider George Tiller has put Fox News Channel's Bill O'Reilly in the media spotlight because of the stories he did about the Kansas doctor over the past few years. Liberal commentators have questioned whether O'Reilly's words, including calling the doctor "Tiller the baby killer," were too incendiary.

Randall Terry . . . launched a new version of Operation Rescue this weekend, calling on activists from across the country to press on despite bad publicity over the May 31 slaying of abortion doctor George Tiller.

Tiller became a tragic figure used to illustrate the dangerous nature of the Christian right. Beyond his unfortunate death is the fact that he died defending the rights of women to choose abortion. This is a big part of what makes him a hero for cultural progressive activists. Individuals are killed every day in the United States, and usually these deaths pass with little notice. Even murders that may temporarily gain notoriety usually do not retain it for long unless the murderer or victim was famous before the act. Neither Tiller nor his killer was famous before the murder, and indeed outside of the circles of cultural progressive activists this crime does not have the attention of most individuals. Yet we speculate that for certain cultural progressive activists the protection of abortion rights has significant symbolic importance in defining them as not sexist or oppressive as the Christian conservatives are. They are able to engage in boundary maintenance in which they reinforce their own in-group while defining who is included in their out-group. This type of identity creation can be a big part of why Tiller has gained such tragic heroic status among many cultural progressives.

Another important symbol that comes up time and again in the primary literature and in some of the respondents' comments concerned an organization called "The Family." The concern emerges from a book written by Jeff Sharlet (2008) that reports on an allegedly secret Christian organization that is a political power broker. The general theme of many of the comments is that this organization secretly controls many of the political conservatives and is bending the political apparatus in our nation to the will of Christian conservatives. It is beyond the scope of this book to assess the accuracy of such claims. But it really does not matter if Sharlet has done an adequate job supporting his charges. These are the sorts of assertions that fit well into the story of conservative Christianity buttressing political conservatives who are ruining society. Regardless of the amount of evidence that Sharlet amassed for his contentions, he has a ready audience that seeks reasons to oppose political conservatism. Linking political conservatism to a fundamentalist religion that few of the respondents respect is a legitimate reason for many of those respondents to dismiss the value of conservative politics and the religion that supports it. How Sharlet's book was noticed by the respondents and how information within it spread among them was not clear from the responses we read, but the value of Sharlet's assertions is clearly seen given the book's fear of the religion-backed political conservatism told throughout this primary literature.

Furthermore, also building on the theme of a culture war is the need to do "reconnaissance." All of the organizations we looked at possessed some form of a "Religious Right Watch." The purpose of such a section was to document some of the fallibilities found among religious and political conservatives. Some of the observations include the following:

> A columnist notes that while much of the media had no trouble detailing the religious commitment of the Muslim killer of an army recruiter, most profiles paint Scott Roeder as a right-wing, anti-government, anti-abortionist, with a prior arrest history and mental problems. His connection with extremist Christian groups, apparently, is irrelevant.[5] The Catholic Diocese of Dallas and a religious order will pay 6 men 4.65 million to settle a suit alleging

they were sexually abused by [undisclosed name] in the 1970s and 1980s.

Samford University ... has canceled an upcoming event featuring Rick Pitino, the University of Louisville basketball coach in the news for a scandal involving alleged adultery and abortion. Pitino, 57, a married father of five, had been booked to speak at a leadership luncheon Sept. 10 at the Baptist College's law school. Pitino, a Roman Catholic, has admitted to police he had consensual sex six years ago with Karen Sypher and paid her $3,000.

The Family Research Council has announced that Gov. Tim Pawlenty, R-Minn, will be a featured speaker at September's Values Voter Summit. The annual conference hosts leaders from the anti-gay rights and anti-abortion movements, and last year was host to the controversial "Obama Waffles" flap.

Minneapolis pastor John Piper seems to have sprouted the idea that God sent a tornado to the Minneapolis Convention Center last Wednesday to express his displeasure that the Evangelical Lutheran Church in America was considering relaxing its teachings on LGBT issues. . . . Despite the weather, the social statement relaxing church teaching on homosexuality passed by exactly one vote. Two days later, under a sunny sky, the ELCA approved a measure to allow gay and lesbian clergy in committed relationships to serve the church.

A Capitol Hill townhouse that serves as a dormitory and meeting place for a band of conservative Christian lawmakers has been linked to a third episode of marital infidelity, this time in a Mississippi court filing by a former lawmaker's estranged wife.

Clearly, some of these observations are presented to poke fun at their cultural enemies. Other observations provide justification to cultural progressive activists that they are on the proper side of the debate. Yet other observations are clearly calls to action in which the writers hope to motivate their readers to become active in some movement to defeat their conservative opponents. Dehumanizing and ridiculing one's enemy serve powerful functions in sustaining support for a social movement. Such actions do not have to be based upon a rational assessment of one's opponents, as exaggerating and amplifying the faults of those opponents serves the purpose of creating consensus and reassurance among the members of the movement. Cultural progressive activists build their legitimization on the idea of rationality; however, like other social groups, they also have to utilize irrational accusations and exaggerations to serve the sociopsychological needs of their social movement.

For those motivated by political considerations, the literature provided for cultural progressive activists provides a diagnostic frame by which they can justify their activism. The literature indicates a story in which Christianity and other conservative expressions of religion support conservative political policies that are damaging all of us. Without such support, it can be hoped that many individuals will perceive the dysfunctional nature of political conservatism and become more willing to help cultural progressive activists create a more harmonious society.[6] The Christian right must be defeated so that a proper political order can be established. Even those who oppose the Christian right primarily for political reasons still link some of their opposition to the religious nature of the group. Antipathy toward both political and religious dimensions of the Christian right is generally linked together, and resentment toward both dimensions appears to be part of the larger collective identity among cultural progressives activists. Thus, as we will find out in the next two chapters, those who oppose the Christian right primarily for religious reasons also link some of their opposition to the political nature of the group.

CHAPTER 5

General Opposition to Religion in Cultural Progressive Activists

Beyond politics, some individuals oppose the Christian right because of its religious nature. One possibility is that some individuals have an exceptional hostility to Christianity. The proposed values and mores within Christianity possibly produce a level of animosity not exhibited toward other religions. Or individuals may have had bad experiences with Christian organizations and project those experiences to Christians in general. This possibility will be explored in the next chapter. However, it is also possible that some individuals possess an animosity toward religion in general. The fact that the Christian right is Christian is not as relevant as the fact that it is a group that finds motivation in any type of religion.

In this chapter we explore the motivations connected to the latter group. It is easy to see how such a group may have developed in the United States. A recent spate of popular atheists' books (Barker, 2008; Dawkins, 2006; Harris, 2005; Hitchens, 2007; Huberman, 2006) has fueled the desire of those who seek to totally reject organized religion. The arguments made in such books can legitimate a desire to limit religion's influence on our society. To the degree that this is true, we should find a significant percentage of individuals who do not trust any religious organization or believe that religious organizations are on balance more detrimental to society than non-religious organizations. This possibility is fed by recent work that suggests an increase in atheists and agnostics in the United States (Kosmin & Keysar, 2008). Such a growing group indicates a larger pool of people who are likely to develop a generalized hostility toward religious expression of any kind.

The analysis we conducted suggested two possible groups that possessed a general animosity toward organized religion. First is the *religion is poison* group. The basic concern of the individuals in this group is the ability of religion to ruin everything it influences. Second is the *religion has been corrupted* group. This group has antipathy toward religion because the group's members believe that religion has gone bad. Perhaps religion at one time had an important function to serve, but now it is more dysfunctional than functional.

Religion Is Poison

In 2007 Christopher Hitchens wrote a scathing attack on religion in a book titled *God Is Not Great: How Religion Poisons Everything*. His work contends that religion is the basis for the world's problems. The sample captured direct and indirect influences of such a philosophy among several cultural progressives. The sentiment that religion ruins everything was clearly demonstrated by some of the respondents. They came to the conclusion that religion in general is a bane in our society.

> . . . sad spectacle of people who don't think, believe nonsense, can't tell truth from fiction . . . beliefs in the bible, a work of fiction, literally drives everything they think and do. (male, 66–75, doctorate)

> Some of them are capable of loving interventions for saving victims of catastrophe, can be generous to food banks, but nothing good they do can undo the great harm they advocate and perpetrate, how can you forgive a lynch mob, an abortion clinic bomber or a doctor killer? (male, 56–65, some graduate training)

> . . . fear-based circular thinking that poisons virtually every aspect of human life—family and personal relationships, work,

appreciation of the arts and culture, sexuality, the life of the mind, self-image, etc. (male, 46–55, master's degree)

I cannot say anything positive about them without risking that it be misconstrued as them having a good quality. Their religion poisons every aspect of their lives. (male, 26–35, master's degree)

I view them as a cancer that poisons American politics and drastically limits our ability to cope with an evolving, irony intended, world. (male, 26–35, doctorate)

Based on such answers and the fact that Hitchens' work either reflects or has influenced the notion of religion as poison, we have named this propensity within the respondents *religion is poison*.

How does religion poison our society according to these respondents? A key way that advocates from this perspective point to is how religion interferes with the ability of individuals to engage in critical thinking. The members of this subgroup were more likely than other respondents to point out how religion appeals to individuals who are not seen as intelligent.

I don't waste my time wrestling with pigs or arguing with fools. (male, 56–65, some graduate training)

Evidence is never an issue with them. They are very dumb and only require their own faith, not reason or evidence. (female, 26–35, some college)

Anybody who believes in a divine savior after the Tooth Fairy & Santa Claus & the Easter bunny have been revealed as childhood myths, is a fool, though she/he have every right to be so. I think they should refrain from political opinions until they fully accept personal responsibility. (male, over 75, some graduate training)

I find myself biased against Christians. I think they are dumb, and I find it very difficult to listen politely to Christian chatter. It annoys me. (female, 36–45, master's degree)

They are their own worst enemies. The stupidity they must display, tends to not allow them much influence with reasoning, or the majority, of people. When you are more than two standard deviations from the mean, by definition you are on the fringes. (male, 56–65, some graduate training)

[Respondent's description of Christian right] Crazy. irrational. anti-intellectual, non-thinking, racists, bigoted, rude, stupid, moronic, anti-Christ-like. misogynistic, biased, creationists, non-scientific, non-reasoned, unfactual, borderline line retarded. (male, 56–65, master's degree)

These quotes indicate that some respondents did not believe that religious individuals have the capacity to engage in intellectual discourse and their ideas should be marginalized. Those in the *religion is poison* group were also more likely to contend that religion in general and Christianity in particular does not promote critical thinking. As such, even if members of the Christian right are not innately less intelligent than other individuals, they are not perceived as knowing how to think about important religious, social, and political issues.

The lack of critical thinking is the defining characteristic. Faith means you will accept no deviation from your belief. You will not explore the possibility of error or even nuance. They look for sins in normal behavior. (male, 56–65, some graduate training)

I tend to view them as uneducated people, or those who don't have the capacity for critical thinking. Perhaps driven by fear. They also feel the need for some sort of birthright, something they feel they have inherited. (female, 46–55, master's degree)

Those associated with the Christian Right tend to polarize on issues based on obscure verses from the Bible. Ideas, taken out of context "drive" an attitude of righteous indignation. The characteristic that creates the polarization comes from lack of critical thinking coupled with mindless emotionalism. (female, 66–75, master's degree)

People with little experience living in other cultures who are thus centered on American cultural ideas. Like anyone in any country who have little understanding of the world outside their immediate experience, they become aggressive in defense of their values, since they place all their identity there. The emotional psychology of this creates non-critical thinkers who are drawn to ideas which please them, rather than the truth. Thus they take the Bible literally, for example. (male, 56–65, master's degree)

Most people I know are Christians and generally tend to be good people. However, when it comes to understanding why they believe in what they believe they generally have no idea and make decisions based on what their church or religious community suggest without critical thought. (male, 36–45, master's degree)

If members of the Christian right were merely allowing themselves to lose their intellectual capacity to religion, then that would be of minimal concern. However, some of the respondents in the general sample were worried that religion's capacity to limit critical thinking creates problems for our society.

[L]ack of critical thinking, meaning replacing biblical nonsense in our public schools instead of science, conservatism to the point of being somewhere to the right of Glenn Beck and making the US a theocracy. (male, 46–55, bachelor's degree)

They threaten to undo much of the cultural progress of the last 500 years by eliminating critical thinking in our schools. (male, 36–45, bachelor's degree)

Their sense of community is a benefit, however, it may be costing this country too much in terms of losing our science/math competitive edge and lack of critical thinking. (male, 46–55, some graduate training)

I think they represent one of the most destructive forces in modern society. They represent irrationality and anti-critical thinking at its worst. (male, 46–55, doctorate)

[Members of the Christian right are] not critical thinkers, too much faith in male authority figures and the GOP, sometimes hateful of the poor, not concerned with military members, conflate fundamentalist Bible theory with Republicanism. (female, 36–45, bachelor's degree)

> My comments go to the Christian Right as a group. I know there are exceptions, but as a group they do not exhibit critical thinking, which is necessary for the advancement of our economy and our well being. "Faith" is the absence of critical thinking. (female, 56–65, doctorate)

These quotes show that poison is a useful analogy for some respondents. Just as poison starts at one place in the body and then works its way through, killing off areas vital to sustaining life, so too, according to these respondents, does religion work through society, destroying individuals' ability to solve society's problems. It may start at a given point, but if it is not contained, these respondents fear, it will greatly damage other vital areas of society. Rationality and education are often seen as the way to deal with the foolishness created by religion. But many respondents do not believe that these tools will be enough to correct members of the Christian right. They perceive such individuals as "brainwashed" and thus unable to deal with reality without imagined beliefs. In fact, comments about the brainwashed nature of the Christian right and how they are like sheep were quite common among all respondents.

> As an extremist cult comprised of below-average IQ lemmings who are comprised of insecure UN-Christian people who have low regard for many personal liberties, and of low-intellect Christians who have been conned by the highly-skilled and crafty propagandists at the oligarchical cult's leadership level into believing that the cult's agendas are biblically-aligned. (male, 66–75, master's degree; emphasis in original)

> Christianity is a social disease, a method to dupe and control weaker minded and desperate people such as occurred with Jim Jones. (male, 26–35, bachelor's degree)

> The Christian Right is able to grow because of a herding mentality of safety in numbers and people wanting to be told what to do instead of becoming informed and making their own decisions. (male, 46–55, some graduate training)

> A mostly brainwashed group who blindly follow unproven and unprovable religious dogma rather than reason. Since they don't use reason, they are essentially sheep being led by the political right who act as sheep herders. (male, 66–75, doctorate)

But the tendency to see members of the Christian right as sheep or brainwashed was exceptionally high among those in the *religion is poison* group. They were more likely to perceive members of the Christian right as sheep who can be easily led by clever leaders.

> I consider a high percentage of the Christian Right as being individuals who are either severely under-educated or trapped by brainwashing. (male, 56–65, doctorate)

> They are unreasonable, idealistic, majority not well educated, uninformed, lemmings (believe what they are told without question). (male, 46–55, master's degree)

> A poorly informed, easily manipulated, emotionally damaged, socially stunted, fearful group of people who seem determined to stay that way. . . . They are sheep. (female, 56–65, some college)

> Follow blindly their spiritual leaders, don't think for themselves. (male, 66–75, bachelor's degree)

> They can be led like sheep. A raving lunatic like Rush Limbaugh can have them head nodding when he contradicts himself between two successive sentences. (male, 56–65, some graduate training)

In this sense members of this group perceive religion as robbing individuals of their ability to accurately perceive reality because it makes individuals more susceptible to bad leadership. Religion is seen as the opposite of critical thinking, which allows individuals to accurately assess a given situation. These respondents perceive themselves as having those skills and look on the misled followers with a mixture of disgust and pity. In this sense, religion is a poison that must be neutralized so that individuals can regain their mental faculties and engage in the critical thinking necessary for them to avoid being misled.

A key reason why respondents in this sample may have such beliefs is their previous encounters with members of the Christian right. They are more likely than other respondents to have had negative encounters that have influenced their perceptions of the Christian right. Some of these encounters have illustrated to such respondents the futility of "reaching" religious individuals with reason. Other encounters have filled the respondents in this subgroup with sadness as they observed some of the ways members of the Christian right were unable to use critical thinking skills.

> Just that I do know some of these people, and have tried to reason with them . . . their answers revolve around something they call "faith," which always ends the conversation . . . sad. (male, 66–75, some college)

> As a college professor who taught critical thinking, I had many students who protested my rule that they could not write essays on religious belief. One in particular complained to the board of trustees that I was denying his First Amendment right to express his opinion. The young man passed the class because he finally wrote a coherent essay; the board members had a hearty laugh over his complaint, and I was glad when the semester ended, but in fact, I felt sorry for the student because his fundamentalist teachings made it impossible for him to think. (female, over 75, master's degree)

> Sad that people have embraced such uncritical thinking and allow themselves to be manipulated by social forces that really could care less about them. (female, 56–65, master's degree)

> A right-wing Christian guy got in a verbal fight with a group of us doing environmental work on campus about recycling. He said that environmentalism was "of the devil" and "of Satan" multiple times. We were so confused, and after a lot of circular nonsense we finally divulged that this man thought that because Jesus was supposedly coming back to Earth imminently, trying to conserve resources was an atheistic action because it expressed a belief that

the world WASN'T going to end very soon with the rapture, which was antithetical to biblical prophecy. I thought that this guy was a lone nut off his meds, but then a quick internet search uncovered hundreds of Pentecostal and other evangelical people who agreed with him! . . . It made me think that they were even more crazy, especially that anti-environmentalism guy. I had thought that recycling was a pretty benign topic even with that group. Apparently not! (female, 18–25, some college)

In these cases, the respondents gained information informing them that members of the Christian right are unable to process information in what they see as a correct manner. Religious, rather than political, ideology is seen as the culprit in most of these cases. The respondents show a concern about the political direction in which many members of the Christian right want to take the nation. It is a political direction that they see as doing great harm to the country. However, the main reason why such an unsavory political direction is possible is because of the terrible influence of religion. Religion is seen as an aspect that weakens the mental capacity of the mind to examine the problems created by conservative political solutions. This weakness is not merely that members of the Christian right have less of an ability to engage in critical thinking. Some of the respondents indicated a concern about the mental stability of members of the Christian right. There was a suggestion from some of the respondents that individuals have to be mentally unstable to accept some of the ideas pushed forth by the Christian right. This was particularly the case for those in the *religion is poison* subgroup.

> When they are in the echo box, they are completely insane. Their thoughts and opinions are not based in any reality that I can discern. (male, 26–35, bachelor's degree)

> Keep them away from me. We used to be able to discuss religion with our friends, but they are now insane. There is no talking to anyone who paints a Hitler mustache on Obama's photo and who spout creationism, ignorant of science. People who lead unexamined lives—spare me. (female, 56–65, master's degree)

> They seem like really damaged people to me in a lot of ways—go to a really fundy church and talk to the people about even non-religious topics—all kinds of crippling mental issues seem to come to the fore. It seems like a need for a really rigid structure of right and wrong from an unquestionable authority. (female, 36–45, master's degree)
>
> Uneducated, blindly following like a cult, not able to consider other ideas, have not studied the bible or religions in real world, just what were taught. Have low opinion, think they are mentally unstable. (male, 66–75, master's degree)

Such comments indicate the lack of respect members in the *religion is poison* group have for individuals in the Christian right. This lack of respect tends to center on the religious ideas of such individuals. Since members of this group have little respect for religion and perceive it as a negative societal influence, there is little wonder that some of these members question the sanity of those who hold onto what they consider to be ridiculous beliefs. But the real concern occurs when religiously induced mental instability influences individuals to make political decisions that affect the rest of society. Some of the individuals in the *religion is poison* subgroup enunciated such fears.

> [I]t's beyond understanding how anyone can believe a single word of the Bible. So a "group" that is so mentally deficient as to believe in the Bible has no place in our government. You are not "Right" and you really should change your moniker to "The Christian Terrorists." (male, 46–55, some college)
>
> People who seek to use Christianity as a political force. I consider them fanatics who are blissfully unaware of their fanaticism, overvalue dogma, and undervalue logic. (male, 18–25, some college)
>
> I don't care what they believe, but I definitely never want to see another unintelligent born-again in a position of political power. (male, 18–25, some college)
>
> The forcing of their theology on a secular world. I don't want to end up like Iran. Their absolutism forced into laws. Intolerance and

> unwillingness to except truth. They are all completely retarded. (male, 26–35, some college)

> The irrational thought that sex is a sin, all atheists are immoral, and pushing their religion into our government when they do not have one single piece of supporting evidence of this god they speak of. (female, 36–45, some college)

Whether it is because of a lack of critical thinking skills or a lack of sanity, religion incapacitates the mind and leads to the adoption of political ideologies that threaten the society and the nation. These ideologies are seen as promoting the possible removal of political rights and imposition of religious ideas that promote political incivility. Thus, religion poisons politics, and by poisoning politics it sets in motion a variety of other social mechanisms that help to ruin our society. Such a sentiment was common among the *religion is poison* respondents.

> Simple minds want to be fed what to believe, includes news, gossip and religion. Tend to vote Republican, xenophobic, see others as "them." Anything different is to be feared. (male, 46–55, bachelor's degree)

> I consider them to generally be irrational in basing their political beliefs upon their faith instead of upon facts and what is just. I find that many members of the Christian Right hold their opinions blindly without understanding all of the actual facts behind the issues. They can only see what they are told by their religious leaders rather than considering what is really fair, and they assume that everyone else is wrong without putting forth an honest effort to understand other people's views. (female, 26–35, doctorate)

> The problem is that since Reagan, these people have been led by people with a political agenda. Christians have long believed that heaven-on-earth will happen when the "right" Christian leads the people politically. (male, 56–65, some graduate training)

> They are a danger to social order, the same way that all easily manipulated populations are. (male, 56–65, some college)

Religion may poison everything, according to Hitchens, but for these respondents the poison generally starts with the rotting of the mind, which then leads to the dysfunctional politics promoted by the Christian right. Whether this is the actual belief of Hitchens is unclear, but this is the general interpretation these respondents demonstrated.

As noted in chapter 3, individuals who belong to this subgroup tend to have more atheistic friends in their social networks. Such a makeup of their social networks may be the result of the mistrust they developed due to previous encounters with members of the Christian right. This personal mistrust of members of the Christian right indicates yet another way in which religion is seen as a despoiling influence in our society. Religious individuals are seen not merely as being wrong politically but also as being morally inferior by members of this subgroup.

> Smug, double-talking, self-righteous, immoral killers to whom the end justifies the means and the end is life as I have known it! They are the world's true terrorists! (male, 46–55, some graduate training)

> I don't want to be around self-righteous people, that are frequently leading immoral lives, judging me. (male, 46–55, some graduate training)

> Insanity, lack of reason, extremism, immorality, willingness to lie, belief that murder is O.K. if it's for their belief. (male, 56–65, some college)

> Just about everything they do or say is based on complete ignorance or unethical and immoral goals. (male, 36–45, bachelor's degree)

These statements make clear moral judgments on the Christian right and engender an image of such individuals as people with little redeeming value. The immorality of the Christian right not only poisons society but makes them distasteful and people to be avoided. Members of the *religion is poison* group were more likely to discuss a desire to avoid contact with members of the Christian right than other respondents.

> Prefer to avoid them. (male, 66–75, high school diploma)

> I attempt to avoid them, as far as personal relationships are concerned. On the other hand, I frequently write letters to the newspaper(s) regarding their activities and their letters. Occasionally, one will contact me by mail to point out that I don't understand "the word of god." (male, 66–75, some graduate training)

> Fortunately I am able to avoid most personal contact with them, otherwise there is short contact w/out discussion of differences. (male, 56–65, some college)

> I have successfully avoided encountering them. (male, 66–75, doctorate)

> A coworker showed me photos of an obviously fresh Flintstones-like brontosaurus carved into an Indian rock art panel in TX. I laughed recognizing the joke; He thinks it's definite proof humans and dinosaurs lived together on a 6000 yr old earth; and we scientists suppress the "truth." I avoid him and his equally ignorant friends. (male, 56–65, doctorate)

> Avoid them, try not to get upset. (male, over 75, high school diploma)

As such, these respondents suggest that religion poisons not just the society but also, in an ironic way, people's souls. For them, religion does not just fool individuals into forming bad political policies, but it also works toward making bad individuals. Many respondents have a strong fear of members of the Christian right. We have documented some of these fears in previous quotes. These fears may be due to the societal effects created by Christian right members.

However, not all of this fear is based upon the political and societal alterations that may develop because of this group. Because bad individuals are seen as a natural consequence of being a member of a religious group, there is little reason to spend time with them.

In fact, individuals in the *religion is poison* group, when asked about what was positive about the Christian right, were more likely than other cultural progressive activists to state that there is nothing positive that could be said about them. With such a complete rejection of the Christian right, members of this group may easily perceive the individuals within the Christian right as having no redeeming value. Since it is religion that is at the heart of their rejection, this indicates a strong reason why some of the members in the *religion is poison* group perceive it to be necessary to avoid religious individuals whenever possible.

When individuals believe that religion is a toxin that ruins our political system and creates ugliness among individuals, such individuals will perceive religion as a force with little, if any, redeeming value. Most respondents seemed to have a "live and let live" attitude toward people of faith. But some of the respondents in the general sample perceived religion as so toxic that they freely expressed a need to rid ourselves of religious individuals. Those in the *religion is poison* group best illustrated this tendency. They envision a society that they believe is not possible if powerful religious influences remain present. Their perception is that by limiting, or possibly eliminating, those religious influences they can create a better society. The Christian right is seen by such individuals as the social force most responsible for the maintenance of the power of religious individuals and for ruining the morality of unsuspecting individuals in our society. For respondents with such beliefs, opposition to the Christian right is a natural way to create a healthier society.

Religion Has Been Corrupted

A second group also fits into the idea that religion in general is the problem. This group is not as convinced as the *religion is poison* group that religion automatically creates problems in society. Rather, members of this subgroup tend to believe that religion can be a benign, and perhaps even helpful, social force at certain times in our society. However, the religion practiced by the Christian right is a corruption of the type of religion that can be part of a healthy society. Thus, we call this group *religion has been corrupted*. It is the smallest of the subgroups, yet it contains some important tendencies that can be seen throughout the entire sample.

There is evidence that members of this group are more likely to have moved away from a neighborhood with Christian right individuals than other cultural progressive activists. This willingness to move away indicates that there are attributes within religion that have influenced them to avoid religious individuals. For example, members of this group are less likely to be married than other cultural progressive activists. Thus, members of this subgroup may be likely to have a nontraditional family formation. This can indicate a reason why they avoid living among the Christian right. Although we did not ask any questions about sexual preferences, several respondents from the general sample indicated that their homosexuality, and the reaction they experience from Christians, is part of what drives their attitudes toward the Christian right.

> Yes it [having Christian right neighbors] would [bother me] because I'm gay and they want me dead. (male, 56–65, bachelor's degree)

> I could go on and on and on about many personal experiences with the religious right in and outside of my own family for the simple reason that I'm gay and have been exposed to my fair share of religious anti-gay bigotry . . . yes I think a lot of anti-gay hatred is born out of religion and have experienced first hand. (male, 46–55, some college)

> We used to have wonderful family get togethers but once I came out as transgendered and gay and now as an atheist they are only polite to me and no longer invite me to gatherings and only speak to me if I speak first. The look of disgust on their face is also something I see regularly. (male, 36–45, bachelor's degree)

> Being told, second-hand, that a so-called "Christian" had condemned me to hell because I am gay. (male, 46–55, some college)

> 1) I was excommunicated from my church for coming out as a gay man after 18 years of marriage and after four years of reparative therapy. 2) I have had people threaten to go to court to have my

children taken away because I am gay. (male, 46–55, some graduate training)

The propensity of such individuals to be judged for their lifestyle and the fear some of them have of violence may be linked to religion's influence on their society. This provides us with potential insight that we may gain from the *religion has been corrupted* subgroup. It is the capacity of religion to be judgmental of deviant lifestyles that at least partially can convince members of this subculture of the detrimental effects of religion. Respondents in general indicate a great deal of concern since Christians are seen as interfering in the lives of individuals.

> They tend not to mind their own business and to interfere in the lives of people with whom they disagree. (female, 46–55, some graduate training)

> I'm accepting of the religious beliefs and practices of the Christian Right to the extent that they do not interfere with the beliefs and practices of others or with the rights of individuals. I am intolerant of religious practices and belief that promote the idea that some people are inherently better than others (based on gender, race, etc.), the idea that a holy book can authorize poor treatment of other humans, or the idea that other religions must be eliminated. (female, 36–45, some college)

> Very willing to interfere in my life, but absolutely rabid should someone interfere in their life. (male, 56–65, some graduate training)

> They have to be countered by every legal means possible when they interfere with the rights of others, particularly atheists, gays and women demonstrating their rights to privacy. (male, 66–75, doctorate)

Christians also are seen as judging those individuals.

> They had better hope that there is no God because if he is as judgmental as they are they are in for real trouble. (female, 66–75, doctorate)

> Making judgments about personal things that are none of their business. (female, 46–55, some college)

> Instead, the Christian Right seems to think that Jesus' message was one of societal segregation, of restriction, and of harsh judgment—both for individuals and for the groups to which they belong—and especially when one does not agree with them. (female, 46–55, bachelor's degree)

> They judge people. At times it seems they have little compassion for people who are different. (female, 46–55, doctorate)

These respondents are not necessarily opposed to all religion but are disheartened by the interference and judgmentalism they see in religion. If religion can avoid engaging in the activities of interference in people's lives and judgmentalism, then religion can be seen as a benign force. In this sense, members of this subgroup can be seen as having more of a laissez-faire attitude toward religion than the *religion is poison* group. Those in the *religion is poison* group see no redeeming value in religion. The problem with religion according to the *religion has been corrupted* subgroup is its tendency to interfere with people's lives. However, this is not the same as calling for religion's eradication, found in *religion is poison* subgroup. This does not necessarily mean that individuals in the *religion has been corrupted* subgroup are more hospitable toward conservative expressions of religion. Because religion is seen as a force that impinges on their lifestyle, the animosity expressed toward religion in general can be just as caustic as that from the *religion is poison* subculture.

These individuals do not tend to focus on just Christianity. They actually were less likely to have animosity toward Christian fundamentalists relative to other religious groups in comparison to other cultural progressive activists. This suggests that they perceive the institution of religion, and not merely certain forms of Christianity, as the problem. However, they were less likely than other cultural progressive activists to desire an apolitical Christian neighbor over a nonreligious Republican neighbor. Although Christianity may not be rejected specifically, it does represent a corrupted religious institution that is to be avoided. These respondents were more likely than other respondents to have lived in a neighborhood with members of the Christian right and to have moved away from that neighborhood. The following quotes indicate the degree to which some respondents in the *religion has been corrupted* subgroup want to remove themselves from living among those of the Christian right:

> I would leave the neighborhood; I wouldn't feel a part of the neighborhood. (male, 56–65, master's degree)

> I don't have young children. If I had young children and my neighbors tried to convert them, I would move. (female, over 75, master's degree)

> If I knew that most of my neighbors were of the Christian right, I would not buy nor rent in the neighborhood. (male, 66–75, some graduate training)

> It would bother me so much I would move. Seriously. I almost took a job in England just because I'm disgusted with the way they are trashing the constitutional separation of church and state in this country. (male, 46–55, doctorate)

It is also noteworthy that these respondents were less likely to live in the South than other respondents. Whether they once lived in the South and moved away cannot be determined by these data, but clearly they now tend to live in areas where relatively few members of the Christian right are close by. Unlike the *religion is poison* group, these individuals are not any more likely to have atheists in their social network than other respondents. They may not be as eager to seek out atheists as a refuge from Christians and thus may have less overall hostility toward religious individuals than those in the *religion is poison* subgroup. In fact, members of this subgroup were more likely than other respondents to see at least some good within the Christian right when asked if there was anything good in the Christian right.

> I agree with their conservative politics. I don't agree with their religious views; however, they don't affect me in my lack of religion. We have other things in common so we tend to live and let live. (female, 56–65, bachelor's degree)

> Their attitudes are built upon superstition, but I may agree with some of their political ideals. (male, 46–55, master's degree)
>
> Somewhat sympathetic about some of their concerns but not accepting their religious beliefs and how some of those beliefs play out in society. (male, 56–65, bachelor's degree)
>
> Some members of Christian right are genuinely nice folks, but many are intolerant and not very smart. (male, 56–65, master's degree)

Such comments indicate that some of these respondents may agree with members of the Christian right on some political issues or appreciate them as people, but they are still disturbed by the religious nature of the group. This may enable some of the respondents in this subculture to avoid demonizing the Christian right enough to have some appreciation for the group, even as they believe that such individuals practice a corrupt religion.

At its core, this is a group that launches a critique at the way contemporary religion is practiced. Religion itself is not seen as problematic, but the practitioners of religion today are the individuals creating the problems. Therefore, such respondents show great concern at how the influence of the Christian right has created a religious institution with, and which causes, many problems. Because of this influence, the members of this subgroup do not want be near members of the Christian right. Their opposition to the Christian right is clearly based on the notion that it is a religious force that is detrimental to society. While the focus on its detrimental effects has been religious, clearly there is also concern from those in the *religion has been corrupted* subgroup about how members of the Christian right have politically misled the nation.

> I feel that the CR is trying to impose their ignorant, narrow-minded views on larger society through political influence on public education and government programs. (female, 46–55, master's degree)

> I think the Christian right is dangerous to the fabric of this nation. When they attempt to foist their beliefs into the politics then they become dangerous. (male, 66–75, some graduate training)
>
> I believe they have sacrificed their own rationality so as to be led by others.... The merging of the religious right with a political party is bad for religion and bad for politics. (male, 56–65, doctorate)
>
> People whose religion means so much to them that they let it determine their course of actions for politics, friends, and community actions.... They can be deceived by evangelists and others due to their superstitions. (male, 46–55, master's degree)

In this sense, we still see how political and religious forces overlap in the assessment of the Christian right. With some notable exceptions, most respondents who discussed the mixing of religious and political perspectives within the Christian right perceived it as problematic. The *religion has been corrupted* subgroup is no different from the other activists in the degree of concern they have for such mixing. They merely focus more on how religion has become corrupted and how this corrupted form contributes to the problems created by mixing religion and politics.

This is one of the smaller subgroups in our study, and many of the other respondents in our sample may not be influenced by this combination of factors. The *religion has been corrupted* subgroup may not have a high degree of influence among cultural progressive activists as a whole. Yet this group demonstrates another way in which some respondents critique religion as an entire entity. Animosity toward the Christian right does not have to be generated by anger at Christianity in particular. Rather, such animosity can also be motivated by an antipathy toward religion in general.

General Opposition to Religion within the Primary Literature

Once again, to understand the social context in which the responses documented in this chapter have originated or have been supported, it is valuable to look at the primary material that many of these members read. As we look at these materials, we will see common themes that link together this opposition to religion. That opposition does not occur in a vacuum but rather occurs in conjunction with a certain image of religion that has developed among many cultural progressive activists. For example, several times the hypocrisy of religion was discussed in these primary sources.

> It's just about the last thing the beleaguered Republican Party needed: a Christian conservative with national aspirations admitting to an extramarital affair with an ex-staffer.

> Political pundits are describing Governor Mark Sanford's admission of adultery on Wednesday as a "confessional" in which he apologized to those of faith and asked for forgiveness. Much of Gov. Sanford's base support and political platform centers on family values and God, and as one pastor put it Wednesday night, it seems more and more of those types of politicians are "biting the dust."

> All [aforementioned Christian congressmen and senators] have recently been implicated in extramarital affairs that casts doubt on their private commitment to the monogamy they praise in public.

Hypocritical words and action provide some respondents legitimacy for rejecting religion. Religion can be seen as an institution making claims that even its followers are unable to fulfill. This makes religion unrealistic and unreliable as a guide for our lives.

Even beyond rank hypocrisy, religion is seen as an institution that continues to harm society. Several times in this literature religion was conceptualized as the major source of evils such as intolerance, ignorance, oppression, and abuse.

> True or untrue, it [religion] is a gratifying, exciting, powerful force, as it was in Nazi Germany, still in present Iran and North Korea, and elsewhere throughout history back to primitive tribes, who at least had the excuse of ancient ignorance.

> A nativity scene is not a symbol of peace. More people have died in the name of religion than for any other reason.

> Religion is a tool that has been used for thousands of years to create a subordinate people. It has installed fear and panic, while creating segregation and isolation.
>
> Faith, despite its abilities to motivate positive achievement, also leads people to become rigid and quashes their motivation to understand the positions of others.
>
> It is the absolutism of all religions which is the bane of all people of this earth.
>
> Religion divides humanity,
> Multiples violence and intolerance,
> Subtracts logic, common sense and reason
> It just doesn't add up.

Thus, religion is seen not as merely creating some of the problems in our society but as the source of most, if not all, of our social problems. An image of religion "poisoning" our society arises from the literature read by many of the respondents. Such notions of religion as poison lead the respondents toward a complete rejection of religion and the advocacy of a society free of its influences. This desire is obviously the complete opposite of the hopes of those in the Christian right.

It must be made clear that this rejection of religion is not limited to Christians. In fact, for many respondents the entire concept of religion is offensive. This rejection of all religion can be seen in some of the literature consumed by these respondents. This literature generally denigrates notions of religion and favors claims of reason as the way to run one's life and to organize society. Reason is seen as the antidote to the poison of religion.

> I think people who despise atheists do so because they're terrified about the weakness, frankly, of their own faith. And we are a rebuke to them that they would rather do without. We introduce a little reality that they'd just as soon avoid.
>
> A lack of rational thought only hinders societal progress. When all other explanations fail, creationists explain that faith along {sic} is the answer to the hardest questions, and the questioning

> a person's faith oppresses them. But the truth will prevail, even if it takes centuries more to eradicate a repressive structure like religion.
>
> It means so much to know that there is an organization of rational people working together to expose the ridiculous notions of religion.
>
> Faith will fade, religions will flower and vanish, but reason remains.

Cultural progressive activists labor to provide a rational legitimization for their antipathy toward religion. They provide it by arguing that religion is on its way out and rationality will soon replace it. Their concern about the Christian right is its propensity to maintain the poison of religion even one minute longer than we have to have it. It is a poison that continues to ruin helpful social institutions, such as our education system, with its efforts to maintain its "illogical" hold on our society.

> A volatile combination of religious fundamentalism and social conservatism has resulted in the virtual strangulation of consideration of principles of education and the pedagogical principles that underlie the topics at hand.
>
> While writing that "only science belongs in science class," McLeroy trots out a series of creationist attacks on evolution that have been repeatedly and forcefully rejected by mainstream scientists.
>
> The same panel members . . . are also arguing that the new standards should emphasize that America's Founders intended to create a distinctly Christian nation based on biblical principles.
>
> The religious conservative bloc of seven really consider their job one of fighting the cultural wars, and education is an afterthought.

Ultimately some nonreligious individuals perceive themselves as victims of the oppressive religious structures and the irrationality of religion in our society. They believe that because of the power that oppressive, unenlightened individuals have, it is inevitable that nonreligious individuals will be victimized. As noted earlier, these cultural progressive activists tend to enjoy several social and demographic advantages in our society but have a minority perspective on religion issues. Perhaps because they are so used to having societal advantages it is difficult for them to understand why they are not supported also in their religious views. The comparison of how they are treated in other societal areas and in religion can help to explain their tendency to perceive themselves as victims. It is also possible that cultural progressive activists are victimized regarding social status, even though they are not when it comes to economic and educational success. After all, understanding oneself as a victim is not necessarily due to objective measures but can also be the result of subjective influences. Indeed, the notion of the irreligious being victimized was supported in several places in the primary literature, feeding readers with ammunition for claiming a victim status.

> Their [atheists'] mere existence was considered an offense to God.

> "In God We Trust" excludes and treats as outsiders the millions of adult Americans, including as many as 15% of all adults, who are not religious, i.e., atheists, agnostics, skeptics and freethinkers, none of whom possess a belief in a god; the mandated language diminishes nonbelievers by making god-belief synonymous with citizenship.

> Bringing your god into this governmental body is telling those who do not worship your god that they are second-class citizens and that their feeling and opinions are not as important as yours.

> [I]f the state of Washington is going to approve religious displays and nativity scenes in state buildings, then state officials know the Foundation will be back to ensure that nonreligious views—which may be as offensive to believers as nativity scenes are to us—will be represented, too.

> Such a practice [prayer at public council meetings] "alienates any non-Christian and non-believers" by turning them into "political outsiders of their own community and government."

This fear provides another reason for the resistance to the Christian right by those who oppose religion in general. This perception of victimization allows cultural progressive activists to develop a need to protect themselves from the excesses of religion. To protect themselves, they must battle the Christian right within the political sphere. Thus, they perceive their actions, no matter how aggressive those actions may seem to religious individuals, as necessary for self-defense. Conceptualizing this shared norm as a persecuted minority allows them to create unity within their ranks and to motivate the members in their social movement.[1] The degree of loyalty toward their social movement is likely correlated with the degree to which cultural progressive activists perceive themselves as persecuted, providing the organizations that support cultural progressives with motivation to maintain the image of religionists as potential oppressors.

Another interesting argument developed in the primary literature was that religion was rejected not merely because of its poisonous effects upon society. There was also a claim that religion corrupts our ability to engage in moral behavior. In other words, irreligious individuals are seen as more moral than religious individuals. Earlier in the chapter we saw that respondents reacted against their perception of religious individuals as being judgmental and interfering in the lives of others. However, a different characteristic of the Christian right was used to indicate its moral bankruptcy. The literature argues that forgiveness is actually an immoral concept that leads to social evil.[2]

> TGIF
> *Thank God I'm Forgiven*
> I must admit it's clever, but it really inviting me to finish the sentence:
> *Because I Don't Want to be Responsible for My Actions.*
>
> It's my understanding that you can be a really despicable human—a serial killer or Halliburton CEO—and if you accept JC into your heart, you'll still go to heaven. So if you got religion, what's the point of being civil.

Rather than helping people to develop into better human beings, the religious person can justify terrible actions since forgiveness is on the way. According to such logic, it makes sense that oppression and abuse are parts of religious faith. A moral person would be able to look at reality without relying on the supernatural and then still act with the moral power to do what is right.

> I don't need religion to complete my life and explain my existence. I am an atheist, I am an evolutionist, I am a great person without religion.

> Regardless of beliefs, personal doctrines or agendas, in the dark of night, everyone wonders if they are doing the right things and if their lives are heading in the right direction. The main difference is that atheists don't ask for absolution or guidance from any supernatural force.

> But I also reject religion and supernaturalism for moral reasons. It allows believers to console themselves that things will all work out in the end, despite all evidence to the contrary.

> Knowing that I have the individual strength of character necessary to overcome any challenge that comes my way is much more satisfying than begging to an invisible man in the sky. God is nothing more than a security blanket or a crutch. When I let go of God, I simultaneously took control of my life, and I refuse to give it up.

In many ways, certain nonreligious individuals who reject religion in general perceive themselves as morally superior to their religious kin. Even those religious individuals who conduct themselves in a morally acceptable way are seen as likely doing it for the wrong reasons. They seek to obtain heaven or fear a nonexistent deity. But nonreligious individuals do what is right merely because it is right. This puts them on a higher moral plane. Ironically, in some ways this may make these culturally progressive organizations guilty of the very judgmentalism that some of the participants in the survey complained about when discussing members of the Christian right. But if religion does not produce even moral actions within individuals, then one may wonder what good it is. To those who reject religion in general, it is not good at all. It is a poison that must be eliminated from society.

Finally, we should present a word about those who perceive religion as corrupted. As mentioned earlier, these individuals are not as hostile to religion in general as those in the *religion is poison* subgroup. But they are saddened by the changes in religion that have led it to become the intolerant and ignorant enterprise we see today. We did not find a lot of evidence that expressed the concern that religion has become corrupted. This may reflect the fact that our analysis indicates that relatively few respondents clearly fit into this category. However, one of our primary sources did contain the following quotation from President Jimmy Carter, who is clearly a person of faith and does not desire to see an end to religion, that distinctly enunciates the concerns of the *religion has been corrupted* group.

> My faith is a source of strength and comfort to me, as religious beliefs are to hundreds of millions of people around the world. So my decision to sever my ties with the Southern Baptist Convention, after six decades, was painful and difficult. It was, however, an unavoidable decision when the convention's leaders, quoting a few carefully selected Bible verses and claiming that Eve was created second to Adam and was responsible for original sin, ordained that women must be "subservient" to their husbands and prohibited from serving as deacons, pastors or chaplains in the military service.

As such there is a small, but viable, group that is concerned with the changes they see in modern religion. They desire to see religion altered but not eliminated. We contend that their concerns are not limited to a single denomination or a single religion, unlike Carter. But rather they are likely to condemn certain fundamentalist excesses of religion regardless of the faith.

General opposition to religion is tied to a larger collective identity that devalues both political conservatism and traditional religion. Many of the issues brought up by individuals who oppose religion in general have political ramifications to them. For example, discussions of religious oppression often were followed by concerns about the separation of church and state. While many of these quotes did not cleanly tie the concerns of the respondents to political action, it is a mistake to ignore the political desires of many respondents. Those who fall into the opposition of religion in general are clearly more active in their opposition to religion than in their promotion of progressive politics. But there is no evidence that they are any less eager to accept political progressiveness than other respondents. In this way, they accept the emergent norm of a more secular and politically progressive society that is part of their cultural progressive vision. However, their focus is much more on dealing with the generalized excesses of religion than on the political sphere that provided the motivation for the groups in chapter 4.

CHAPTER 6

Cultural Progressive Activists and Critics of Christianity

As mentioned in the previous chapter, animosity toward religion does not have to be generalized. In fact, we found that some of the hostility directed toward the Christian right is specifically due to misgivings about Christianity. When that is the case, then the subgroups described in the previous chapter are inadequate for understanding all of the religious reasons why individuals oppose the Christian right. There is a need to comprehend opposition based upon hostility toward Christianity itself.

We have termed those who have a unique opposition toward Christianity as *critics of Christianity*. At this point we use the term only to define individuals whose animosity toward Christians and Christianity motivates their hostility toward the Christian right. Since we asked the respondents questions about politically active Christians, we may assume that the way critics of Christianity are being defined in this context concerns their hostility toward Christian involvement in politics. However, that may not be the best way to conceptualize them since the Christian right is tied to conservative politics. We speculate that this hostility is directed toward politically conservative Christians and not just political activism in general. As such, we have little reason to believe that such individuals would oppose the Christian-based political activism of Martin Luther King in the same manner that they oppose the Christian-based political activism of James Dobson.[1]

However, as we will show, that animosity toward Christianity rather than toward political conservatism is the more powerful shaper of the attitudes of some respondents. They likely reject the political conservatism among members of the Christian right, but it is the Christian beliefs manifested among members of the Christian right that really fires up their hostility. However, the source of their hostility to Christianity varies among the respondents. It is the similar, but distinct, sources that determine the two subgroups of critics of Christianity documented in this research.

Christianity as Unevolved

The first group of critics of Christianity consists of individuals concerned with the lack of progress tied to the influence of Christianity. The members of this group perceive Christianity as a religion of the past that threatens to take society backward. They are also concerned that Christianity is hindering progress in society. So even if Christians do not take society backward, they do not allow society to progress at the rate these respondents believe it should. As such, we have named this subgroup *Christianity as unevolved* in that the respondents look to Christianity specifically, and not just religion in general, as the barrier to social progression.

The premise of such respondents is that Christianity is a regressive societal force. As stated above, there are two clear ways in which this regressive force is detrimental. First, respondents from this group worry that Christianity threatens to take us back to earlier and more barbaric times.

> Some of this group wants to establish a theocracy and to have all laws and rules confirm to Biblical law. They will use any means to accomplish their goal to undermine democracy, so that their theology can dominate. (male, over 75, master's degree)

> Believe in the bible myth as opposed to scientific inquiry, treatment of women as second class citizens. They have opposed every

> progressive movement this country has gone thru. If it were up to them we would still be burning witches in Salem. (male, 46–55, bachelor's degree)

> Has the Christian Right (a misnomer for sure), not learned from the Middle Ages and what happens when the Church runs the government!! (female, 66–75, bachelor's degree)

> Their 14th-century mind-set, their religious beliefs about imaginary beings such as gods, devils and witches, their socially backwards views on abortion, birth control, and the place of women in society, their partially successful attempts to convert the U.S. military into a religiously fundamentalist organization, etc., etc. (male, 66–75, some college)

> Their culture evolves at a slower pace than progressives and therefore they cling to 1st century religious superstition and let these beliefs influence decisions that affect society as a whole. (male, 56–65, some college)

Some individuals may desire the "good 'ol days." Clearly these respondents are not such individuals. They see previous times as unenlightened and backward. They conceptualize our past cultural heritage as one of intolerance, ignorance, and cruelty. Christianity can be seen as a philosophy focused on the past and perhaps attempting to bring that past back. The traditional expressions of Christianity typical of the Christian right can be seen as part of this tradition of worshiping the past. Some of the respondents fear such a tradition and want to escape the past.

Second, many respondents from this group perceive Christianity as a threat to our future. For them, Christians and Christianity may stand in the way of the natural progress of our society.

> They are a detriment to society because they resist positive change toward more freedom of thought and action. (male, 46–55, master's degree)

> I am very disappointed when the Christian Right slows our scientific and health progress because of their religious beliefs. (male, 56–65, bachelor's degree)

> It is beliefs like theirs, a sort of redux of the Inquisition, that contributes to civilization's difficulty in moving forward and changing the ignorance, disease and poverty that afflicts so much of the world. They are not a solution; they are part of the problem. (female, 66–75, bachelor's degree)

If the past represents an unenlightened and socially confining time, then for these respondents the future can be seen as enlightening and liberating. But according to these respondents the Christian right threatens to stop us from enjoying such a future. While some of the concerns brought up by the respondents involve the political movement generated by the Christian right, there are also concerns about the traditional social norms and religious beliefs that members of the Christian right want to establish. As such, this is not merely a political argument about the direction of our government but also an argument about the general direction of all sectors of our society. In the minds of the respondents, it is about whether we are going to move forward to an age of enlightenment or be stuck in the tribal bickering and ignorance that we currently experience.

A common complaint among many activists is the argument put forth by some Christians about the religious nature of the United States. Individuals within this group do not perceive this characteristic as desirable or accurate. They angrily contend that we are not and never have been a "Christian nation." While some of this argument is directed at the contemporary need to find a way to incorporate those of different religions and faiths, there is also hostility toward the idea that the United States was founded as a Christian nation and remains so today. In fact, for many respondents in this group, this is merely one more example of how the Christian right has distorted reality.

> Erroneously using the notion that the U.S. is a "Christian nation" to justify positions and actions. (male, 46–55, master's degree)

> A friend sent me e-mail messages concerning the "fact" that America was a Christian nation. When I responded with information from the Constitution and the writings of the founding fathers, he was offended. (male, over 75, master's degree)

> There should be a law prohibiting them from proliferating the lie that the USA is a "Christian nation." (male, 56–65, bachelor's degree)
>
> Fundamentalist Christians who have a dominionist worldview, desire to implement Biblical law as law of US, hold that US is a "Christian nation." Very scared that they will stop at nothing to take over US to remake it as "Christian nation." I am distrustful, outraged, and sickened by the blindness of the majority that support their political agenda. (female, 56–65, bachelor's degree)
>
> The Christian Right is attempting to politically force their views of a largely {sic} Old Testament with some New Testament on a civilian population. They want to create an obedience and law based New Jerusalem of the USA. They want to establish a so called "Christian Nation." (male, 56–65, doctorate)

This complaint becomes one more way in which such respondents believe that the Christian right is stifling knowledge and growth. But it is more than the contention of bad knowledge. It allows these respondents to make the claim that Christianity has never been central to the formation of rights and freedoms in the United States. With such legitimization, any role that Christianity has played in establishing the development of Western civilization can be denied. This claim frees the respondents to envision an evolutionary process without significant input from Christianity.

The notion of societal evolution is a powerful one among individuals who are part of the *Christianity as unevolved* group. Indeed, among many respondents there was concern about the attack of the Christian right on the teaching of evolution. Although biological evolution and societal evolution do not necessarily share the same supporters, clearly within these respondents there is a significant subgroup that perceives it to be important that society engages in a process of societal evolution as well. This philosophy fits well into a secularist perspective whereby human society is constantly improving through the acquisition of knowledge and education. Education can be seen as a way in which individuals in society can experiment with innovations and thus find ways for our culture to evolve. Respondents in this group see Christians as barriers to this improvement with their hostile approach toward education and societal experimentation.

> They frighten me. In a time when our schools rank nearly dead last in science, they want to present creationism as a true science. Our children deserve better. (female, 36–45, high school diploma)

> Believe in the bible myth as opposed to scientific inquiry, treatment of women as second class citizens. They have opposed every progressive movement this country has gone thru. If it were up to them we would still be burning witches in Salem. (male, 46–55, bachelor's degree)

> Religious conservatism that want to have a system of government ruled by ancient religious ideas that are totally out of touch and unrealistic towards the personal freedoms that everyone deserves to have apart from religious ideals and allows people to express their individuality thus promoting the change and progress that has advanced society and actually helped make life better for many people. (male, 36–45, some college)

These comments indicate that some respondents clearly see Christianity as a barrier to creating a better society. The degree to which the Christian right seeks to inhibit the type of societal changes desired by respondents who fall into the *Christianity as unevolved* group inspires the members of that group to go to war with the Christian right. Respondents in the *Christianity as unevolved* group are less willing to have an apolitical Christian as a neighbor than an irreligious Republican. Thus, hostilities do not tend to center on political desires but on the different visions that members of the *Christianity as unevolved* group have for societal evolution in comparison to the Christian right. Political issues are just part of the larger contest between worldviews animated by a humanist philosophy versus a belief in a supernatural vision for our society.

A couple of social factors may shed further light on the dynamics of individuals within this group. They are more likely to have born-again individuals within their social networks and are more likely to live in the South than are other respondents. Undoubtedly these demographic factors work together since individuals who are conservative Christians are more likely to reside in the South than in other areas of the United States. The exposure to Christians on a daily basis may help to shape their antipathy toward Christians. It is possible that such exposure provides evidence to these respondents that Christians support mores that are socially retrogressive. Some of the respondents in this subgroup freely commented on how their experiences with Christians showed them that such individuals have an unenlightened view of reality.

> I grew up in a southern Baptist home my entire life. I was "born-again" at 5 years old, not really knowing what I was committing to, but certainly knowing that I didn't want to burn in hell, so I chose accordingly. As I grew older, went to college, and ultimately formed my own belief system, I realized how one sided and narrow most of my teaching was growing up. . . . I always attended a mainstream, large, usually wealthy organization. I did have friends in the small fundamentalist schools/churches and they were even more adherent to some of the most primitive rules. (male, 26–35, bachelor's degree)

> My sister (a devoted Baptist) insisting her daughter be taught pseudo-science. In her words the subject was not open for discussion for an oppositional point of view, even from a family member. At that point, I realized the scope and height of the wall Christians build to keep them from "thinking outside the box" (scratch box and insert "bible book binder"). (male, 36–45, bachelor's degree)

> A young street preacher living at a motel in small town in Northern Arizona that our motorcycle group (7 men) stayed overnight at one summer. We got into an evolution debate and he invited himself over to our group having cocktails (whiskey and beer) on the common patio, bible in hand. I, as the resident atheist of our group, destroyed his arguments with Dawkins, Harris, Dennett and Hitchens. I do believe his faith was relatively new and had kept him off drugs (of which I commended him), but his ignorance of science and religious history was typically appalling and he frequently protested that he was more into "heavenly knowledge"

rather than "worldly knowledge." That cop out I also destroyed, allowing him to come to the realization himself that he was truly a slave wrapped in golden chains that "feel good" most of the time, but are still chains. (male, 56–65, bachelor's degree)

We were debating abortion in high school (this was mid-eighties . . . I'm sure you could not mention that now) and one fundamentalist said that abortion was wrong, even if the mother will die. I thought, and still do, that that gal is a four star idiot . . . but I know she was just parroting what she was hearing at church. (female, 36–45, master's degree)

A traveling evangelist came to campus. He set up his "soapbox" outside of the Student Union, and preached from that spot for a week. I went by one day, with several of my friends, to listen to him. I was struck, unfavorably, by amazement to hear him tell the crowd that all of the females should cease attending college, should cease any pre-marital sexual relationships, and should go home to live with their parents as dutiful daughters until such time as each joined herself in marriage as a dutiful wife with a good Christian man. . . . I am confident that this man was a member of the Christian Right, and that he still is. (female, 46–55, bachelor's degree)

Given such experiences, it is not surprising that certain respondents are concerned about the Christian right gaining power in our society and imposing values that such respondents find reprehensible. Respondents with negative encounters with members of the Christian right may interpret what is a neutral incident as a negative one or may actually experience what is clearly a negative encounter. Regardless of whether the incidents above are determined by their interpretation or not, the end result is a reinforcement of the belief about the regressive nature of Christian fundamentalism. Even though these individuals are more likely to be Christians than other cultural progressive activists, their interpersonal contact with members of the Christian right is a big source of their hostility regardless of their own Christian belief.

Contact theory suggests that contact with out-group members produces opportunities for individuals to develop tolerance toward those members (Caspi, 1984; Pettigrew, 1998; Yancey, 2007). However, for some activists such contact serves merely to reinforce previous concerns about the out-group. Since contact is theorized to produce only positive relations when it occurs under the proper conditions (Caspi, 1984; Dixon & Rosenbaum, 2004; Pettigrew, 1998), there may be value in future work that determines when contact between cultural progressive activists and the Christian right encourages tolerance and when such contact exacerbates the current cultural conflict. With this current sample, we can see how such contact may exacerbate the negative perceptions that respondents have about the goals of the Christian right. Yet this negative assessment of the regressive goals of the Christian right does not necessarily indicate that there is personal animosity directed toward members of the Christian right. In fact, individuals in this subgroup were more likely to state that they had no problem living in a neighborhood with the Christian right. When this acceptance of potential Christian right neighbors is combined with the fact that these individuals have a higher percentage of born-again individuals in their social networks, it is clear that they are more likely to enjoy friendships and relationships with individuals who are members of the Christian right. It is plausible that intergroup contact has little effect on their willingness to assess Christianity as an outdated belief system, but it does help them to appreciate Christians as individuals.

Christians as Political Oppressors

The second group of critics of Christianity is less open to interpersonal relationships with conservative Christians. They are more wary of this religious group and more fearful of the intentions of Christians as individuals, as well as their aims as a group. This group is concerned that Christians seek to force their will on others in society. Thus, they conceptualize *Christians as political oppressors*, which is the title we provide for them. For this group Christianity is a problem because it is an enabling force for a political ideology that the respondents see as oppressive. It is tempting to see this as part of the groups motivated by political concerns. While this group does have serious political problems with the Christian right, their greater concerns are centered on the nature of Christianity and its ability to sustain oppressive political structures. They focus more on the religious foundations of dysfunctional political systems rather than the systems themselves.

Part of this religious, as opposed to political, hostility can be seen in the low opinion that members of this group have for Christians. As we mentioned in the previous paragraph, they are less likely to have Christians in their social network than those in the *Christianity as unevolved* group. Their perception of members of the Christian right helps drive this difference. For example, members of this group are more likely to complain about the tendency of the Christian right to be judgmental than other cultural progressive activists.

> Dogmatic, ideologues, intolerant, often very negative view of others' beliefs and views. Unwillingness to have an open mind and honest dialogue with others. (male, 56–65, master's degree)

> They are judgmental and blind to their own faults. (male, 36–45, bachelor's degree)

> It is a tossup between judgmentalism and intellectual dishonesty. Having assumed the mantle of their God, they feel the right to judge others by their understanding of that mantle. They are willing to ignore facts/history to support their beliefs. Of course, in this they are simply human. (male, 56–65, bachelor's degree)

This is similar to the complaints of the *religion has been corrupted* group. And like members of that group, these activists had negative perceptions of Christians as individuals. But unlike members of that group, they were not likely to see good within the Christian right. Rather, they tended to have a very dark perspective that they linked to all Christians. As such, they attributed very negative characteristics to Christians as individuals. For example, intolerance is another characteristic that individuals in this group attributed to members of the Christian right.

> Rigid belief that they are right and you are wrong and have no respect in diversity of opinion. . . . Would squelch all dissenting opinion as immoral. (male, 56–65, master's degree)

> Strict belief in their interpretation of the Bible; intolerance of other religions not strictly theirs; intention and efforts to impose their religion on society in any way, including use of government. (male, 66–75, master's degree)

> Dogmatic, ideologues, intolerant, often very negative view of others' beliefs and views. Unwillingness to have an open mind and honest dialogue with others. (male, 56–65, master's degree)

> People who see only Black vs. White, Right vs. wrong, and feel entitled, nay feel a duty, to force their views on others. . . . Judgmental Fundamentalists who believe all others are depraved and deserve their hell-bound status. . . . They are entitled to their views, but must not be allowed to fulfill their agenda of forcing their views everyone else. They want the symbols of their religion posted publicly, but would deny that option to all other viewpoints. Tolerant, caring people must oppose their agenda. (male, 46–55, doctorate)

Given the fact that 61.3 percent of all respondents made at least one complaint regarding the intolerance of the Christian right in their statements, it is quite noteworthy that members of this group were more likely than other cultural progressive activists to make such complaints. This finding indicates an especially high propensity of individuals in the *Christians as political oppressors* subgroup to conceptualize intolerance as a major feature of the Christian right. Finally, it is noteworthy that one of the reasons why individuals in this group were less willing to live in a neighborhood with members of the Christian right is a fear of proselytizing.

> I'm a rational person. I don't want to hear any more about magical thinking, Jesus, or hell. The person on the Christian Right has as his purpose on this earth to save all the unbelievers, so in his mind he isn't going to (go) quietly into that good night without first trying to convert me. (female, 66–75, bachelor's degree)

> Part of their mandate includes converting non-believers and because I'd be forced to be surrounded with their culture. (male, 56–65, bachelor's degree)
>
> They would be on my case to convert me. (male, over 75, some graduate training)
>
> Yes, because I'd get really tired of listening to them try to "convert" me. (female, 36–45, master's degree)

Members of the *Christians as political oppressors* subgroup are not any more fearful of proselytizing in general than other respondents. However, the idea of living near Christians disproportionately produces such fears for members of this group. This is clearly a group that does not relish the idea of interacting with conservative Christians. Avoidance of Christians is a defining characteristic of this group and a major reason why we conceptualize this group as critics of Christianity.

Perhaps their mistrust of Christians is due to the fact that they had fewer interactions with fundamentalists at an early age than did the other respondents. However, members of this group are more likely than other respondents to be Christians themselves. This leads to an interesting note about some critics of Christianity in that they themselves are Christians. They are also more educated, have higher incomes, and are older than the other respondents in our sample.[2] The educational difference may be the most important demographic factor, as it suggests that those who are Christians are unlikely to have fundamentalist or evangelical beliefs. They are also more likely than other cultural progressive activists to have Jewish friends in their current social networks and in their networks at age 15. They are also more likely than other respondents to have friends who are spiritual but not religious. This indicates that those who are Christians are more likely to practice a Christianity that is more interfaith in nature than the religion practiced by members of the Christian right. Some of them may have a Christian faith that is more focused upon religious tolerance and societal progressiveness than other Christians. Those who have this faith are likely embarrassed by some of the activities of the Christian right. Indeed, many of the Christians in our overall sample did indicate such embarrassment.

> Jesus teaches us to love our enemies. The "Christian" Right makes me ashamed to be a Christian more than anything else in the entire world ever could. (female, 26–35, master's degree)

> Nothing they do, think, behave is at all very Jesus-like. They are the opposite of Jesus' way of thinking and being. I'm embarrassed to be linked to them when all we share is the title of "Christian." The church I go to now is so unlike them. We are a progressive church, Christian, yes, but loving, caring, accepting, respectful, and tolerant of all faiths and people. (female, 46–55, bachelor's degree)

> I consider myself to be a Christian, and I am ashamed of the Christian Right in its intolerance and hypocrisy. I don't want to be mistaken as that kind of Christian, yet I don't want to relinquish the name "Christian." I want moderate Christians to take back the name "Christian" from the right. I believe it is our duty, just as I believe it is the responsibility of moderate Muslims to take back the name "Muslim" from terrorists using that name to hurt people. (female, 46–55, doctorate)

> I really have nothing positive to say about the Christian Right. They have given Christianity a very bad reputation and have made moderate Christians like myself embarrassed to admit that we are Christians, fearing we will immediately be lumped together with the Christian Right. (female, 66–75, bachelor's degree)

> I am ashamed to admit to being Christian because of the political stigma attached. (male, 26–35, master's degree)

This embarrassment and this desire to distance themselves from the Christian right explain their desire to fight against them. By engaging in such a fight, they are able to define themselves as not members of this group and develop a Christian identity that is more comfortable for them. This type of conflict is reminiscent of the conflict between mainline and progressive Christianity based on notions of social justice and fundamentalist or conservative Christianity based on the ideals of evangelism and conservative religious theology. The fact that members of this group are older than other cultural progressive activists may indicate that they are more aware of earlier conflicts between mainline and fundamentalist Christianity that occurred in the middle of the 20th century. They may have even been very active in those conflicts. We need to be careful to note that this mainline/fundamentalist conflict was not the motivating force for all individuals in the *Christians as political oppressors* group. Indeed, even in this group only 11 percent are Christians of one type or another, as opposed to the rest of the sample, which is 9 percent Christian. So for the vast majority of critics of Christianity there is not a struggle to define their own Christian identity as separate from the Christian right.

There is more evidence that *Christians as political oppressors* oppose a particular type of Christianity rather than the Christian faith in its entirety. For example, they are more hostile to Christian fundamentalists relative to other religious groups than are other cultural progressive activists. They also rank Muslims higher than fundamentalists at a significantly higher rate than do other respondents. Furthermore, unlike the *Christianity as unevolved* group, members in this group are more willing to have apolitical Christians as neighbors than are irreligious Republicans. Indeed, members of this group are more likely to attribute negative personal characteristics to potential Republican neighbors than are other respondents. This seemed to be especially the case when the respondent himself or herself identified as Christian, but it was generally true of individuals in this subgroup regardless of whether the respondent is a Christian or not. Belonging to this group seems to make a respondent especially likely to attach negative personal characteristics to potential Republican neighbors.

> In my experience, persons with strong political views of this nature often make comments that are ignorant, angry or offensive. (male, 46–55, some college)
>
> Since I am still a Christian, I'd rather live next to another Christian, as long as that person is not of the Right Wing. A Republican

> with no spiritual bearing is likely to be rather uncompassionate. (male, 46–55, doctorate)
>
> Vocal Republicans tend to be confrontational besides being opinionated. (male, 36–55, bachelor's degree)
>
> A vocal republican would be worse because they are mean and narrow minded. (female, 66–75, bachelor's degree)
>
> I would probably have a more difficult time discussing ideas of a political nature with hard Right Winger because of the brashness and pomposity that I've come to expect on that end of the political spectrum; and I admit my defense would be up as I would expect to not be accepted by my neighbor should my ideas not match up with his or hers. (male, 26–35, some graduate training)
>
> I would rank the vocal Republican lower as I find them generally selfish and without a desire to help the less fortunate. (male, 36–45, master's degree)
>
> Vocal Republicans are generally obnoxious, and vocal Christians can't do much to bother me because I, myself, am Christian. (female, 46–55, master's degree)

These respondents do not necessarily mind having a Christian as a neighbor, but it is the combination of conservative activism and Christian faith that disturbs them. Fundamentalists, especially those who are politically active, and not Christianity in general, is what angers them.

Given this reality, we can now see how the characteristics of members in this group fit in with their perspective of certain Christians. The Christians they do not like are intolerant, a feature they likely tie to political conservatism. The same can be said for their concern about the judgmental attitudes of the Christian right. This judgmentalism is likely tied to a perception of political arrogance. Yet this is not merely a political assessment. There is a fear of proselytizing that is one of the fears of having Christian right neighbors. Such proselytizing can also be a potential way in which members of the Christian right are seen as intolerant and judgmental. This concern is generally tied to a fundamentalism that seeks to impose its particular notion of Christianity upon others. Thus, this is not a category compelled by purely political concerns; rather, these respondents fear a political ideology motivated by religious fervor.

When we examine the characteristics they fear, we are in a position to see that their concern is about the ability of Christians to oppress others. Because of their interfaith social networks, it is likely that these respondents are worried about the imposition of conservative Christianity upon non-Christians. Such individuals may envision an interfaith society in which a tolerant form of Christianity is merely one of many forms of religious expression. The Christian right is a threat to this interfaith society since they support political positions that are conceptualized as intolerant by members of this group. Yet political concerns do not appear to be the greatest fear of members in this group. For example, they are less willing than other cultural progressive activists to use laws against members of the Christian right because of their fears that such laws will have a negative impact on free speech rights.

> Liberty means we allow all ideas, even ideas we abhor. Now when they seek to overthrow the Constitution, then we have a problem, but that is a question of being vigilant, not authoring new laws. (male, 46–55, master's degree)

> No, they have a right to their beliefs and freedom of speech, as much as I or anyone else does. Their problem is they think their way is the only way and do not want to accept that there are other acceptable and viable opinions and options. (female, 46–55, bachelor's degree)

> Despite their oppressive and fascist views, it is as much their right to express their views as it is anyone else's. To legislatively restrict their actions as a specific religious group is inappropriate and an anathema to the principles of a democratic society. If we elect their leaders as our national and regional leaders, and if we allow their opinions to shape public policy, then we have no one to blame for their dominance in the political arena but ourselves. (male, 46–55, doctorate)

> There is a law: it's called the First Amendment to the U.S. Constitution, also known as Article One of the Bill of Rights. It guarantees freedom of religion to those who chose to believe in the supernatural, and freedom from religion to those who choose instead to believe in reality and reason. It simply needs to be enforced. (male, 46–55, bachelor's degree)

> People are free to believe as they choose—but not infringe on MY right to do the same . . . so no, I would not favor enacting "laws" to harm members of the Christian Right. (male, 56–65, some graduate training; emphasis in original)

Even though they have severe political disagreements with members of the Christian right, they are more cautious about imposing political restrictions upon members of this group than other cultural progressive activists. This group has an overarching concern about political and religious freedom that they fear will be lost if the Christian right gains power. But according to these respondents fear of political imposition by the Christian right cannot be eliminated by limiting their political expression. Such an attitude indicates a limitation of the political fears that such respondents have as they likely believe that bad political ideas will be defeated in free and open communication.

However, the greater concern seems to be tied to the religious imposition of the Christian right. It is that imposition where they fear that judgmentalism and intolerance can have the most powerful effect. These individuals may fear the interpersonal interaction that members of the Christian right have with those of other religions and how this interaction imposes upon the rights of members of those religions to fully enjoy their own faith. At that point Christianity may become a source of political oppression, but it is the religious imposition that creates the greater concern for these respondents. As with the other groups, for this group it is not a simple choice of whether religion or politics is the bigger worry. Members of this group do have antipathy toward Republicans. But their hostility toward fundamentalists indicates that religious concerns are more central to their activity against the Christian right than is political activism.[3] They fit well into the notion of having hostility toward Christianity, although it is a certain type of Christianity that this hostility is directed toward.

Critics of Christianity and Primary Literature

Just as there are stories in the primary literature that support those who oppose the Christian right because of conservative politics or opposition to religion in general, there are also important messages for those who oppose Christianity specifically. It should not come as a surprise that Christianity faces unique opposition from some of the activists. The flaws of Christianity, as the dominant religion in this society, are going to be more apparent to cultural progressive activists than the shortcomings found in other religions. As such, Christians are more likely to engender the ire of cultural progressive activists than adherents of other religions.

But beyond the distinct characteristics within Christianity, there is also a story about the imposition of Christianity on our society. Clearly some of the respondents indicated a fear about the undue influence that Christians have in our society. This fear is echoed in much of the primary literature we found that served these respondents. Before we get to those fears, we should first discuss that much of the primary literature discussed the *Religious right* instead of the *Christian right*. In the last two chapters, this difference was not important. However, since the focus of this chapter is the cultural progressive critique of Christianity, it is important to note this distinction. But despite this terminology, it is clear that in the minds of the writers in the primary literature, they still have the idea of Christian activists in mind even as they use the term *Religious right*.

> The single greatest threat to church-state separation is the movement known as the Religious Right. Organizations and leaders representing this religio-political crusade seek to impose a fundamentalist Christian viewpoint on all Americans through governmental action.
>
> Backed by national Religious Right organizations, proponents of these ideas seek to drive evolution from the science classroom

and replace it with their interpretation of the Bible. If they succeed, church-state separation and sound science education may be irreparably harmed.

There is {sic} no signs that the Religious Right is moderating its agenda. The movement seeks to scale back church-state separation and bring in a government that reflects "Christian" values. In keeping with fundamentalist theology, activists seek to ban all abortions, deny civil rights protections for gays, fund religious schools and other ministries with tax dollars and teach Bible and creationism in public schools.

As reflected in the primary literature, for many individuals, religious activism is equated with Christian activism, and this is reflected in the primary literature of cultural progressive activists. Given the reality that Christianity is the most prominent religion in the United States, this should not come as a surprise. Even when there is an interfaith element within religious conservatism, there is still usually deference given to Christianity. Conservative religious Jewish personalities such as Michael Medved and Dennis Prager still tend to indicate a great deal of respect for Christianity (Medved, 1992; Prager, 2004). The main difference between the attitudes that buttress critics of Christianity and those that support hostility toward religion in general is the focus of the former on Christianity. However, it is quite possible that this focus is due to the religious context in the United States, as critics of Christianity may become "critics of Islam" if they lived in the Middle East.

Nevertheless, there are unique aspects connected to the ideas critics of Christianity articulate about the United States. Much of the struggle of critics of Christianity is against the centrality of Christianity as a governing force within the United States. As such, a key concept that is part of the critics of Christianity is the notion that the United States is not a Christian nation. The denial of the argument that the United States is a Christian nation is an important political assertion by some respondents. Some of the primary literature concentrates on finding historical arguments that justify their claims that the United States was not founded as a Christian nation. They refer to the writings of historical figures such as Thomas Jefferson, James Madison, and George Washington as they see fit to reinforce their claim about the non-Christian founding of the United States. Some of them also refer to the Treaty of Tripoli as evidence of the non-Christian origin of the United States. Thomas Jefferson's letter to the Danbury Baptists is almost "sacred scripture" to some of these advocates.[4] In short, the critics of Christianity advocate an interpretation of U.S. history that allows them to minimize the Christian influence on its origin. We are not historians and thus cannot speak to the accuracy of their interpretations; however, there are clearly important religious and political implications to these interpretations. Such interpretations allow critics of Christianity to minimize the historical contributions of Christians and eventually the value of, at least conservative, Christianity today.

One of the complaints of the respondents with a critic of Christianity perspective is the scientific and educational neglect of Christians. As noted above, many of them also are concerned with the inaccurate history perpetuated by many Christians. This concern is echoed in the primary literature they read.

> Our forefathers, being educated and thinking . . . tried to set up a government of the people, by the people and for the people, so that absolutist thinking did not dominate our country.
>
> Religious freedom is a celebrated American tradition. Our Founders knew that mixing religion and government only caused civil strife, inequality and very often violence in pluralistic societies. For more than 300 years, church-state separation advocates have fought to keep the tradition moving forward. Thanks to these efforts Americans enjoy more religious liberty than any people in the world.

Religious freedom is an important value for critics of Christianity in that it also speaks of being free from religion. For these advocates, it is vital to indicate that such a freedom has been part of our society from its very beginning. Thus, they eagerly have entered into an argument about the historically Christian nature of our society and make a consistent argument that the United States was not set up as a Christian nation.

There are important contemporary ramifications behind this historical argument. If the United States was set up as a Christian nation, then critics of Christianity can be painted as radicals who want to change the basic nature of our society. But if it was set up under the umbrella of religious freedom, then it is the critics of Christianity who are fighting to preserve the basic nature of American society. Of course in that case it would be cultural conservative activists who would be the radicals attempting to alter the basic nature of American society. Therefore, a common theme within some of the readings is the argument that the Christian right is altering the basic nature of our society with their assertions about the primacy of Christianity. These readings contend that by pushing Christianity into such a central position, many in the Christian right are going down a path that is different from the one that was historically set by earlier Americans.

> Baptists have, since their earliest days, been advocates of religious liberty and its corollary, the separation of church and state. But different groups of modern-day Baptists in the United States interpret church-state separation—and the Constitution's provisions for it—in different ways.
>
> The Texas religious-right leader who is working hard to wed Christian fundamentalism to law and government, . . . [and] who calls separation of church and state a "myth," will help guide the revision of social studies curriculum standards for Texas public schools.
>
> Social conservatives are already moving to censor discussion of important civil rights leaders in the standards, while promoting dubious arguments that suggest the nation's Founders intended for our government and laws to be based on fundamentalist Christian biblical principles.

The critics of Christianity perceive the notion of a Christian founding to the United States as a myth. The result of that myth is the development of a society in which there continues to be abuses and ignorance perpetuated by members of the Christian right. Critics of Christianity can perceive themselves as the antidote to the dysfunctions promulgated by the Christian right.

Of course the contemporary problems created by the Christian right are not seen as limited to the promotion of an inaccurate history. Critics of Christianity are naturally concerned about the efforts of the Christian right to continue to invade the sanctity of church-state separation. This concern is also reflected in the primary literature.

> That doesn't mean council members can't pray; just do it before you come into the council chamber. Do it in private, do it in a separate room, do it in unison with others if you like. But once you enter the council chamber, you're not there to pray; you're there to govern by the consent of the governed, the people who elected you.

> The war for the soul and the government of America needs more Christian soldiers, Rev. Rick Scarborough, head of the Pearland-based far-right Vision America, and other speakers told about 100 attendees of the "Hope for American Rally."

> A well-organized and well-funded campaign is under way to undermine the separation of church and state in America's public schools. Aggressive religious pressure groups are pushing school boards nationwide to change the curriculum to conform to their doctrines.

This literature clearly plays on the fears that many cultural progressive activists have about the separation of church and state. These fears are that if those two institutions do not remain separate, the church will eventually take over the state. Accordingly, the literature suggests that if we are not careful, this invasion will lead to a Christian government that will endanger the rights of all non-Christians, who will be forced to pay homage to a religion that they do not believe in.

> The Ten Commandments are a sacred text in the Jewish and Christian faiths, but not for all Oklahomans. The government

cannot endorse one religious belief over others, nor can it prefer religion over non-religion. The legislature did exactly that when it approved this monument, and its begging for a legal challenge.

Men and women of many faiths and none have served our country honorably and died to preserve our rights. A Christian symbol cannot memorialize them all.

The Religious Right seeks to reorder society by insisting that the country embrace a rigid set of rules based on a narrow definition of Christianity. The movement leaders would use the power of government to force all of us to follow its dictates. This is the Religious Right's greatest mistake—and its biggest threat.

The fear of a Christian takeover of the United States may arguably be the biggest fear of critics of Christianity. Given their general antipathy toward conservative Christianity, such a reality would force them to live in a society that is counter to most, if not all, of what they believe. While some of the primary literature offered critiques of non-Christian religions, there was a clear fear enunciated in the literature of all of the problems that are found within Christian institutions. Note how the writings work to engender this fear, from the description of Dobson's "empire" to the comparison to Stormfront, a white supremacist organization, to the description of Liberty, a conservative Christian college, as politically oppressive, to the description of a secret Christian society by Sharlet.

> In the book *The Family: The Secret Fundamentalism at the Heart of American Power*, author Jeff Sharlet examines the power wielded by the secret Christian group known as The Family or The Fellowship.
>
> When Liberty University withdrew recognition from the student-run College Democrats earlier this year, left-leaning organizations quickly lashed out against the fundamentalist Christian school, accusing it of banning the club and saying that a person couldn't be a Christian and a Democrat. Since then, a new policy was instituted by the university to regulate political student clubs, thus giving the College Democrats the opportunity to

operate without hindrance once again when the new school year begins next month.

What do Pastor Rick Scarborough of the Texas-based organization Vision America, Cynthia Dunbar of the Texas State Board of Education and people at the racist Web site Stormfront have in common? They all believe President Obama is lying about being a natural-born citizen of the United States.

Although he poses as a {sic} avuncular family counselor, [James] Dobson and his empire spread Religious Right propaganda and extreme rhetoric . . . he attacked the concept of tolerance, calling it "kind of a watchword of those who reject the concepts of right and wrong. . . . It's kind of a desensitization to evil of all varieties." Two years before that, an FOF magazine attacked the Girl Scouts for being agents of "humanism and radical feminism."

Fears of a Christian takeover are clearly stroked by this literature. If the above quotations are too subtle, then other examples show how readers of this literature are clearly and sufficiently warned of the possibility of a Christian usurping of power.

The original idea was to create a funding pool that would subsidize the Religious Right's courtroom activity, and as its Web site proclaims, "reclaim the legal system for Jesus Christ."

To the Religious Right, education not infused with fundamentalist dogma is useless and an affront to God.

Religious Right groups have a specific set of goals for American life. The {sic} speak openly of "taking back" America, of asserting control over the lives of every single citizen. They have an agenda, and they want action on it.

Modern Religious Right groups might not press overtly for writing their understanding of Christianity into the Constitution, but their agenda, if implemented, would force Americans to live under a system of laws based on fundamentalist interpretations of the Bible.

While there are critiques of other religions, the idea of a religious takeover is generally preserved for Christians. This focus on Christianity is clearly a consequence of its relative influence and status as the majority religion in the United States.

As we have seen within the other major categories, there are also themes among the critics of Christianity concerning the mixture of politics and religion. On their surface, the issues brought forth by critics of Christianity seem to focus only on the religious nature of the Christian right. In reality, the fears of Christians are connected to fears about their potential political might and influence. Thus, the concerns are connected to an interaction of religion and politics. This propensity can be seen in some of the writings.

> In the 1990s, Religious Right forces regrouped under TV preacher Pat Robertson's Christian Coalition. This organization focused heavily on local politics, playing {sic} special attention to public school boards. Its supporters brazenly demanded an end to public education and the "Christianization" of politics.

> The Republican Party has become the first religious party in U.S. history.

> Reconstructionism, which openly opposes democracy and calls for a harsh Old Testament-based theocracy, has never been a large movement. The main groups promoting it, the Chalcedon Foundation and American Vision, do not have large budgets but are recognized as having established the framework for mixing religion and politics that many Religious Right leaders cite as a model for their activism.

> The Religious Right seeks to build church-based political machines to help elect ultra-conservative candidates. Movement leaders want to forge a voting bloc based in conservative churches that are so powerful no GOP aspirant to public office can ignore it.

It is likely the case that many critics of Christianity would have concerns about Christianity even if the intermingling of politics that has been part of the Christian right did not exist. The disdain that some of the critics of Christianity have for supernatural beliefs would produce such concerns. However, the political action of the Christian right provides an added sense of urgency and danger to these cultural progressive activists and helps to provide legitimization to their activism. Christian and political conservatism are linked in the opposition of critics of Christianity to the Christian right. This fits with the general trend already observed among the previous two groups and suggests that part of the collective identity of cultural progressive activists is a mixing of religious and political objections to the Christian right.

In sum, this group of cultural progressive activists finds the major source of their motivation to counter the Christian right in their fears concerning a particular adaptation of Christianity. Their reaction to Christianity is tied to a historical understanding of the religious and political history of the United States that differs from that of cultural conservatives. From their perspective, the common misunderstandings of our nation's history and the proper role of Christianity today help to perpetuate the abuses and attempts at governmental takeover that are promulgated by the Christian right.

Summary of the Major Themes from All Three Groups of Cultural Progressives

In the past three chapters we have looked at the source of resistance to the Christian right from three different origin points. Chapter 4 looked at motivations created by political opposition, chapter 5 explored motivations created by hostility toward religion in general, and this chapter examined motivations generated by anger toward Christianity in particular. By exploring these different sources of motivations, we were able to appreciate some of the diversity and complexity of cultural progressive activists. This is not a monolithic movement, but rather there are a variety of different philosophies and ideas that provide motivation for the activism of cultural progressives. However, at this point it is useful to analyze some of the similar themes that tie members of the movement together. These ties provide the overarching themes that provide unity within the movement and engender a common understanding and language that cultural progressives use to empower their movement.

A clear theme we have already established is the fear of mixing religion and politics. Hostility toward political conservatives and hostility toward the highly religious comingle with each other, and it is taken for granted that the mixing of both forces is a big part of the problem. Separation of religion from governmental mechanisms is accepted as an important solution among cultural progressives. While atheists and agnostics are overrepresented in our sample, some of the cultural progressive activists do subscribe to a traditional supernatural Christian belief. Yet no matter what their individual beliefs may be, the respondents of our survey indicated overwhelming support for the separation of church and state. As such, they are particularly wary of a political movement that found its legitimization within religious beliefs. The reason for this wariness may vary depending on the general motivation of the respondents. For those with political motivation, the fears may come from the degree to which conservative politics may gain support from religious theology. For those mistrustful of religion in general, there is a powerful dream of a secular society, and religion is seen as "poisonous" to that dream. For critics of Christianity, there are concerns about how the historical and contemporary nature of Christianity may influence the larger social and political reality. But the same antipathy toward the mixing of religion and politics is shared by respondents in all three categories.

A second common theme shared by members of all three categories is the notion of the importance of rationality. Cultural progressive activists generally argue that they are the proponents of rationality and are in opposition to the superstitious arguments of their more conservative opponents. Indeed, many of them alluded to a perception of a societal evolution in which supernatural belief is to be replaced with rationality. The desire to be perceived as rational came out often in the description of the encounters that these respondents had with members of the Christian right as they often recounted how they outthought and outdebated their hapless Christian right opponents. For those with political motivations, this rationality is seen as leading to better political outcomes and thus is more beneficial to everyone in society. Those who oppose religion in general see the value of rationality in their critique of religion as an irrational institution. Critics of Christianity are particularly sensitized to the irrational aspects of Christianity. Cultural progressive activists envision themselves as rational actors who are attempting to infuse society with rational instead of traditional and often fear-based institutions.

A third theme is the value of limiting the influence of religion within our society. For many of the cultural progressive activists, religion should be limited to one's home and church. Some of the cultural progressive activists even question whether it is ethical to "brainwash" one's own children to adhere to a supernatural faith. Regardless of whether a respondent goes that far in his or her opposition to the influence of religion, there is clearly a desire to limit the influence of religion within the public and political spheres. Such desires are clear in the motivation of those driven by politics as they perceive religion as problematic to the creation of a healthy political order. This desire also feeds those who oppose religion in general since they desire religion to have as little influence in society as possible. Finally, critics of Christianity desire to see Christianity have a limited influence and argue that historically this has been the case for Christianity. An important tenet that the respondents agree upon, and that is supported in their primary literature, is that the United States was not established as a Christian nation, and thus Christianity has never been the core foundation of American values. This argument helps to legitimate a deemphasis of religion in the public sector. The reduction, or even removal, of religion from the public sphere is a powerful desire among many cultural progressive activists as they generally accept individuals practicing their religion privately but want religion to have little influence outside of private practice.

A final theme to be brought out is the value of progressive politics over conservative politics. A few respondents identified themselves as Republicans, and others mentioned that they respected the fiscal conservatism or muscular foreign policy supported by members of the Christian right. But the overwhelming number of respondents indicated a powerful progressive desire on a variety of political issues. Even those indicating some political conservatism tended to oppose the conservative stances on social issues such as abortion and same-sex marriage promulgated by the Christian right. But generally respondents also indicated hostility to the Christian right when it came to issues such as foreign policy toward Israel, environmentalism, the death penalty, health care, and so on. Political progressiveness is obviously a motivator for those who oppose the Christian right for political reasons. Political progressiveness also helps to shape the opposition of those who reject religion in general since religious nonbelief is often connected to political progressiveness (Christiano, 2000; A. B. Cohen et al., 2009; Layman & Green, 2005). Critics of Christianity also support political progressiveness as they often rail against the theological and political conservatism of certain Christians. Political progressiveness is an ideal commonly accepted by cultural progressive activists and motivates their fight against the Christian right.

These themes indicate taken-for-granted "truths" that have been adopted by the respondents. The respondents discuss them as if they are self-evident and have no further need of discussing the accuracy of these assertions. Indeed, the respondents discuss these themes in a manner indicating that only the uneducated or the foolish could disagree with them or believe in the doctrines of the Christian right.

> A good friend, an attorney and former colleague, came to visit and we argued about George Bush; her Christian Right sympathies came out. I suddenly saw her as foolish and the friendship ended. A similar incident happened with another colleague, a geologist whom I used to respect. (female, 56–65, master's degree)

> The Christian Right is a dangerous group that has played upon the emotions and fears of a large number of people who are either too uneducated, or too lazy to think for themselves. (female, 46–55, master's degree)

> They spend their money and waste their lives supporting their leaders, foolishly expecting their reward after death. Meanwhile, the leaders frequently live very extravagantly on the followers' money. Relying on ancient, superstitious writings that promise life everlasting after death, and giving a lot of your money (that

168 || WHAT MOTIVATES CULTURAL PROGRESSIVES?

you may not be able to afford to give) to your church is irrational. (female, 46–55, master's degree)

Tend to be poorly educated and poorly informed of worldly events and other cultures. Close-minded and incapable of logical, rational, well-reasoned argumentation. (male, 56–65, doctorate)

They think the world is only 6,000 yrs. old, and try to explain that . . . they are fools, and that it makes no sense to argue with them. (male, 56–65, high school diploma)

Uneducated in the ways of thinking, fearful, not balanced or rational, followers of dogmatic people, afraid to acknowledge any flaw in biblical theology/writings or leaders. (female, 56–65, master's degree)

With their eyes firmly fixed on their imaginary sky-god, they either have no sense of the harm they are causing the real world around them, or worse are delighted at that harm, because it somehow proves them right. How else do you make sense of all those fools who believe they can completely ruin the only planet we have and not worry because their sky-god is going to give them a brand-spanking new one once they finish destroying it? (female, 56–65, bachelor's degree)

More uneducated, looking for simple answers to complex questions, decisions based on fear rather than rational [thought]. (female, 26–35, bachelor's degree)

The major task for cultural progressive activists is to "enlighten" those who are not adequately informed about the value of these assertions. Such statements indicate the presuppositions many cultural progressive activists have about what is the right way to think. Confidence in their societal perspective is important for helping cultural progressive activists to justify their social movement and become the source of the norms that provide a simplified perspective for the social complexity and complicated issues members of the movement face.

The reality that there are millions of Americans, many of them highly educated, who are political conservatives or believe in the supernatural or believe in the value of religion in society or that religious values should be part of the government does not dissuade these respondents from taking for granted the accuracy of these themes. Such confidence is valuable for the tasks of group cohesion and maintenance of the ideology that sustain a social movement. In many ways, the assumptions made by cultural progressive activists about the efficacy and value of a secular society as opposed to a religious society are just as unprovable as the assumptions about the value of a religious society made by the Christian right. But it is upon such tenuous presuppositions that social movements are built.

CHAPTER 7

The Framing of Cultural Progressive Activism

Over the past three chapters we have allowed cultural progressive activists to enunciate their concerns and frustrations with the Christian right. From those enunciations we have seen the values and norms generally supported by cultural progressive activists. These values and norms represent a given understanding of society, religion, and government. This understanding helps to sustain a social movement in that it provides societal resources for a certain segment of the United States. As we documented in the third chapter, cultural progressive activists in our sample tend to be more educated, wealthier, more white, and less religious than other individuals in the United States. As such, they are part of a general subculture served by the perspectives put forward in the preceding chapters.

In this chapter we look more deeply at the themes documented in chapter 6. This will help us to understand the collective identity that unites cultural progressive activists. We then explore the types of collective action frames emerging within this subculture that legitimate this social movement and support the desires of individuals within the movement. This will provide insight into the ideas emerging from cultural progressive activists and how they are shaped by the group interests tied to members of this movement. Finally, we explore the paradox of a movement that prides itself on rationality and yet is tied to values that serve its own interests. Rationality becomes a tool that cultural progressive activists use in their struggle to legitimate their movement, rather than an end in itself.

Basic Emergent Norms of Cultural Progressive Activists

Our exploration of different political and religious motivations helps us to identify certain themes that tend to drive cultural progressive activists. We conceptualize these themes as emergent norms that help to provide simple answers to the complex social reality in the United States. Now we look more deeply into each norm so that we can understand the role they play in producing a collective identity among cultural progressive activists. The power of these norms is such that it matters little whether individuals oppose the Christian right for political reasons, because of a general antipathy toward religion, or because they are critics of Christianity. These emergent norms represent certain presuppositions about social reality that are accepted with little question among cultural progressive activists. The opposition to the Christian right is based upon those presuppositions.

The first emergent norm comes from the fear of mixing religion and politics. This fear is connected to the general pattern of many respondents to link conservative political ideology with religious activism. The use of religion for the promotion of progressive political values is rarely, if ever, condemned by any of the respondents. It is only the mixing of political conservatism and religious ideology that is problematic for respondents. Promoting conservative, but not progressive, politics through religion is what cultural progressive activists oppose. Given this propensity, we can now identify this emergent norm as the expectation that religion within conservative political activism is wrong and harmful to society.

The mixture of political and religious conservatism is taken for granted by many respondents. Indeed, several respondents had a difficult time envisioning a political conservative who is not also religiously motivated or vice versa.

> Well, first of all I don't think there is such a thing as a Republican who is not a Christian. (female, 46–55, bachelor's degree)
>
> Republicans and Christians are the same people. (male, over 75, some college)
>
> I've never met . . . a Republican who is not Christian. (female, 46–55, bachelor's degree)
>
> I see Republicans and Christians as the same thing because the GOP is dominated and controlled by them. (male, 36–45, some college)
>
> I can't believe there would be a non-Christian Republican, or an apolitical Christian in TX. (female, 26–35, master's degree)
>
> I think a "vocal Christian who is apolitical" is an oxymoron. If I assume "vocal Christian" means "evangelical," that's not apolitical and I really dislike evangelicalism. (female, 56–65, some graduate training)

Such a propensity indicates that respondents often conflate religious and political conservatism in a way that enables them to see these social forces as identical to each other. Since this is a highly educated subgroup, it is likely that some respondents are aware of religious individuals who are politically progressive or apolitical. However, the general image of the Christian right activist who simultaneously promotes both religious and political conservatism creates a powerful stereotype adapted by many respondents. That image allows the respondents to possess a common enemy to be faced by cultural progressive activists. They can identify themselves by making sure that they do not have the qualities of the stereotypical image of the Christian right. Fear of the mixing of conservative religion and politics serves the social movement by creating an enemy to be part of the out-group and the development of an in-group identity based on the rejection of utilizing their religious beliefs when making political assessments.

It is in this context that ideas about the separation of church and state can be understood. The primary literature devoted a great deal of space to the rightness of church/state separation. Furthermore, many respondents also articulated church/state separation as an important issue that influenced their perspectives. Fear of violations of church/state separation led some respondents to oppose the activism of the Christian right as it concerned sex education, the teaching of evolution, and their general intrusion into politics.

> Denial of scientific evidence/evolution. Stance on sex education, pushing of religious studies/attitudes in public schools. (male, 66–75, master's degree)

> They want public schools to teach the bible and creationism. Plus they advocate abstinence only for teens. (female, 56–65, master's degree)

> Opposition to abortion or even the kind of age-appropriate sex education that would make abortion less necessary.... Historical revisionism, including fake quotations from our nation's founders designed to undercut the separation of church and state. (male, 56–65, bachelor's degree)

> The irrational thought that sex is a sin, all atheists are immoral, and pushing their religion into our government when they do not have one single piece of supporting evidence of this god they speak of. (female, 36–45, some college)

> They are eager to impose shoddy sex education and Creationism on all children. (female, 56–65, bachelor's degree)

As these quotes, and many others we could have included, indicate, there is a clear resistance to religious activism when it intrudes in the public sphere. The envisioning of conservative religion and politics is not merely a minor part of the beliefs of cultural progressive activists. It is a core issue by which they can justify the superiority of their ideas over those ideas driven by religion, which in the eyes of many respondents is a great source of irrationality.

In fact this leads to the second important theme we noted, which is the importance of rationality. Rationality is taken as a given with many of the respondents. Many of the respondents have a difficult time understanding why individuals are unable to perceive the correctness of their political and social positions. They possess an understanding of rationality that implies that the truth of social and political reality can be objectively determined if an individual is willing to ruthlessly apply the principles of rationality to a given social problem.[1] A second emergent norm is the application of rationality as the way to solve social and political problems in society.

Rationality is a valuable emergent norm as it allows members of this social movement to easily legitimate their assertions. The picture often painted by the respondents is that individuals would clearly perceive the proper course of political, social, and religious action if they merely allowed rationality to dominate their decisions. The fact that some members of the Christian right are intelligent and/or educated but did not accept such a course of action is often disturbing to some respondents.

> Hard to believe that otherwise intelligent people would still believe in fairy tales. (male, 56–65, bachelor's degree)

> An otherwise rational friend suggesting she agreed with Sara Palin's incredible assertion that health reform would include "death panels." It just made me concerned that their numbers include educated (nice in most other ways) people . . . not just those who would kill abortion providers and homosexuals. (male, 66–75, master's degree)

> A former coworker left the company to pursue a Ph.D. in Theology. He was a software engineer and one of the most brilliant and logical thinking people I have ever met. During his last visit I was shocked to hear him trying to explain Creationism to me as a valid, scientific, theory. The man is now completely brainwashed and is but a thin shell of the person he used to be. It was like conversing with a wind up doll. Pull the string, and get the canned, pre-programmed answer. (female, 56–65, some college)

These respondents are confused by the seeming intelligence of some Christian right members because of the assumption that there is an objective answer to how individuals should understand these social and political issues that can be rationally derived. Thus, the presence of individuals who display intelligence but do not come to those conclusions violates the understood social reality of such respondents. Furthermore, individuals who do not utilize rational responses are perceived as making problems worse. Thus, the emergent norm of rationality has located the source of the problems in our society. That source is the unwillingness or inability of certain individuals and groups to apply the principles of rationality to address social and political issues.

> The Christian Right appears to be composed mainly of lower-middle class, blue-collar Caucasian workers with limited formal education who use their limited mental abilities to come up with illogical arguments, and then angrily enforce their positions with fear and intimidation. (male, 56–65, master's degree)

> I fear their influence in our government, our military and society as a whole. They are . . . unable to think rationally. (male, 66–75, some graduate training)

> Texas, and other states dominated by the "Christian" Right, must wrest control of education and social welfare from these rigid, irrational hands. Texas in about 15 years will be a third-world country—uneducated and unhealthy. . . . The idea that my grandchildren, other people's children will not learn honest science, history, or sex frightens me. (female, 66–75, some college)

> [Those of the Christian right are] indoctrinated at an early or a very emotionally vulnerable age or time. Largely uneducated and hence unable to evaluate dissenting opinions or see fallaciousness of pastor pronouncements. Tend toward absolutism and have inability to participate in objective discussion. (male, 66–75, master's degree)

> Largely uneducated, white, male dominated, female subservient. Suburban. Narrow minded sheep mentality . . . clinging to old religious ideals of bible such as male superiority, spare the rod, spoil the child crap. (female, 46–55, some college)

Since the respondents envision themselves as having a powerful ability to apply the principles of rationality to these issues, they can set themselves up as the individuals who need to make important societal and political decisions. Rationality becomes a norm that allows the respondents to claim priority of their social worldview over the social worldview of religious or political conservatives. Rationality becomes an important value within the collective identity of cultural progressives since it legitimates their rights to make societal decisions.

The assumption of rationality and objective answers is not always accepted. A great deal of work in the sociology of knowledge challenges the idea that such objectivity is possible (Berger & Luckmann, 1967; Bloor, 2001; Kuhn, 1962; Mannheim, 1954; Polanyi, 1958; Popper, 1959; Swidler & Arditi, 1994). Furthermore, the idea of objectivity has also been challenged by feminists (Haraway, 1991; Rosser, 1990; D. E. Smith, 1972) and Afrocentrist (Collins, 2000; M. Hunter, 2002; Lugg, 1998) scholars on the bases of the importance of sex and race in shaping our abilities to understand objective reality. Given such a critique, and the reality that cultural progressive activists come from a given racial, economic, and educational social position that likely shapes their outlook on objectivity, the claims of the respondents can be fairly challenged by such assertions. The ability to objectively apply rationality has to be seen as an assumption incorporated into the perspectives of cultural progressive activists in such a way that many of them do not understand the tenuous nature of that assumption. Instead, they accept that their ability to objectively apply rationality, and ignore the social dynamics that shape their viewpoints, is greater than the ability of those they oppose and use that assumption to legitimate the social and political solutions they prefer.

The third theme tied to the perspectives of the respondents is the value of limiting the influence of religion in our society. Given the irreligious makeup of the respondents, it is not surprising that traditional religion is given a low value. In fact, for many respondents traditional religion is perceived as a competitor to the ideas that they would like to support. For some respondents, the way they identify themselves is likely tied to their irreligious outlook on life.

> But the disconnect that I perceive between historical and experiential reality, and the beliefs of Christians, makes it much harder

for me to conceal my (admitted) disdain for their views, and in my experience Christians are often hostile or at least cold to open atheists such as myself. (male, 18–25, master's degree)

A year ago, I came out as a Freethinker to my still staunchly Catholic mother. She informed me that I was going to hell. We rarely speak anymore. (female, 46–55, master's degree)

I've had my life or physical harm threatened more than once by fundamentalist Christians simply because I was an unabashed atheist and would not back down from my disdain for irrational belief. (male, 56–65, some college)

Yeah, because after awhile they would either be ignoring me or harassing me as an anti-theist.... However, as Prof. Dawkins has eminently shown, there is no logical pathway from atheism to violence but a very real logical pathway from religion to violence. (male, 56–65, bachelor's degree)

Since I am an atheist activist, I have a lot of encounters. One lady said it is a shame I will never know how loving God is because I am going to burn in Hell. Another guy decided, without ever having met me before, that I am unhappy and filled with darkness. Both these people amused me, and I was amazed at how quickly they decided they knew all about me only because they knew I am an atheist. (female, 46–55, bachelor's degree)

By seeking to minimize the impact of religion on society, such individuals can maximize their social value as those who refuse to put up with the nonsense of religion. The respondents often portray religious individuals quite negatively, which helps them to shape an identity in which not having a traditional religious faith is seen as a social good. Furthermore, since religion is often seen as a source of oppression and a barrier to societal progress, respondents can perceive themselves as victims of religion. Such victimization is useful for respondents in justifying receiving redress and respect because of their grievances. But to justify such rewards, religion has to be attacked and its potential influence challenged. Thus, an emergent norm has developed in that traditional religion is seen as dysfunctional to society and its potential impact must be limited.

The problem of the influence of religion is not limited to political activism. For some respondents the very existence of religion is problematic. These respondents did make statements concerning the elimination of religious individuals or Christians. However, this should not be seen as being indicative of the general attitudes of all respondents. More common are statements about the need to limit the influence of interpersonal religious interaction. Some statements about the need to limit religious influence can be seen in the concern many respondents have about proselytizing.

> I'd say enforce what's already there, including the bit about not proselytizing in the military. (male, 66–75, doctorate)

> Proselytizers at the door. When I told one that I was not interested in his message, he demanded to know why not. I replied that as long as it was a free country I owed him no explanation. (male, 66–75, master's degree)

> I am fearful of its growing political power, its heavy proselytizing especially aimed at young and uncritical minds. (female, 66–75, some college)

> Call it paranoia, but I would spend a lot of time concerned that they were trying to convert my children. (female, 26–35, doctorate)

Proselytizing can be seen as a problem if it is envisioned as rude and disrespectful to those who are not interested in Christian faith. However, it is also seen as a problem because it may allow Christians to become more influential by converting individuals to their way of thinking. Therefore, proselytizing is a problem because it may allow more individuals to become Christians and spread the "poison" of religion throughout society. However, some respondents go even further than this. They object to the religious socializing that many parents provide for their own children.

> They insist on indoctrinating their children, as though the mind of a child is somehow a possession of the parent rather than the seat of an individual consciousness that needs to be brought up to accept that this world is not, universally, a Christian one, and it never will be. (male, 36–45, master's degree)

They are allowed to reproduce and indoctrinate their kids. It's one thing to be irrational and shy away from a realistic world view, but to mentally handicap your children is shameful. (male, 26–35, bachelor's degree)

I feel that the fundamentalists are so controlling that they want to seize the children of their followers and condition and indoctrinate them to carry out their poisoned agenda for humankind. Family members are split between loyalty to their polyester preachers, who have gotten their educational tactics right out of the inquisition, and allowing others to interact with their children to break them out of the fear trap they have created for them. As a family member, it is very painful to see how they terrorize their children and if you say anything, you are ostracized. This is damaging not only to the children but to the whole social and family fabric of society. (female, 66–75, some college)

I think it's born out of an environment where the superstition is passed down to children when they are most vulnerable to suggestions from parents. The result is a total distortion of the world view and disrespect of human value which is forced to submit to the will of the so-called god which is a total fabrication during a time when human beings were ignorant of how the universe works. (male, 46–55, doctorate)

Not all, or even most, respondents went as far as wanting to discourage Christian parents from socializing their children, but enough of them enunciated such a perspective to suggest that this "solution" is not stigmatized by the larger cultural progressive movement. Cultural progressive activists who would accept that Christians should be able to socialize their children are not likely to reject those who enunciate such sentiments. In fact, Dawkins (2006), who is well respected among cultural progressive activists, argues that religious socialization is child abuse. The acceptance of the idea that Christians should not socialize their children in religious matters may exist since this socialization allows Christians to maintain their numbers and influence in society. Some respondents believe that without the manipulation of religious socialization, the irrationality of religion would eventually disappear. Objections to religious socialization are linked to the desire for a fading away of religious societal influence.

Not all respondents perceive religion as evil. Many acknowledge that religion can be beneficial for certain individuals. Other respondents have religious faith themselves. But religion is at best seen as an optional aspect for some individuals in society and at worse can be seen as a major source of the inability of society to progress. Religion provides the possibility for a theocracy, and that possibility is a danger that has to be constantly monitored. While there is possible good that can come from religion for some individuals, respondents perceive the way religion is practiced today as problematic, and thus it is a force to be reduced and, if possible, stopped.

The opposition to religion is an important emergent norm widely accepted by cultural progressive activists. It contains the important assumption that religion does not have overall positive effects in society. This theme is seen in some of the primary literature that explores the dysfunctions of religion or highlights the "evil" acts perpetrated by religious individuals. Naturally, this literature, and the comments of the respondents, tends to dismiss academic literature that indicates possible societal benefits of religion (Brooks, 2006; A. B. Cohen, 2002; Dew et al., 2010; Ellison & Levin, 1998; Ferriss, 2002; Larson et al., 1992; Larson et al., 1998; Levin & Vanderpool, 1992). Whether religion is ultimately beneficial or harmful to society is a question that has not been unilaterally determined by scientific means. So the notion that religion is detrimental is an assumption that is taken for granted. The respondents generally perceive the fallibility of religion not as a presupposition but as an obvious reality. This perception feeds into the social interests of this highly educated, politically progressive, and irreligious subculture that would envision religion as an ideological competitor. Opposition to traditional religion is part of an emergent norm that feeds into the social and political desires of cultural progressive activists. In doing so, it serves to link the members of this social movement together, regardless of their own personal religious beliefs.

The final emergent norm comes from the theme of valuing progressive political perspectives over conservative political perspectives. Consistently, respondents promoted politically progressive ideas on a wide variety of issues. In fact, when one of the respondents identified as a political conservative, she made the observation that this was unusual by stating, "I'm an odd duck! ... an Atheist Conservative." This theme leads to an emergent norm that values progressive political ideology. To be more precise the norm is the desirability of politically progressive ideology.

It should not be surprising that cultural progressive activists tend to be political progressives. Previous research has documented that the highly educated (Bolzendahl & Myers, 2004; Revenson, 1989; Unnever & Cullen, 2007) and irreligious (Gallup & Lindsay, 2000; Glaeser & Sacerdote, 2008) are more likely to have progressive political attitudes on a variety of issues. Since these are two of the categories that cultural progressive activists are drawn from, it is natural that political progressiveness would be a major unifying factor within this subculture. Such an ideology offers solutions to social and political problems. For the cultural progressive activists, these solutions are seen as a natural answer to those problems. However, many individuals in the United States are political conservatives who do not accept the solutions so easily promulgated by the respondents. This opposition allows the respondents to create an identity boundary by defining themselves as distinct from such conservatives. They perceive distinctions that are not merely linked to political disagreement, but rather those distinctions illustrate for them the very dysfunctional character of conservatives.

> Republican has a totally different perspective on people's rights, the environment, and the role of government. Generally is not compassionate towards poor people in the society. (male, 56–65, master's degree)

> My most memorable encounter is actually my experience of having a very close friend who was a member of the Christian Right. What struck me the most was the incredible dichotomy of her person (Honest and kind and sensible to a fault) and her politics (Mercilessly bloodthirsty, underhanded and extravagant). (male, 18–25, some college)

> Republicans are a lot about hate and fear, too. However, they also put down the most vulnerable in society for their own gain. (female, 36–45, master's degree)
>
> The vocal Republican is probably only cheap/greedy. (male, 46–55, doctorate)
>
> Republican concepts . . . promote personal greed, widespread discrimination, and lack of concern for the citizenry. (female, 46–55, master's degree)
>
> I look at Republicans as greedy, self-centered individualists who think only of themselves at the expense of everyone else. Republicans are able to not only watch people suffer and die, they could actually hasten it with equanimity if they knew they'd be making money off it. (male, 56–65, master's degree)

In this way political conservatives are not merely seen as being wrong but are, for some respondents, conceptualized as having undesirable personality characteristics as well.

Since political progressiveness is deeply embedded within the social and demographic groups where we tend to find cultural progressive activists (i.e., the highly educated, the irreligious), efforts to support politically progressive ideas also lend support to those groups and serve the interests of cultural progressives.[2] The respect given to political progressiveness, as opposed to political conservatism, is at least partially linked to the promotion of social interests of individuals in certain social groups. Cultural progressive activists generally assume the superiority of politically progressive ideas but may not always realize that this superiority is assumed and not proven. Political progressiveness allows cultural progressive activists to create politically conservative villains, provide answers to political problems, and provide a way in which cultural progressive activists can be unified by accepting a common belief about social reality. In this way, political progressiveness is integral to an emergent norm that serves to advance the social movement of cultural progressives.

These emergent norms are not mutually exclusive. Indeed, it is easy to see how they work together to reinforce each other. For example, the valuation of rationality helps to support a critique of religion—buttressing that emergent norm as well. Political progressiveness contains within it the desire to separate church and state, which is indicative of individuals who fear the mixing of religious and political conservatism—allowing both of these emergent norms to strengthen each other. Naturally, there are other ways in which these emergent norms reinforce each other, but what is important to note is that these norms work together to help create a coherent collective identity that serves the members of this social movement. It is an identity of individuals who disdain traditional religion, want to keep religion in a proper place outside of the public sphere, value rationality as a way to solve problems, and have come to the conclusion that most of these solutions fit within a politically progressive framework.

Collective Action Frames Used by Cultural Progressives

In chapter 2 we pointed out that social movements develop collective action frames in which they can promote the perspectives shaping their movement. In the previous section we have explored the emergent norms that are taken for granted by cultural progressive activists. These norms help to create certain images of cultural progressive activists and of their opponents in the Christian right. They also help to legitimate the aims and goals of the movement. How to justify the movement and what it desires to accomplish can be seen in the way members of the movement create collective action frames that help them to interpret, prognosticate, and outline the necessary action to be taken (Snow & Benford, 1988). Emergent norms can be used to screen out interpretations, prognostications, and actions that do not fit with the collective identity of a given social movement. Once those parameters are set, then collective action frames can be established to inform members as to the reasons why their movement is important and the sort of actions that have to be taken to promote it.

The first type of collective action frames to be established is diagnostic in nature. These are the arguments about what has gone wrong and the source of the injustice. From the emergent norms we can see that the problem is believed to be created by the unethical and/or unwise mixing of bad religion and politics. This mixing is seen as allowing irrationality to become commonplace within our society and lead to the promotion of regressive political action. Members of this social movement perceive themselves as trapped by these religiously and politically conservative and restrictive social forces. They interpret the intrusion of conservative religious ideology into the political sphere as the source of many of the larger problems in our society.

> They are anti-choice, pro-death penalty, largely pro-gun, against social programs, anti-science, in favor of tax breaks and other political favors for the rich, and seek to allow their religious views to dominate American government. (female, 26–35, high school diploma)

> I am very indifferent towards the Christian Right. They have every right to practice their religious beliefs, just as every other person has a right to practice their particular religion or no religion. I only object when someone else tries to impose their belief system on me through government legislation or other means. The Christian Right does not appear to understand how crucial it is for the separation of church and state to be maintained, not only for the survival of religion in this country, but for the very survival of our form of government and our country. (male, 56–65, some graduate training)

> I object to their lack of appeal to reason. I object to the selective weeding out and subjective interpretation of portions of the bible that are used to support their views. I disagree with their political stances—all the ones I'm aware of. (female, over 75, some graduate training)

> They are pushing the most horrendous legislation in education, laws, personal freedom. They are rabid anti-gay, anti-any progressive religious group, are sanctimonious, push anti-sexual

education, evolution, open understanding of history and feel that their religion gives them the RIGHT to decide who can live and die-war. (female, 56–65, master's degree; emphasis in original)

A group determined to turn the country into a theocracy.... The main characteristic is the willingness to push their view of their god. Abortion, prayer in schools, intolerance of differing views and a general condemnation of secular values are some examples I see. (male, 56–65, some graduate training)

... primarily, trying to get me (the public) to force through legal means (e.g. legislation) to recognize, practice, proselytize and support, through public monies, their version of Christianity or their underlying unknown motives (including their push into the military and forcing others to practice the above) and trying to create punishment for those that do not (through military command, legislation, economic boycott if you are not Christian, etc.). For instance, the right believes in the death penalty. They want abortion outlawed as murder. Therefore they will have women, doctors, nurses assisting in abortion then killed by the state or federal governments.... Their inability and refusal to use rational thought to come together to solve societal problems, poverty, global warming, etc. (male, 46–55, doctorate)

As these quotes indicate, these respondents perceive a variety of social and political problems that are connected to the conservative religious and political influences imposed on society. Instead of rationality being the dominant characteristic of our society, these respondents fear that irrational religion has too great an influence in our society. While some respondents oppose religion in just about all of its expressions, many merely want conservative religion to stay in the home and churches. Several respondents expressed that they would be comfortable coexisting with religious individuals if religion stayed out of the public sphere.

It is not only the good of society that motivates these respondents. Many of them perceive themselves as being trapped in such an irrational and oppressive social situation. This perception is curious since we have already established that most respondents enjoy majority group status as it concerns income, education, sex, and race. However, while the percentage of irreligious has recently grown in the United States (Kosmin & Keysar, 2008), many of the atheistic or agnostic respondents are outnumbered by those with traditional religious beliefs. The impact that individuals with traditional religious beliefs have on our society provides such respondents with a mechanism by which they can experience cultural victimization. Many respondents conceptualize themselves as having suffered some degree of persecution for their religious and/or political beliefs.

> The Christian right and I have never gotten along. In small town Texas, they persecute anyone that is different. (male, 18–25, some graduate training)

> My household is pretty liberal, both politically and religiously. We already are discriminated against due to us being an interracial couple, and because of our liberal views in a conservative area of the country. I don't want to begin to imagine what kind of discrimination and hatred we would be subjected to if we were surrounded by members of a radically conservative religious and political movement such as the Christian Right. (female, 26–35, some college)

> [T]hey would most likely tear down my Dem yard signs and kill my cats. I too am very vocal. (female, 56–65, master's degree)

> The Christian "wrong" seem hell-bent to take over this nation and persecute everyone who does not conform to their illogical anti-life views. (male, 66–75, some college)

> They want the "end times" to come when anyone not Christian either converts to Christianity or dies. I have no doubt if they get impatient they will take action against those of us who are not Christian. (female, 56–65, some graduate training)

> Realized some of these people are so brainwashed that they would burn people at the stake if that were acceptable today. All the while believing that they were the best people of society. Uneducated nasty ignoramuses. (female, 46–55, doctorate)

Whether the respondents have an accurate perception, despite their potential societal advantages outlined in chapter 3, of being victimized is a subject that can be investigated in future research. However, their claim of victimization is important for helping respondents to indicate that they have suffered an injustice for their social status. With this image of injustice, the respondents have greater justification for making claims about the larger society.

An important part of the diagnostic that cultural progressive activists apply for their social movement is tied to a different vision for society. One does not have to accept the fears many respondents have of a theocratic takeover of our society to understand that members of the Christian right desire a society that is governed by traditional values and norms. They perceive these values and norms as a way to create social order. Cultural progressive activists chafe at the notion of having such a social order imposed upon them. They envision a society where lifestyle innovation and freedom are highly valued. They view the lack of such innovation and freedom as problematic. The role of science is also in conflict between these two groups. Members of the Christian right are more likely to look toward scientific innovations that support the traditional order they support. Cultural progressive activists see science as an end unto itself, although the case can be made that they do not always support the sort of scientific freedom they espouse (see, e.g., Yancey, 2011). Thus, another part of the perceived problem is the lack of science and rationality currently in our society.

It is in the effort to characterize the Christian right as evil that many cultural progressive activists fail to fully utilize the rationality they claim drives them. For example, about 10 percent of the respondents mentioned that racism is a problem in the Christian right. Of that 10 percent, about a quarter of them alluded to the racial makeup of the Christian right as being part of the problem. These respondents have a perception that the Christian right is "too white" and that this is reflective of racism within the group. However, we have seen that almost 94 percent of this sample is white, and this is a sample that is overrepresented by those living in the South, which is more racially diverse than most other regions in the United States.

While we do not have a representative sample, it seems unlikely that cultural progressives have a high percentage of people of color considering the different types of groups from which we obtained our sample, and in none of these groups were people of color more than 20 percent of the sample.[3] We have no data about the Christian right, but we highly doubt that they are "whiter" than cultural progressive activists given such a high percentage of whites among that latter group. The claim that racism is exhibited by the whiteness of the Christian right is logical only if there is also acknowledgment that cultural progressive activists also may have such problems due to their own overwhelmingly white social networks. Not one of the respondents pointed out such a problem among his or her in-group. While only a small minority of cultural progressive activists pointed out racism as a problem of the Christian right, it should also be noted that only 10.1 percent of the respondents openly identified proselytizing, 7.0 percent openly identified their backward nature, and 4.4 percent identified their sexual repressiveness as a problem of the Christian right. Such low numbers are indicative of the fact that we asked the respondents open-ended questions about the Christian right instead of directly asking about such characteristics as a part of the Christian right. As these are also common stereotypes of the Christian right, it is plausible that much more than 10 percent of cultural progressive activists also accept the notion of a racist and white Christian right even as they work within overly white culturally progressive organizations.[4] The need to demonize the Christian right, rather than provide a rational assessment of those who are members of the Christian right, is the best explanation for the notion that the Christian right is too white and this whiteness leads to racism.

Understanding the diagnosis of cultural progressive activists allows us to explore the next set of collective action frames, those focused upon possible solutions or prognostic frames. Obviously an important part of the solution involves political and legal action. Since the problem is located in the bad influence of the Christian right on the political process, the solution must reside in confronting such individuals with the same process. As a result of this type of collective action frame, many of the respondents talk about becoming active to confront the Christian right. But what is even more insightful is that all of the organizations we examined also discussed freely in their literature ways in which they are developing legal and political challenges to the Christian right.

> [Name of organization] established as a national group in [year], has brought more than 40 lawsuits to protect the constitutional principle of the separation between church and state.

> So we started this website, started assembling resources, and started reaching out to let people know that we were here. Over the years we've built a network of individuals . . . and organizations dedicated to energetically opposing efforts to Christianize our government and our culture.

> [Name of organization] will monitor the situation and will not hesitate to report churches to the Internal Revenue Service is they use their tax-exempt resources to intervene in any election by endorsing or opposing candidates.

> . . . acts as the . . . watchdog, monitoring far-right issues, organizations, money and leaders. The organization has been instrumental in defeating initiatives backed by the religious right . . . including private school vouchers, textbook censorship and faith-based deregulation.

These citations indicate the importance of developing a collective movement. The respondents gain from these primary sources an understanding that they need to work together if they are going to be able to confront the problems they see with the Christian right. Financial and political support is seen as necessary to achieve victory.

In order to justify such action, an opponent has to be seen as powerful enough to warrant such attention. Indeed as both respondents and writings in the primary literature discuss the Christian right, they paint a picture of a political and legal powerhouse.

> They are the most powerful and evil people I have ever met. (male, 56–65, bachelor's degree)

The [name of Christian right organization] which works with the [National Day of Prayer] Task Force and has a $32.7 million annual budget [!], put up an online video with a practically tearful call to believers to fight [name of organization] by sending them money. We're in a "David and Goliath" fight. (primary source support letter)

Unreasonable fearmongers whose conservative intolerant agenda might change public policy and social attitudes to the degree that it harms the greater good. Their powerful rants might influence enough non-thinking followers and their voice grows to marginalize and shut out other points of view. (male, 36–45, bachelor's degree)

The United States is home to dozens of Religious Right groups. Many have small budgets and focus on state and local issues; the most powerful organizations conduct nationwide operations, command multi-million-dollar bank accounts and attract millions of followers. They have disproportionate clout in the halls of Congress, the White House and the courts, and they wield enormous influence within the political system. (primary source article)

Religion is like kudzu; if you don't constantly watch it and prune it back it will take over everything around it, strangling every other plant it touches. If allowed to grow unchallenged, the Christian Right will take over our political system, education system, legal system, financial/banking system, health care system, merchandizing . . . everything it can control . . . and it will destroy everything it touches. We must pass laws (or enforce laws that already exist) that eliminate its influence in all those areas of public life I mentioned. (male, 66–75, high school diploma)

We wanted to oppose the growing strength of the Christian right and the accelerating pace of its theocratic agenda . . . we continue our work because the Christian right continues *its* work, unabated, on the state and local levels and, without missing a beat, in augmenting the ranks of Christian Zionists, who envision Israel as the scene of the End Times. (primary source website; emphasis in original)

Even when discussing their possible victories over the Christian right, they still remind each other that they have a powerful and wicked enemy. This allows the organizations that support this social movement to gain a higher degree of support from the members of this movement. It also allows members to justify sacrificing their time and money to provide support for the actions taken on their behalf.

It is in the context of such assertions that we can understand why many of these groups are almost eager to seek out political conflict. Protests about a church using a public building in a small town in the Midwest do not seem to affect cultural progressive activists living in the Northeast. Yet engaging in such a legal battle may provide a symbolic victory over the powerful Christian right political and legal machine. Placing a representation of atheism next to a Christian manger scene at a state capital also provides an important symbolic assertion about the presence of the irreligious in society. Even the push for same-sex marriage takes on symbolic importance since traditional religious organizations are at the forefront of preserving the standard of one man–one woman marriage. These sorts of legal and political scrapes serve the highly educated, irreligious subculture that buttresses this movement by helping them to perceive that they are helping to usher in the new rational, irreligious, and politically progressive society many of them desire. The relative aggressiveness of these organizations on political and legal issues that seem irrelevant to those of us not in the middle of the cultural war is not misplaced. Rather, it serves to show the sort of actions that are seen as necessary for holding the Christian right in check, no matter where the Christian right may attempt to assert its influence.

An interesting caveat needs to be made concerning political action. Most respondents perceive their political activism as defensive and not aggressive. We asked the respondents about what sort of political action needed to be taken to deal with the Christian right. We deliberately kept the question vague to allow the respondents to generate their own responses and not react to suggestions we gave them. Indeed, many respondents had a tough time answering the question because of its vagueness. However, among those who did answer, we found that 61.3 percent of the time the respondents did not want to pass any extra laws to deal with the Christian right. Many commented that they would not mind passing laws that infuriated members of the Christian right but did not want laws to directly affect members of the Christian right. We suspect that some of the comments allude to the possibility of legal changes that may have a disparate impact upon the Christian right. In other words, they support changes that are, technically, religiously neutral but are more likely to affect members of the Christian right than non-religious members of society. Several respondents indicated such a desire even as they commented that they wanted no special laws for the Christian right.

> No laws that single them out, but certainly laws that (for example) require health professionals to treat everyone and fill prescriptions, prevent intimidation and bullying (e.g. at abortion clinics, in schools), etc. (male, 36–45, master's degree)

> We cannot pass any laws that would tend to prohibit free speech, but we could certainly pass a hate crime bill; and that would affect the "Christian" Right. (male, 66–75, doctorate)

> No, they are free to believe as they wish, but I would like to see something that forbids anyone to indoctrinate their children into their religion. The child should be allowed to make his or her own decision when they are old enough to understand what they are doing. (male, 36–45, some college)

> If this means limiting them in some way that no one else is limited, then absolutely not. That would be suppression. If this means something regarding separation of church and state that happens to affect them, then yes. (female, 36–45, bachelor's degree)

> I don't think we should pass laws that are directed towards any particular group of people. However, if a particular *good* law happens to negatively affect practices or beliefs of the Christian Right, but protects the freedom of most Americans, then I would be in favor. (female, 46–55, bachelor's degree)

However, generally there is a not a great appetite for laws that directly influence the Christian right. The lack of a desire for such laws can help to create a collective action frame in which the respondents see themselves as only victims, and not perpetrators, in the ongoing political conflict.

Finally, there were only sporadic assertions about interpersonal solutions. Several respondents commented on how they avoided the Christian right, but such avoidance was not supported by the primary literature, and so we hesitate to include such avoidance as part of the prescriptions put forth and widely accepted by cultural progressive activists. Some commented on little ways they resisted the imposition of religion such as their reaction to a statement like "God bless you" after sneezing or whether to capitalize *God* when writing. But generally there was little push for interpersonal actions, and most of the assertions concerned political and legal action taken against the Christian right. Although there were plenty of expressions of hatred toward members of the Christian right, the emphasis on interpersonal freedom and innovation supported by cultural progressive activists may make it intellectually unviable for these individuals to systematically support interpersonal rejection of members of the Christian right, although we suspect that such rejection does occur. The one exception to this is that a few respondents did indicate a desire to try to convince some Christians to abandon their religious beliefs. In an ironic sense some individuals often engaged in the proselytizing that many of the other cultural progressive activists often complained about.

> We must remain vigilant and proactive against their trying to push their religious agenda. We cannot eliminate them, but our voice must be even more vocal. . . . I feel that popular movies (aimed at children and young adults) are needed. Things like free Willie-but with scientists or open-minded Christians being the hero are the way to change a culture. . . . This costs tons of money but can also make money if it is a popularist film with a HIDDEN AGENDA—not like Michael Moore but entertainment. (female, 56–65, master's degree; emphasis in original)

> I have been working for years to have included, as mandatory, in high school curriculums, the scientific study of the world's great or major religions, and the study of the non-religious

alternative—skepticism, or the application of reason, rather than "blind faith," which is the basis of all religions. I am convinced that about 98 percent of all high school students would come away from such a course as skeptical thinkers; in other words, as atheists. Of course, this is simply a wild dream of mine and would never actually happen in "real life." (male, 66–75, master's degree)

My friend announced to a stranger that SOME people don't believe all this beauty was part of a plan. The person to whom we were talking said, with a sneer, that THEY think they have all the answers. So I said that no, people who study science knows that we are far from having all the answers but that is why the ancient people came up with religion to answer the things that were not answerable at that time. . . . I already knew that their desire to believe was strong and comments from me would have little effect BUT, you never know when a seed of thought might germinate. (female, 46–55, master's degree; emphasis in original)

I've de-converted two of them to some form of agnosticism. It felt great to see the peace of mind it has brought them. (male, 26–35, some graduate training)

Finally, motivating cultural progressive activists is important, and motivational collective action frames have to be taken into account. We have already seen some of the motivation in the justification for the solutions proposed by cultural progressive activists. However, the motivation goes beyond these solutions as many respondents indicate their fears of what may happen if they do not get involved and stop the Christian right. Some of these fears come in the concern of some respondents to the possible takeover of our society by the Christian right. Indeed, it is quite common for the Christian right to be compared to the Taliban and other oppressive regimes.

They are a sanitized version of the Taliban, relying on misinformation & faith to manipulate the people to do whatever the witchdoctors tell them. (male, 46–55, master's degree)

The Christian Right is discrimination by another name. Because someone does not think, act, and believe like they do, that person is inferior. Therefore everyone else is a second class citizen.

> This group is no better than the Romans who persecuted the Christians, the Catholics during the Inquisition, and the Nazis in the 1930's. (female, 56–65, some college)

> What can you say about fanatics? Christian fanatics have not yet reached the stage of active persecution but it is only a matter of time to where they become as bad as the Islamic fundamentalists. (male, 56–65, master's degree)

> They are dangerous!! They are already as bad as the Taliban with money and politics and someday they will kill as easily as the Taliban!!! Some day, killing abortion doctors just won't be enough bloodshed for the right. (male, 46–55, some college)

> Becoming Nazis would be an improvement. (male, 26–35, some graduate training)

> They have perverted all things Christ like. They are to America what the Taliban is to the Muslim world. They are religious terrorists. (male, 56–65, master's degree)

Furthermore, there is a fear of theocracy often mentioned by the respondents. These respondents do not tend to use the term *theocracy* as hyperbole. The respondents are not merely discussing Christians moving into political power and passing a few undesirable laws but the removal of personal and religious freedoms. As such, they envision a real theocracy of politically based religious oppression and violence.

> They are bigoted, and wish to make their bigotry and interpretation of the Christian religion into law. Moreover, the extremes in their party wish to ignore the Constitution and replace it with a Christian Dominion resembling the Taliban or Iraq's theocracy. (male, 18–25, some college)

> Americans who want to overturn basic American freedoms and turn the United States into a "Christian" theocracy. (male, 36–45, bachelor's degree)

> Their belief in theocracy, in Christian supremacy, and in hatred for their fellow man. They belief in legally enforcing moral

standards on how people use their own bodies, or how people speak. I'm speaking of gay rights, abortion rights, death penalty, state endorsed and enforced prayer and rituals, the use of terms like "socialist" to mean "evil," the right wing militias/terrorists, the murders of Matthew Sheppard, Dr. Tiller, Bill Sparkman, and the shooting at the Tennessee Valley Unitarian Universalist Church. (male, 26–35, some graduate training)

They would like to turn this country into a theocracy and do away with freethinking. (female, 56–65, some college)

My most memorable encounter was a book banning crusade that took place in my school district when I was a freshman in high school (1994–1995 school year). The Christian Coalition had elected a stealth slate of candidates to the school board in the previous election, which subsequently drew up a list of books they wanted banned from the English curriculum. Most of the books were challenged for sexual content. However, most of the books challenged were also written by ethnic minorities, which led my parents to suspect that racism may have played a role. This was the first political controversy that I had ever been involved in, and it is largely what is responsible for my opposition to the Christian Right. I learned first hand what it might be like to live under a theocracy, and I didn't want that to happen in America. (male, 26–35, some college)

Some of this group wants to establish a theocracy and to have all laws and rules confirm to Biblical law. They will use any means to accomplish their goal to undermine democracy, so that their theology can dominate. (male, over 75, some graduate training)

Despite the rationality professed by these cultural progressive activists, some of them cling to the notion that a religious takeover of society is possible and even likely to soon be a reality. There is no real evidence that a Christian takeover of the United States to the degree of imposing a religious theocracy on par with the Taliban's previous dominance in Afghanistan is possible in our contemporary society. Fears of such a takeover do not comport to the given political and legal reality in the United States. If such claims are not merely rank hyperbole, then these claims do indicate a distorted perception of political reality in the United States. But the fear is not completely illogical. It serves as a powerful motivating collective action frame that compels many of the respondents. The unrealistic concern about a theocracy is logical in that it helps to motivate the social movement that serves cultural progressive activists.

It is also the case that there is a positive vision that powers the motivation of such respondents. Participation in this social movement is seen as desirable since this can be a movement that can help to bring in a progressive and enlightened society. To be sure the respondents were more likely to comment negatively upon the imposition of the Christian right than the possibility of bringing about an enlightened society. This may be because of the way we asked questions about the Christian right and not directly about hopes of a future society. However, the primary literature read by cultural progressive activists also was much more highly focused on the negative aspects of the Christian right than on a positive future. As such, it is quite likely that the negative costs of not opposing the Christian right are generally emphasized over the positive vision enunciated by some cultural progressives. Regardless, we did get glimpses of a possible progressive and enlightened society from some of the respondents, even though usually such visions were cast as a celebration of the end of the Christian right.

> The world would be better off without religion, including the Christian right. It would be a better world of all religion was replaced by secular humanism and rational thought. (male, 36–45, bachelor's degree)

> In a perfect world, my neighbors would all be interesting, well-informed, atheist, and college educated. They would be concerned for the environment, interested in preserving bio-diversity, reasonably anti-war and concerned about human-rights. They would not impose their moral beliefs on others—they would be supportive of two gay friends getting married, or of a lesbian couple having a baby. They would be supportive, and never judgmental, of a woman contemplating abortion. They would want only science taught in science class. They would not force their atheism

on others with symbols or monuments on public property. Such would be my perfect neighborhood. To be surrounded by the Christian Right, on the other hand, would be akin to finding oneself in an insane asylum. (male, 46–55, bachelor's degree)

The world will be a more peaceful, loving, educated planet when these people fade into inevitable obscurity. (male, 46–55, some graduate training)

The hope for a positive future, when the Christian right has been neutralized and "rationality" is the dominant value, is distinctly part of the ways in which cultural progressive activists find motivation for their actions. However, the more powerful type of motivation for them was driven more by fear than by hope. Thus, we have a social movement that is based upon defeating the Christian right more than establishing a new and better society.

The emergent norms and collective action frames we have discussed so far help to establish a certain vision of society for cultural progressive activists. They also help to create imagery about the Christian right and of cultural progressive ideals. As such, these are the foundations on which cultural progressive activists can create the identity generated by their social movement. That collective identity meets important needs for cultural progressive activists and helps us to understand the nature of this social movement. In the next section we explore this collective identity and its implications.

Collective Identity of Cultural Progressive Activists

From these emergent norms and collective action frames a certain type of collective identity emerges to define cultural progressive activists. Cultural progressive activists have developed an identity based on the values of rationality, irreligiosity, and progressive political action. Their perception of themselves is one in which they are a rational core that is working to stop the encroaching irrationality that is promoted by the Christian right. They contrast themselves with what they perceive as irrational and religiously based actions from their political and religious opponents. In this way they have an identity of being the leaders to produce a coming golden age of rationality and political/social progressiveness.

Even though irreligiosity is a value among many respondents, we must be clear in that we do not argue that most respondents believe that religion has to be eliminated. Indeed, there is a disagreement among respondents as to whether religion should be encouraged or not. Some respondents openly pine for the elimination of religion. Others see value in religion for individuals and even endorse what they perceive as the true values of religion, which they see as different from the values of the Christian right. However, what these respondents do agree upon is that religion should not be a dominant societal force. Regardless of the personal religiosity of a respondents, they tend to support the notion that religion should have little effect on political matters. Cultural progressive activists also tend to dismiss the notion of religious truth being exclusive to any given faith. In this way they advocate a rejection of aspects of religious traditionalists. It is in their opposition to religious traditionalists, represented in this society as usually Christian traditionalists, that the respondents find agreement. Rejection of notions of a preeminent place of religion in society and of traditional religious notions is an important part of the collective identity of cultural progressive activists.

This collective identity indicates that cultural progressive activists utilize their impressions about rationality, lack of traditional religiosity, and political progressiveness to evaluate a given person or social institution. Most respondents focused upon creating images that emphasized these qualities within themselves. We have already documented that several respondents emphasized their irreligiosity as part of their identity. We have also seen that those who do have Christian religiosity often emphasized their separation from traditional Christians. Likewise, other respondents emphasized the importance of defining themselves by perceiving themselves as rational and/or politically progressive.

> Almost any progressive law is viewed by the Christian Right as affecting them negatively, so, since I believe in progressive causes, I would say that yes we should pass such laws, but not because they're specifically aimed at the Christian Right. (male, 56–65, master's degree)

> For at least my last 50 years of rational thought, I have never let incidental contact with any fundamentalist turn into a "personal encounter." I walk away. (male, 66–75, doctorate)

> It bothers me when ANY person is irrational and relies on faith over reason. Many of these people think I'm immoral and/or unfit for US citizenship because I'm an Atheist. (Bush I actually said that) It's just about impossible to get along with these people when they think I should subsidize their religion, bow to their will, or "go back to Russia." (male, 56–65, bachelor's degree; emphasis in original)

> Ours is the only yard on our street with campaign signs for progressives come election season, but here in Texas supporting progressives (even if there is one on the ballot) is kinda futile, but we still try. (male, 46–55, some college)

In the subculture of cultural progressive activists, being seen as rational, politically progressive, and not traditionally religious is highly valued, and individuals go out of their way to emphasize these values. They are values used to assess whether events, people, or organizations are beneficial or dysfunctional. Thus, being seen as rational, politically progressive, and not traditionally religious is a critical core of the collective identity of cultural progressive activists.

The tenets within collective identity play an important role in serving cultural progressive activists. We can understand the role it may play if we remember that this is a highly educated and irreligious group. Rationality helps to support the identity of the highly educated who emphasize science and reason. They are able to use notions of rationality to justify their societal position and legitimate their work. Reason and education are to be emphasized over traditionality and religion, and that emphasis can be used to justify more resources for educational institutions. Likewise, a deemphasis on traditional religiosity also serves the cultural progressive activists who are irreligious. For such individuals, ideological competition with traditional religious organizations is made easier if religion is devalued. The valuation of irreligiosity helps to raise the status of irreligious members of cultural progressive subcultures.

Finally, we have noted that political progressiveness tends to be favored by those who are highly educated. Such progressiveness is often tied to a more open and less traditionally restrictive society. The idea of evolving to such a society requires leaders who are highly educated. Furthermore, politically progressive ideology generally supports a larger governmental role. The highly educated can find a larger public sector useful as it creates the need for educated experts to run that sector. Politically progressive philosophy may have a natural home among the highly educated since this philosophy increases the need for the highly educated to play an important role in our society.

All of the components (i.e., emergent norms, collective action frames) that contribute to the collective identity of cultural progressive activists are interrelated to each other. We realize that this explanation may be somewhat confusing. For those who are more visual in their understanding, we have constructed a graph that places these components together (see figure 7.1).

The collective identity of cultural progressive activists meets important economic and social needs for the members of the subculture that supports this ideology. It is a subculture that envisions itself as based on an ideology that is steeped in rationality, yet in reality it is an ideology that has developed, at least in part, to meet the social and economic needs of cultural progressives. Understanding this dynamic enables us to comprehend the illogical assertions made by some of the respondents such as the nonexistence of conservative Christians who are not also Republicans or the emergence of a Christian Taliban. The same sociological dynamics that drive other social movements also empower cultural progressives. Even social movements that deeply value rationality are unable to escape the sociological dynamics that create the need for a collective identity to pull members of the movement together, create stereotypical images of perceived enemies, and support a worldview based on the social needs of the members of the group. Attempts at rationality do not eliminate the sociological dynamics that obscure the ability of social movements to create rhetoric and perspectives that objectively reflect social reality.[5]

THE FRAMING OF CULTURAL PROGRESSIVE ACTIVISM || 203

FIGURE 7.1
Graph Representing Components of Collective Identity of Cultural Progressives

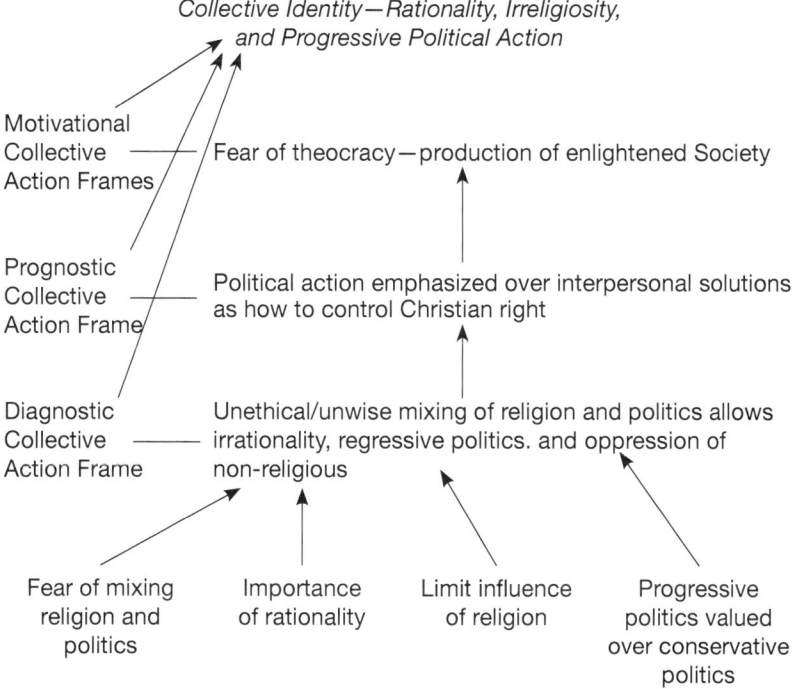

CHAPTER 8

Cultural Progressives in the Continuing Culture War

Studying social movements and the individuals in them often creates a paradox. On the one hand, we know that there have to be overarching beliefs or justifications uniting individuals together into a social movement. On the other hand, there is a danger of overlooking differences between the members of social movements as we seek to find these common links. Understanding the social movement created by cultural progressives presents the same set of challenges. Cultural progressive activists are a group with diverse interests. They have differing perspectives on religion and on how to address their concerns about the Christian right. It is a mistake to think of them as monolithic in their opposition to the Christian right. However, it is also true that they tend to come from a certain segment of our society. It is a segment that is highly educated, whiter, wealthier, more irreligious, and more politically progressive than other segments in the United States. As such, there are certain propensities that they share from what they have learned in the similar subculture they inhabit.

Over the course of this book we have struggled with this paradox. Our work has allowed us to locate seven different groups that help to explain the type of opposition cultural progressive activists have toward the Christian right. Those groups indicate a mixture of political and religious motivations that differ between respondents. While there are distinctions among these different groups, certain themes emerged time and again. These themes come from a collective identity that ties members of this social movement together. Despite their diversity, they do tend to share certain societal values that unite them as a social group. While cultural progressive activists do not agree on all issues (e.g., many of them are militant atheists while some profess belief in a loving God), they do have certain common values that, if violated, would likely invite scorn from other cultural progressive activists. It is by understanding those values that we gain insight into this social movement and obtain a better understanding about their actions and the arguments put forth by the members of the group.

Three important principles emerge time and again through this research as being central to the collective identity of cultural progressive activists. Those principles are rationality, irreligiosity—or at least nonacceptance of traditional religiosity[1]—and progressive political activism. We have pointed out that these principles are useful for serving the social interests of the highly educated and irreligious—individuals who are attracted to this movement. As such, this is a social movement that has developed ideas that meet the sociopsychological needs of the members of the group. Although the members of the group perceive rationality as the driving force behind their movement, the reality is that members of this social movement are no more immune to the social forces that establish a biased perspective of the movement and of society than members of other social movements. The collective identity of cultural progressive activists is no more inaccurate about social reality than the collective identity of other social movements. However, it is not necessarily any more accurate than those formed in other social movements.

For example, we have documented that individuals who are cultural progressive activists are wealthier, more educated, more likely to be male, and more likely to be white than other individuals in society. Yet many of them put forth a narrative in which they are seen as victims because of the actions of the Christian right. It is true that many cultural progressive activists are irreligious and Christianity is the majority group religion in the United States. Based upon their religious orientation, it is plausible that many cultural progressive activists are indeed being victimized by a lack of social acceptance. However, it is relatively difficult to find individuals who do not possess some quality that may link them to a minority group status. In the United States, the percentage of the population that is white, male, wealthy, highly educated, and Christian is relatively small and growing smaller with each passing day. Given this reality, why would such an educated and wealthy group that is mostly white and male focus on their one aspect of minority status to perceive themselves as victims? Protection of the collective identity that drives this movement provides a powerful, although not necessarily only, explanation for the focus some of the respondents have on their own victimization in spite of their relative societal advantages.

We have already explored one of the principles that feeds into the propensity of some respondents to have a perception of themselves as victims of the Christian right, which is the irreligiosity of cultural progressive activists. However, the ideal of progressive political activism is also a factor as well. At the time of this writing we have a relatively politically liberal president and a Democratic Senate. Yet this progressiveness in the United States is weak compared to that in other Western democracies. Several respondents indicated that they were sympathetic to a more European type of society, which is generally much more politically and culturally progressive than the United States. If a European type of liberalism is more attuned to what the respondents desire, then they may be experiencing a degree of frustration that produces some of their perception of victimization. Furthermore, many of the respondents despaired over the level of irrationality they perceived in the United States. Several of them commented on their concern about the lack of and type of education Americans are receiving. The idea of rationality has also produced a degree of frustration within the respondents that may contribute to their perception that they are victims. Even with a Democratic president and Senate, the enlightened, rational, and politically progressive society cultural progressive activists want may be a long ways away. And the main culprit standing in the way of that society is the influence of the Christian right to inhibit science, education, and rationality. In this way, the respondents can perceive themselves as victims of the Christian right and as marginalized in their efforts to produce what they believe is best for society.

All of this concern is well placed. However, it does not remove the fact that they are still highly educated and relatively wealthy, male, and white. As individuals, they have more power, on average, than other individuals in the United States. They may experience a certain amount of societal rejection or ambivalence due to their religious beliefs, but many of them have channels of power that are denied to groups that are traditionally seen as marginalized such as the homeless, immigrants, racial minorities, and so on. Their perception of marginalization is likely tied to the ideas that make up their collective identity at least as much as a dispassionate assessment of their social position. Even though this is a group that prides itself on being rational, in reality the members of this social movement are just as vulnerable to having their ability to objectively assess their social situation shaped by subjective sociological forces as members of other social movements. They are part of a social movement that finds it useful to perpetuate a certain vision of victimhood, and the respondents tend to support such an image even though they themselves possess a central and salient position in society. It is true that perhaps cultural progressive activists do not possess as much power as they may desire and likely believe that they, and their social movement, are entitled to more societal influence. But such is the lament of nearly all activists within various types of social movements. The needs of the social movement can often blind the adherents to the movement to the social reality they face and instead persuade those adherents to a perceived reality that better serves the movement.[2]

The Continuity of Cultural Progressive Activist Collective Identity

The core of the collective identity of cultural progressive activists can be summed up as rationality, irreligiosity, and political progressiveness. While we have identified three core principles within the collective identity of cultural progressive activists, it is important to note that these principles do not operate in isolation. They are not mutually exclusive ideas that compete with each other. To fully understand the collective identity of cultural progressive activists, it is vital to understand that these ideological constructs mutually reinforce each other. Doing so allows cultural progressive activists to find agreement with each other and to unite against a common enemy who is the antithesis of the rationality, irreligiosity, and political progressiveness that they seek to promote.

For example, the ideal of political progressiveness paints a world whereby religion is separated from the concerns of the government. In this way, political progressives are less likely to envision an intrusive role for religion than their politically conservative counterparts. Such political goals mesh well with the ideals put forth by the norms of irreligiosity in that religion is downplayed in society. Furthermore, there is the well-accepted conflict between science and religion, and part of this conflict can be tied to whether rationality or religious belief is going to be the dominating force in our society. The deemphasis of religion that serves the norms of irreligiosity and is part of a politically progressive mind-set also supports a norm of rationality, if rational thinking is perceived as being the opposite of religious thinking. According to many of the comments cited in the earlier chapters, it is easy to see that many respondents have a dichotomous notion of religion and rationality.

As such, the ideals of rationality, irreligiosity, and political progressiveness reinforce each other. Cultural progressives active in this social movement find ways of communicating these values to each other. Often they find ways of communicating these values so that all three of these principles are assumed. For example, many of the respondents discussed the value of critical thinking. The general idea of critical thinking is that this is a more rational way of conceptualizing one's ideas, and so the ideal of rationality is automatically operationalized when a respondent discusses critical thinking. Yet often the respondents discussed the inability of religious individuals to engage in critical thinking. Religion is seen as the opposite of critical thinking, and irreligiosity is also conceptualized as an important aspect of critical thinking. Many respondents also implied that their progressive political stances were the results of critical thinking. In this way, critical thinking is also tied to the respondents' propensity to support political progressiveness. The term *critical thinking* can be used to activate all three of the core principles that make up the identity of cultural progressive activists. Such terms can provide shortcuts that allow members of this social movement to quickly communicate their values to each other.

Just as the ideals that cultural progressive activists favor are easily linked together, the opposites of these ideas are easily linked together as well. Adherence to a traditional application of a Western religious faith violates the ideal of irreligiosity generally accepted by cultural progressive activists. Furthermore, traditional faith is often seen as a competitor to scientific knowledge (Cho & Squier, 2008; Gould, 1999; Smedes, 2008; Staver, 2010) and linked to a greater acceptance of conservative political ideology (Bonanno & Jost, 2006; Guth & Green, 1990; Miller & Wattenberg, 1984). This indicates that the ideals of rationality and political progressiveness are violated as well. The image of the Christian right put forth by cultural progressive activists tends to be a person who illustrates these perceived detrimental values. It is in this context that all of the other charges made by the respondents about the Christian right, such as bigotry, racism, sexism, mental instability, hypocrisy, proneness to violence, evilness, and so on, can be understood. These charges stem from a larger master image of an irrational religious and political conservative who is everything that the cultural progressive activist opposes. Naturally, cultural progressive activists will easily agree with almost any negative attribution that can be linked to the Christian right.

The image of the Christian right as the opposite of the ideals possessed by cultural progressive activists allows them to create an enemy. Having this image is important because it helps them to define themselves as they can use the image as a negative reference group. Since they are not members of the Christian right, they can perceive themselves as tolerant instead of intolerant, rational instead of irrational, progressive instead of conservative. In other words, the image of the Christian right created by cultural progressive activists is vital for helping those activists to define themselves. But what may be even more significant for cultural progressive activists is their perception of the relative effectiveness that the Christian right has in promulgating their values of traditional religion, irrationality, and conservative political activism. Here the concerns of so many of the respondents about the "brainwashing" of simple-minded individuals and/or the proselytizing that has taken place feed into the fears of cultural progressive activists. These concepts serve to produce fear among cultural progressive activists about the growing power of the Christian right. It motivates them to support their organizations, attend rallies, file lawsuits, and endure the other costs that are important for developing this social movement.

There are important implications linked to the image of a powerful, intolerant, conservative, and irrational Christian right. Many of our respondents indicated not only a strong dislike for members of the Christian right but also that they actively seek to avoid contact with individuals associated with the Christian right. In fact, 6.8 percent of the respondents volunteered that they would immediately move from a neighborhood if too many members of the Christian right became their neighbors. While this is a small percentage, the actual percentage is undoubtedly higher since we did not directly ask them about moving, only about how they would feel living in such a neighborhood. Furthermore, many of the respondents who would not move stated that they would still attempt to avoid contact with their religious and politically conservative neighbors. The animosity that respondents feel toward the Christian right is not merely political. It is often visceral and leads to a social distancing that perpetuates any misunderstanding that they may have of the Christian right and that the Christian right may have of them. Many respondents do not personally know members of the Christian right and do not want to know members of that hated religious and political group. To the degree that social animosity in our society has a religious and political basis, our research indicates that it is at least partly driven by this desire for social distance. An important implication of the culture war is this social distance that likely perpetuates the levels of stereotyping and misunderstanding that have developed between the members of the conflicting parties in this war.

Understanding the fears generated by the image of the Christian right within this social movement enables us to more fully understand the types of actions often taken by cultural progressive activists. One may wonder why such relatively powerful individuals are concerned about issues such as religious monuments in small towns, the phrase "in God we trust" on U.S. money, or a prayer at a football game that they will never attend. All of these can be seen as symbolic fights against that irrational, religious political conservative who has been built up as an oppressive enemy. Losing to such an enemy is unthinkable for cultural progressive activists. Even the loss of small battles may signal to them that the overall war is not going well. Therefore, many cultural progressive organizations have emerged to maintain a legal and political presence and to engage their foes. To individuals who are neither cultural progressive activists nor members of the Christian right, such legal or political fights may seem like wastes of time and resources. But for those engaged in the culture war, the stakes are simply seen as too high, and the battle must be fought.

The Ongoing Culture War

Much of the previous work on the culture war has focused upon cultural conservative activists (Burack, 2008; Gilgoff, 2008; Lienesch, 2007; McConkey, 2001; Wilcox & Larson, 2006). A great deal of this work documents the degree to which those conservatives are committed to their causes. Such research indicates that cultural conservative activists' commitment is tied to their social identity, which is deeply felt and not going to wane any time soon. In this research we have found evidence of a similar type of commitment on behalf of cultural progressive activists. These individuals have developed a collective identity based on rationality, irreligiosity, and political progressiveness. The strength of the identity of some cultural progressive activists is such that they are almost required to engage in the prognostic frames of political and legal activism. This action helps to reinforce their sense of being a good person through their rationality and political perspective. The loss of such an identity would be devastating to the perception of morality for such individuals. Like cultural conservative activists, the commitment of cultural progressive activists is deeply felt, tied to their social identity, and not going to ebb soon.

For cultural progressive activists, losing the culture war is unthinkable. Story lines about theocracy and returning to Dark Ages have developed within this social movement and serve to create sufficient fear to motivate the members of the movement into action. Whether it is realistic to think that conservative Christians could actually create a new theocracy whereby all individuals would be forced to obey Christian law is not important. The fear of this possible reality is a powerful motivator for cultural progressive activists. When the cultural progressives in our study write about their fears of such a possible reality, we believe that they are earnest in their concerns. So for them, losing the culture war and having to live under "Christian rule" is a fate that must be avoided at all costs. Commitment to the causes espoused in this social movement varies among the respondents. But enough respondents indicate a high enough level of commitment that there is little reason to believe that this activism will disappear in the near future.

We did not study the perspectives of cultural conservatives in this current research effort. But assuming that the cultural conservative activists are motivated by the same level of fear as cultural progressive activists, then it is clear that we will continue to see conflict over the cultural and political issues that animate both sides of this culture war. Some previous work argues that notions of a cultural war are overblown (Demerath, 2005; Fiorina, 2005). These scholars suggest that most Americans do not concern themselves with the cultural issues that are the focus of both cultural conservative and progressive activists. Our research is not based upon a probability sample, and we are not in a position to comment upon how many individuals in the United States have adopted the attitudes of the respondents in this survey. However, the existence of organizations discussed in the first chapter indicates that these individuals are not without institutional power. Furthermore, cultural progressive activists continue to win legal victories and have the resources to continue fighting in the legal and probably political realms for some time to come.[3] Given this reality, we contend that it is unwise to dismiss the importance of the ongoing culture war. Assuming that cultural conservative activists also have the resources to work toward realization of their legal and political objectives, it seems certain that cultural progressive activists will continue to marshal their forces against them. From their perspective, failing to engage in battle with their hated enemy invites disaster and creates the possibility of an unfathomable future. All indications are that there is a culture-war-like mentality among certain cultural progressive activists that is not going away soon. If that is the case, and assuming that such a mentality is also present among cultural conservative activists, then the culture war is clearly here to stay.

Since the culture war is likely to continue, it is useful to "handicap" the ability of cultural progressive activists to continue their engagement in this war. As noted earlier, some cultural progressive activists emphasize the tremendous power and influence of the Christian right. Doing so enables them to claim the mantle of victimhood and to make claims on the members of their social movement and on society as a whole. However, the story is more complicated than that. We have already documented that cultural progressive activists tend to have a great deal of social and material resources as individuals. They are better off economically and educationally and more likely to have majority group status in race and gender than other individuals. This indicates that they have a great deal of resources at their disposal. They obviously have disposable income to contribute to their social and political causes. Several of them indicate that they were teachers and professors, which indicates the possibility of influencing the thinking of the younger generations. However, the organizations they have established may not have been around long enough to have the necessary experience to always be able to engage in their chosen legal and political battles with a great deal of skill and knowledge. Furthermore, cultural progressive activists do not have the decentralized and widespread institutions, such as churches, to allow them to get their message out to the general population. But this is not a group that is clearly outmatched by the superior forces of the Christian right. While those in the Christian right have some advantages in their struggle against cultural progressive activists, it would be inaccurate to perceive those activists as mere victims in this ongoing conflict.

It is the case that a majority of individuals in the United States identify themselves as Christians, although it may not be the case that a majority of Americans accept the traditionalist interpretation of Christianity supported by the Christian right. Nevertheless, concerning religious identification, cultural progressive activists are in the position of a minority. Legal victories may sometimes create a public policy backlash that makes it more difficult for them to achieve their political and social agenda. For example, early legal victories supporting same-sex marriage have led to a series of political defeats as many states have passed resolutions or changed their constitution to prohibit such marriages. The advantages they have with their superior social and economic status may be counterbalanced by their loss of status as religious minorities. However, since there may be a growing number of individuals who have little or no religious identification, cultural progressive activists may find themselves well positioned for gaining more public support and can find it easier to obtain more members for their organizations in the future. If such new members have the same economic and educational resources as current cultural progressive activists, then this will be a social movement that will enjoy a considerable level of economic and educational resources in the future.

Will cultural progressive activists eventually win their long struggle with cultural conservative activists and create their vision of a rational and politically progressive irreligious society? Such predictions are probably better left to futurists and prophets rather than sociologists. Some empirical research has indicated that on certain political issues, such as same-sex marriage, the ideals of cultural progressives are becoming more acceptable among younger cohorts (Lewis & Gossett, 2008; Sherkat, de Vries, & Creek, 2010). On their other hand, there is evidence that these same younger cohorts have become relatively conservative on other cultural issues such as abortion (Carlton, Nelson, & Coleman, 2000; Carter et al., 2009). There is not a clear trend in which one can definitely acknowledge the inevitable victory or defeat of cultural progressive activists. This may indicate that the answer to the question is somewhere in the middle. It may be unlikely that cultural progressive activists will ever gain a complete victory over their hated cultural and political rivals. They are not likely to be able to re-create a European type of society here in the United States. On the other hand, we see that they have the resources to maintain a long-term fight with their rivals and will gain victories along the way. Their fears of a future theocracy or society that is totally dominated by Christian are likely unfounded. More likely is that there will be more acceptance of nonreligious ideas and individuals in the foreseeable future and cultural progressive activists will find ways to create their own subculture and niche in our society.

The Future Study of Cultural Progressive Activists

This work fills an important hole in the previous literature on the culture war. It has presented important research on the motivations, typology, and collective identity of cultural progressive activists. Previous work has either focused upon cultural conservative activists or produced a comparison of both groups. We contend that there is at least as much value in doing work that focuses upon the perspectives only of cultural progressives as there is on developing work concerning cultural conservatives. The fact that we could not find any other research on this subject is an indication that this is a gap in the research literature that cannot be filled with one study. To this end, we welcome future research that attempts to meet such empirical needs. In the concluding section of this book we take the opportunity to suggest where such future work may go.

We did not use a probability sample in this particular study. As such, we can discuss only cultural progressive activists and not cultural progressives in general. Understanding cultural progressive activists does provide some insight into cultural progressives, but it is not clear how much the two groups overlap in their social and demographic characteristics, much less their social attitudes. We are quite confident that some of the trends we document will hold up once a probability sample is collected, but we acknowledge that there is no true replacement for quantitative work based on a probability sample. Our findings concerning income, education, race, and sex are overwhelming, and we believe they would be substantiated through the collection of a probability sample. But such a sample would more accurately document the degree to which cultural progressives are overrepresented in these important demographic and social categories. Such a sample may also shed light on other important demographic and social differences between cultural progressives and other individuals in society. For example, regional and urban/rural distinctions are also likely to be captured by such an investigation.[4] Finally, the collection of such a sample will also provide researchers, through the use of carefully designed quantitative questions and qualitative interviews, with the ability to assess the degree to which the social attitudes documented by our work are part of the social attitudes of cultural progressives in general or merely of those who are politically active.

Of course there already is work that has documented the social location of the political support for cultural issues such as abortion, stem cell research, and homosexuality (Carter et al., 2009; Hicks & Lee, 2006; Loftus, 2001; Nisbet, 2005; T. Smith, 1998). But such work cannot by itself indicate whether individuals with a progressive political perspective on these issues also have developed an identity in which they perceive themselves at war with the Christian right. One of the difficulties in conducting this quantitative research is determining who is a cultural progressive. The definition we used to operationalize which organizations served cultural progressives was to see if they made a statement regarding resisting the religious or Christian right. But this is a measure that weeds out those who have cultural progressive beliefs but are not politically active in supporting those beliefs. To capture those individuals, as well as the activists documented in this book, such a concept can be operationalized as a series of questions that assess the attitudes of respondents toward important cultural issues. We could then assess the attitudes of all cultural progressives toward either the Christian or religious right. This would allow a researcher to capture sentiments against either the political or religious aims of this group regardless of their level of political activism. In such a manner we could then assess whether the negative attitudes picked up in our research are a feature of those who are politically active or of cultural progressives in general.

We also contend that work with cultural progressive activists would benefit from a more intentional questioning of members in those groups. Our research design allowed us to engage in preliminary exploration of some of the ideas of those in this subculture. However, it is a design that did not allow for sufficient opportunities to follow up and dig deeper into perspectives that need further clarification. Personally interviewing members of this group would provide insightful analysis as to how these activists perceive their social and political identity. Such interviews would also allow researchers to assess the processes by which these activists developed their current attitudes. We could investigate whether their personal experiences with members of the Christian right led to such animosity or whether they have been socially isolated from members of the Christian right, which has allowed them to develop stereotypes and fears about this group. Such interviews could also further differentiation of the contrasting motivations of cultural progressive activists beyond the simple descriptions we have with our seven groups. For example, we could find out if there are qualitatively different perspectives from the *sexual progressive* and *religion is poison* cultural progressive activists. Even though there is a great deal of overlap between the members of different groups, there are likely to be differences that are important to understand so that we do not make the mistake of linking all cultural progressives to a monolithic experience.

Nevertheless, it is the common threads that tie together the various subgroups of cultural progressive activists that may produce the most generalizable results. For example, the legitimatization of irreligiosity by cultural progressive activists may be the same regardless of which subgroup they belong to. Such a rationale may serve to be a unifying ideology among cultural progressive activists.

It is plausible that such legitimatization does not greatly differ regardless of the religious identity of a cultural progressive activist. Cultural progressive activists who are "born-again" may agree more with atheist cultural progressive activists as it concerns the role of religion in society than with culturally conservative individuals who identify themselves as born-again. Likewise, there may also be great insight gained from exploring how the legitimization of rationality and progressive political action is shared by cultural progressives in the different subgroups. Learning how such values are legitimated and sustained among cultural progressives would provide valuable information about this segment of our society.

Our research is a valuable starting point for understanding cultural progressives and the social movement they have created. There is clearly a need for further work, but we suspect that conducting such research may be difficult since many researchers likely identify with cultural progressive activism. They, like cultural progressive activists, tend to be highly educated and politically progressive. In fact, many researchers may be members of the organizations that serve cultural progressives. Both of us identify with neither cultural progressives nor the Christian right organizations that they are battling. This has given us an outsider perspective that is quite useful in conducting this type of research. Yet there is also a lot to be gained by mining the efforts of movement insiders who also happen to be researchers. Those insiders may be in a position to interpret the perceptions of cultural progressive activists and cultural progressives themselves that escape the examination of those outside their social movement. Given the current dearth of research on cultural progressives, we welcome such insiders to either engage in participant observation or conduct the type of quantitative and qualitative research we have outlined in this section. Only with the efforts of insiders and outsiders can a social movement as important and influential as that supported by cultural progressives be fully understood.

Appendix

Obtaining a Sample

The heart of this research is a questionnaire sent out to members of a variety of groups that are noted for their opposition to the Christian right. The questionnaire can be seen in table A.1. SurveyMonkey, an online survey website, was utilized. We located several cultural progressive groups and contacted them. In every case we sent a link to a contact member of the targeted group and had him or her send the survey out to the members of the group. The advantage of doing this is that we obtained no list of potential respondents and were better able to maintain the anonymity of the respondents.[1] The downside is that we do not know how many individuals received our link and cannot calculate a response rate.

We used a variety of local and national groups. One group is a national group known for its promotion of atheism. Another group is a national group known for its progressive political activism. A third group is a regional group that concentrates on issues of education. Finally, we sent the survey link to a local activist group that sent it out to other local groups and social contacts that our contact believed would fit the definition of cultural progressive. While we acknowledge that we did not obtain a probability sample, we did make efforts to gain some diversity in our population by religious ideology, level of political concern, and region. We are certain that we did not succeed by region due to the large number of individuals we surveyed from the South. However, we do believe that we found an adequate number of individuals who are highly concerned about the Christian right for political reasons and an adequate number of individuals who are concerned due to religious reasons.

In addition to our survey, we also subscribed to a variety of different news and electronic letters. Each of the three major groups in the previous paragraph supplied this primary material. We read all of the materials for a given period of time to get a sense of the messages that were being sent out to the members of the group. The time frame depended on how frequently the primary sources were sent out. For example, one organization used a daily electronic journal. We monitored it for three months. Another organization sent out a monthly paper newsletter. It was monitored for an entire year. The periodicals were coded according to the general theme of each article. As we looked through the codings, we were able to gain a general perception of the attitudes of the leaders of the social movement of cultural progressives. Articles and readings that were purely informational and that did not attempt to persuade the reader about a given point were not necessarily coded. One of the periodicals also contained letters to the editor. We looked through those letters as well for clues as to what drives cultural progressive activists. Although the letters do not directly come from cultural progressive organizations, the fact that the editors of the periodical allowed them to be printed indicates that the writers had compatibility with the aims of the organizations. This is reinforced by the fact that few, if any, of the letters were critical of the organization.

Finally, one of us attended a training workshop for one of the groups mentioned above. It was the only time we interacted face-to-face with some of the cultural progressive activists at an event. He kept notes during the meeting, and we discussed his experience. Fortunately, this visit occurred before the survey was conducted and allowed us to develop some understanding of what some cultural progressive activists want.

Coding of the Short-Answer Responses

The coding of the questions was straightforward and allowed for a quantitative assessment of the group as a whole. Each open-ended response was coded by one researcher. Each attribute was coded as a dichotomous yes or no in regard to that particular response. This allowed us to enter the answers into a statistical program. Each attribute was assessed on its own, and for many responses several attributes were coded as *yes*. However, we strove not to code the same phrase or word in a response with more than one attribute. Thus, a respondent who defined the Christian right as "murderous" would likely have that response coded as *defined as violence* but not as *dangerous*. If the respondent defined the Christian right as *dangerously murderous*, then that answer was coded as both *defined as violence* and *dangerous* since there were different parts of the answer that matched the two attributes. If the response did not fit into any particular codes, all of the attributes for that given response were coded as *no*. But because of the extensive nature of our coding system, this was an uncommon occurrence. Table A.2 contains an explanation of each attribute linked to each question.

Once all of the answers were coded, we created a series of variables that combined some of these variables. For example, the measures *defined as crazy, crazy creates attitude, crazy*, and *crazy is negative* were combined together for a measure in which the respondent received a score ranging from 0 to 4. However, none of the respondents were coded as a 1 in all four measures, but six of them were coded in three of the categories and thus were coded as 3. This gave us a master variable that assessed if, and how often, respondents commented that mental instability or craziness is a feature of the Christian right. The same procedure was used to create similar variables based on intolerance, against science, ignorant, stupid, evil, hypocrisy, trying to take over, violence, backward, claiming victimization, proselytizing, and sexuality.

We also used the same techniques to create such variables for *master bad politics*,[2] *master bad religion*, and *master religion is bad*. Variables that did not fit into any of the above categories were left by themselves when used in our factor analysis. But these last three variables were critical for determining the typology used to examine the motivations of the respondents. We conducted principle axis factor analysis by taking each of those three variables and adding the variables of each question to the analysis one at a time. Each of those three variables was analyzed one at a time so that we could gain a sense of which factors were explanatory of those who opposed the Christian right for political reasons in our first series of analyses, who opposed them because of a general opposition to religion in our second series of analysis, and who opposed them because of the Christian nature of the group in our third series of analysis. We added the codings of each question to the *master bad politics, master bad religion*, and *master religion is bad* variables one at a time. Dummy variables that did not load highly in the analysis were dropped, and then the variables from the next question were added in. But the *master bad politics, master bad religion*, and *master religion is bad* variables were kept when used at the base variable and carried on to the next analysis. Finally, we also loaded a series of general attitude variables and some demographic variables. Thus, a series of factor loadings was discovered for each of the theorized reasons why individuals have hostility toward the Christian right: political motivations, hostility toward religion in general, hostility toward Christian specifically. The final factor analysis and the loadings of the remaining variables can be seen in table A.3.

We made reasonable interpretations about the variables that loaded with our three base variables. Three factors loaded for the analysis that began with the *master religion is bad* variable. But the last loading is built upon those who do not have belief in the supernatural. Furthermore, the variable *religion is bad* did not load highly on that factor. That factor was dropped, and the other two factors were named *religion is poison* and *religion has been corrupted* in our efforts to speculate about the results. All three factors were kept in the loadings that started with political aspects, and these factors were named *political activist*, *sexual progressive*, and *feminist*. Both factors were kept in the loadings started by the *bad religion* variable, and those factors were named *Christianity as unevolved* and *Christians as oppressors*.

The next step was to use these measures to determine which factor applied to which respondent. To do this we took the loading coefficient for each of the variables kept in each loading and applied it to the score of the variables. Most of the variables have a dichotomous 0 or 1 score, so either the value of the coefficient was added to that factor's score or nothing was added to the score. For the master variables of certain characteristics (e.g., against science), the value of the coefficient was multiplied by the number of times a respondent scored in that variable. So if the respondent mentioned the Christian right being stupid two times, then .61 (.305*2) was added to the *religion is poison* factor. Once this was accomplished, we simply looked to see which factor had the highest score to get a rough determination of which factor best explained the attitudes of the respondents. This provided us with a basic breakdown of what motivated the respondent and led to the creation of table A.3.

As noted in chapter 4, there was a great deal of overlap among the characteristics of individuals in the different factor loadings. Table 4.1 indicates the degree of interconnectedness of the different factors when using the raw scores of the factor loadings for each respondent. These correlations are so high that it is not surprising that many respondents scored relatively highly on multiple factor loadings. As a result of these correlations, at times we decided to use all respondents when discussing the different characteristics of each factor and not just the ones assigned in the table. We reason that a respondent may score higher in a particular group such as *political activist* than another respondent and yet because the first respondent scored even higher in *sexual progressive*, then he or she would not be listed as a *political activist*. Yet there is no reason why the first respondent does not represent *political activist* just as well as the second respondent given the higher scores. The few respondents in some of the factor loadings also justified the limited use of all respondents in the discussion of some of the groups.

With the factor loadings now applied to each respondent, we were in a position to assess whether certain demographic and social characteristics were correlated to certain types of motivations within the respondents. This analysis allowed us to discover trends such as the gender imbalance toward females among *feminists*. Such analysis allowed us to further understand the dynamics that undergird the different subgroups discovered in this research. So we tested the scores of the respondents against a variety of demographic and coded variables. We used the dichotomous score that determined which group the respondent was placed in to set up our correlations tables. For example, those labeled as *feminists* were significantly more likely to be females as opposed to males ($r = .051$, $p < .05$), although this was not a powerful correlation. So sex influences whether a respondent is likely to be part of the *feminist* category. Likewise, we tested for other correlations to better understand the differences between the respondents in the contrasting groups. The quantitative operationalizing of the different subgroups allows for a statistical analysis of the differences between the subgroups, which helped to explain why these groups were able to attract cultural progressive activists.

We admit that this is not as precise of a methodology as one may hope. For example, our interpretation of the factor loadings is debatable. But this methodology does provide us with some demarcations between the respondents and helps to illustrate a major point of this research, which is that there is diversity among those who oppose the Christian right. Just as it is a mistake to stereotype all members of the Christian right with broad generalizations, it is also a mistake to use a broad ideological brush to understand cultural progressive activists. Some individuals react the way they do because of certain political concerns, while others have apprehension about the religious nature of the Christian right. Such differences come out in this work, even though much of these political and religious concerns overlap each other. Whether our interpretation of the nuances in these political and religious differences is correct should be a feature of future work.

Yet even with these differences, we found a great deal of overlap between the members of these groups in how they perceived the threat of the Christian right. The evidence of that overlap increases our knowledge stock of cultural progressive activists as it suggests an overarching vision that partially animates the concerns of our respondents, although the contrasting ways they react to that vision are part of their larger diversity. These data provide us with an understanding of the ideological core that ties together different concerns about the Christian right.

TABLE A.1
Questionnaire for Online Survey

1. We'd also like to get your feelings about some groups in American society. We'd like you to rate it with what we call a feeling thermometer. Ratings between 50 degrees and 100 degrees mean that you feel favorably and warm toward the group; ratings between 0 and 50 degrees mean that you don't feel favorably toward the group and that you don't care too much for that group. If you don't feel particularly warm or cold toward a group you would rate them at 50 degrees. Also if you do not know anything about a group you would rate them at 50 degrees.

   Mormons _____   Atheists _____

   Hindus _____   Fundamentalists _____

   Agnostics _____   Jews _____

   Muslims _____   Catholics _____

   Non-Fundamentalist Protestants _____

2. Think back to a time when you were in high school. About what percentage (from 1 to 100) of your friends do you think were in the following religious groups?

   Atheists or Agnostics _____   Jews _____

   Born Again Christians _____   Christian, but not born again _____

   Spiritual, but not religious _____ Other _____

3. Now think back to a time when you were in college or just after high school. About what percentage (from 1 to 100) of your friends do you think were in the following religious groups?

   Atheists or Agnostics _____   Jews _____

   Born Again Christians _____   Christian, but not born again _____

   Spiritual, but not religious _____ Other _____

4. Finally, think about today. About what percentage (from 1 to 100) of your friends do you think are currently in the following religious groups? (If you are still in college then please skip this question.)

   Atheists or Agnostics _____   Jews _____

   Born Again Christians _____   Christian, but not born again _____

   Spiritual, but not religious _____ Other _____

5. How would you define the Christian Right?

6. Please describe your general attitude toward the Christian Right.

7. Is there any specific characteristics of members of the Christian Right or political issue that they support that drives this attitude?

8. What is the most positive thing you can say about the Christian Right?

9. What is the most negative thing you can say about the Christian Right?

10. What is your most memorable personal encounter with a member of the Christian Right.

11. What happened in that encounter and how did you feel about that experience. Please list more than one such encounter if you so desire.

12. Did that encounter alter how you perceived members of the Christian Right? If so then how did it do that?

13. Imagine that you choose who is going to be your neighbor. Please rate the desirability of having one of the following individuals as your neighbor.

    A vocal Republican who is not a Christian _____

    A vocal Christian who is apolitical _____

14. Which of the two hypothetical neighbors do you desire less and why do you have a lower desire for the neighbor you ranked lower?

15. Would it bother you if most of your neighbors were members of the Christian Right and if so then why?

16. Do you think that we should pass laws that would affect members of the Christian Right? If you do want to pass such law(s), what would they be and why?

17. Are there any comments about the Christian Right you would like to add that you did not get a chance to in any of the other questions?

18. Sex

    ___ Male   ___ Female

19. Age

18–25	26–35	36–45	46–55	56–65
66–75	Over 75			

20. Race

White	Black	Hispanic
Asian	Native American	Middle Eastern
Multiracial	Other	

21. Education Obtained

    Not High School   High School Diploma   Some College
    Bachelor's Degree   Some Graduate School   Master's Degree
    Doctorate

22. Income

    Under 30K   30K–75K   75K–125K   Over 125K

23. What region of the country do you live in?

    ___ East North Central (Wisconsin, Illinois, Indiana, Michigan, Ohio)

    ___ Middle Atlantic (New York, New Jersey, Pennsylvania)

    ___ New England (Maine, Vermont, New Hampshire, Massachusetts, Connecticut, Rhode Island)

    ___ South Atlantic (Delaware, Maryland, West Virginia, Virginia, North Carolina, South Carolina, Georgia, Florida, District of Columbia)

    ___ West South Central (Arkansas, Oklahoma, Louisiana, Texas)

    ___ East South Central (Kentucky, Tennessee, Alabama, Mississippi)

    ___ Mountain (Montana, Idaho, Wyoming, Nevada, Utah, Colorado, Arizona, New Mexico)

    ___ Pacific (Washington, Oregon, California, Alaska, Hawaii)

    ___ West North Central (Minnesota, Iowa, Missouri, North Dakota, South Dakota, Nebraska, Kansas)

24. How would you describe your own religious faith?

    ___ Non–Born Again Christian   ___ Born Again Christian

    ___ Jewish   ___ Muslim

    ___ Eastern Religion   ___ Spiritual, but not Religious

    ___ Agnostic   ___ Atheist

    ___ Other

TABLE A.2
Descriptions of Codes Used for Short-Answer Questions

The question of "How would you define the Christian right?" was coded with the following attributes in mind.

1. *Defined as evil*—The respondent indicated that the Christian right is somehow evil or dangerous to society in general. The code was also used if the respondent referred to oppressive groups such as the Taliban or Nazis when discussing the Christian right. However, this is different from the problems (i.e., Takeover, Violent) indicated in other attributes. They may have discussed the Christian right in ways that show that the Christian right have no redeeming values ("they should all just go away"). The notion of the Christian right as traitors is also used in this category.
2. *Defined as stupid*—The respondent indicated that the members of the Christian right are unintelligent or stupid. The respondent may have indicated that the members are unable to use reason or logic.
3. *Defined as ignorant*—The respondent indicated that the members of the Christian right are ignorant or undereducated. This is differentiated from stupidity as it is linked to a lack of knowledge rather than an inability to reason. At times respondents indicated that the members of the Christian right are willfully ignorant and at other times they suggested that the members simply have not been taught. The code was also used to indicate that members of the Christian right were trying to stifle the acquisition and promotion of scientific knowledge as this can be seen as encouraging ignorance.
4. *Defined as against science*—The respondent indicated an aversion to the Christian right because they resist the development of science. Resistance to creationism was categorized in this variable unless there was clearly some other dynamic (such as violence toward creationists) that better captured this variable. But also if the respondent believed that the Christian right resists science in general or is unwilling to allow scientists the freedom to do their work, then this code was used.
5. *Political definition*—The respondent indicated that the Christian right is involved politically in ways that are harmful to society or in ways that encourage political conservatism.
6. *Defined as intolerant or bigoted*—The respondent indicated that the Christian right encourages intolerance or bigotry. Usually

the respondent used these terms directly, although at times the respondent indicated that the Christian right is not open to alternatives. In those cases we also coded the response with this attribute. Finally we found that when the term *bigotry* was used it almost never was tied to racial bigotry. If it was, then this code was not used unless there was another reason to use the code.

7. *Defined as crazy*—The respondent indicated that the Christian right fosters some degree of mental instability or craziness. This is differentiated from stupidity as we looked for indications that the respondent thought that mental illness is a feature within the Christian right. The notion that the Christian right is deluded was also coded as craziness.

8. *Defined as immoral*—The respondent indicated that the Christian right is made up of individuals who are immoral. We used this code when individuals were described in ways that did not fit in the other categories. Thus intolerance could be seen as immoral, but if that was the only description this code was not used, but the "Defined as intolerant or bigoted" code was used instead. However, there were other attributes such as racist, arrogant, and selfish that did not fit into the other codes, and thus we used this code to define them.

9. *Practical definition*—If the respondent attempted to provide a practical or "textbook" definition of the Christian right, this code was used. We did not use it if there was a general rant against the Christian right disguised as a definition. But if there was a real attempt to define this specific group, and not a general evil or a dysfunctional group, then this code was used.

10. *Defined as religious extremist*—The respondent indicated that the Christian right is made up of those who distorted religion in general or Christianity specifically. Concepts such as fundamentalist or biblical literalist were tied to this code since such concepts are generally seen as pejorative to individuals who resist the Christian right.

11. *Defined as extremist*—If the respondent simply used the word *extremist* without any qualifying adjectives, this code was used since it was unclear what type of extremism (i.e., political, religious) was being talked about.

12. *Defined as hypocrisy*—The respondent indicated that the Christian right is made up of hypocrites or tends to promote hypocrisy. If the respondent used the word *hypocrisy*, this code was used. But it was also used if the respondent discussed the inability of members of the Christian right to live up to their own moral code or

incongruence of the ideology and lifestyle or reality in the Christian right.
13. *Defined as trying to take over*—The respondent indicated that the Christian right is a threat to democracy and/or is trying to set up a theocracy. It also was used if the respondent indicated attempts at imposing Christian values.
14. *Defined as violence*—The respondent indicated that the Christian right promotes and/or engages in violence. This was linked to individuals' actions of violence rather than arguments that the political direction of the Christian right leads to international or national violence. References to groups such as the Taliban and Nazis were not automatically coded as violent since there can be other aspects of these groups that are undesirable.
15. *Defined as backward*—The respondent indicated that the Christian right is trying to lead the society backward. We did not use this as it concerns scientific progress but rather if the respondent indicated that the social changes championed by the Christian right were those that would take the country back to "the 1920s" or the "Dark Ages."
16. *Defined as claiming victimhood*—The respondent indicated that the Christian right is trying to claim to be victims in society or that they are making claims of being oppressed.
17. *Defined as proselytizers*—The respondent indicated that the Christian right is trying to proselytize others into their beliefs. This is differentiated from taking over as it concerns the efforts of individuals to convince other individuals of the rightness of the Christian right cause. Takeover attempts concern the imposition of Christian values by use of the government or social pressure.

The statement of "Please describe your general attitude toward the Christian right" was coded with the following attributes in mind.
1. *Evil*—Respondent indicated that the idea of the Christian right being evil is responsible for attitude toward Christian right. See above for the definition of evil. The only exception to the above definition of evil is that the word *dangerous* was not used in this variable since it was used in the variable about fear.
2. *Intolerance/bigotry creates attitude*—Respondent indicated that intolerance and/or bigotry is responsible for attitude toward Christian right. See above for definition of intolerance and/or bigotry.

3. *Ignorance creates attitude*—Respondent indicated that ignorance is responsible for attitude toward Christian right. See above for definition of ignorance.
4. *Stupidity creates attitude*—Respondent indicated that stupidity is responsible for attitude toward Christian right. See above for definition of stupidity.
5. *Crazy creates attitude*—Respondent indicated that craziness is responsible for attitude toward Christian right. See above for definition of crazy.
6. *Attitude of fear*—The respondent indicated an attitude of fear toward the Christian right or that the Christian right is a threat to the rest of society. Respondent may also have stated that the Christian right is dangerous, which implies that we should fear them.
7. *They are wrong creates attitude*—Respondent indicated that the incorrect stances of the Christian right is responsible for attitude. The incorrect stances may be on political or religious issues, but the fact that members of the Christian right promote those stances accounts for the attitude of the respondent.
8. *Respondent has bad attitude toward Christian right*—If the respondent used terms or concepts that are not in this list of attributes, then this code was used as a catchall for bad feelings toward the Christian right.
9. *Negative*—Respondent used the word *negative* to describe attitude toward Christian right.
10. *Hatred*—Respondent used some term indicating hatred (i.e., distain) of the Christian right or indicated that the Christian right is not liked.
11. *Pity*—Respondent indicated a certain degree of pity toward the Christian right. Respondent was not necessary sympathetic toward members of the Christian right but saw them in an inferior social and/or intellectual position. Sometimes this was an expression of condescension.
12. *Tolerate*—Respondent indicated a willingness to tolerate the Christian right.
13. *Avoid them*—Respondent indicated a desire to avoid contact and sometimes even knowledge of Christian right.
14. *Some good*—Respondent qualified negative attitude toward Christian right by indicating that there are issues of agreement or that some of the people in the Christian right are good.

15. *Hypocrisy creates attitude*—Respondent indicated that hypocrisy is responsible for attitude toward Christian right. See above for definition of hypocrisy.
16. *Mistrust of Christian right*—Respondent indicated a lack of trust for members or leaders of the Christian right.
17. *Bad religion*—Respondent indicated that the fact that the Christian right is based on religious beliefs is part of attitude toward group. Respondent indicated that religion in and of itself is bad and thus is the problem.
18. *Religious aspects*—Respondent indicated that religious aspects of the Christian right are part of attitude toward the group. These religious aspects may be a belief that the Christian right has corrupted good religion or may be an assertion that religion in general is a problem.
19. *Political aspects*—Respondent indicated that political aspects of the Christian right are part of attitude toward the group. Generally it is a political stance taken on a specific issue or in general that the respondent is reacting negatively to.
20. *Backwardness creates attitudes*—Respondent indicated that backwardness of Christian right is responsible for attitude toward Christian right. See above for definition of backward.
21. *Violence creates attitudes*—Respondent indicated that violence was responsible for attitude toward Christian right. See above for definition of violence.
22. *Victimization creates attitudes*—Respondent indicated that victimization is responsible for attitude toward Christian right. See above for definition of victimization.
23. *Attempts to take over society create attitude*—Respondent indicated that concern about the Christian right taking over society is responsible for attitude. See above for definition of takeover.
24. *Proselytizing creates attitude*—Respondent indicated that proselytizing is responsible for attitude toward Christian right. See above for definition of proselytizing.

The question of "Are there any specific characteristics of members of the Christian right or political issues that they support that drive this attitude?" was coded with the following attributes in mind.

1. *Political difference*—The respondent brought up political issues other than the issues stated below as the driving force behind attitude.

2. *Gender issues*—The respondent brought up concerns about equality of females, other than the issue of abortion, as the driving force behind attitude.
3. *Religious intrusion*—The respondent brought up the corruption of good religion or the misuse of religion as the driving force behind attitude.
4. *Intolerance/bigotry*—The respondent brought up intolerance/bigotry as the driving force behind attitude. See above for definition of intolerance and/or bigotry.
5. *Church/state issues*—The respondent brought up the intrusion in education or government as the driving force behind attitude. We also coded attempts to push creationism under this attribute.
6. *Ignorance*—The respondent brought up ignorance as the driving force behind attitude. See above for definition of ignorance.
7. *Antiscience*—The respondent brought up antiscience as the driving force behind attitude. See above for definition of antiscience.
8. *Stupidity*—The respondent brought up stupidity as the driving force behind attitude. See above for definition of stupidity.
9. *Crazy*—The respondent brought up crazy as the driving force behind attitude. See above for definition of crazy.
10. *Homophobia*—The respondent brought up issues related to homosexuality or same-sex marriage as the driving force behind attitude.
11. *Abortion rights*—The respondent brought up issues of abortion as the driving force behind attitude.
12. *Stem cell*—The respondent brought up issues of stem cell research as the driving force behind attitude.
13. *Sexuality*—The respondent brought up traditional sexuality as the driving force behind attitude. This should not be confused with issues of homosexuality, which are captured in the homophobia attribute, but rather it indicates concern that the Christian right is not open to modern norms of sexuality and is trying to impose traditional sexual mores. We also used this attribute to indicate concern about sex education.
14. *Violence*—The respondent brought up violence as the driving force behind attitude. See above for definition of violence.
15. *Backward*—The respondent brought up issues of the Christian right being backward as the driving force behind attitude. See above for definition of backward.
16. *Victimization*—The respondent brought up the claims of victimization by the Christian right as the driving force behind attitude. See above for definition of victimization.

17. *Hypocrisy*—The respondent brought up hypocrisy as the driving force behind attitude. See above for definition of hypocrisy.
18. *Bad character*—The respondent brought up bad characteristics (racists, arrogant, etc.) not already directly noted in the other attributes as the driving force behind attitude.
19. *Takeover*—The respondent brought up the attempts of the Christian right to take over society as the driving force behind attitude. See above for definition of takeover.
20. *Proselytizing*—The respondent brought up proselytizing as the driving force behind attitude. See above for definition of proselytizing.

The question of "What is the most positive thing you can say about the Christian right?" was coded with the following attributes in mind.

1. *Nothing*—The respondent indicated that there was nothing positive to be said about the Christian right or his or her only comment was just another complaint about the Christian right.
2. *Backhand compliment*—The respondent gave a compliment that could be seen as sarcastic ("they keep their lawns mowed").
3. *Added complaint*—The respondent added a qualifier to an otherwise positive compliment (they have honest beliefs but their beliefs are just wrong). In this situation both this attribute and corresponding attribute connected to their positive compliment were coded.
4. *Numbers are decreasing*—Respondent indicated that the best thing to be said about the Christian right was that they were decreasing in numbers and/or power.
5. *Good works*—Respondent indicated that the Christian right sometimes does good work for society or community such as feeding the hungry.
6. *Have human rights*—Respondent indicated that the Christian right had the right to their opinion or actions.
7. *Well organized*—Respondent admired the organization or community that the Christian right has created.
8. *Community*—Respondent indicates that the Christian right were good at creating a community and meeting people's needs for community.
9. *Honest beliefs*—Respondent noted that at least some members of the Christian right believed that what they were doing was the right thing to do and/or would help make society better.

10. *They are Christians (or spiritual)*—Respondent indicated that at least the members of the Christian right had religious faith.
11. *Some good beliefs*—Respondent indicated that some of the beliefs (e.g., environmentalism, taking care of poor) of the Christian right are worthwhile.
12. *Morality*—Respondent indicated that at least some members of the Christian right were moral and/or nice individuals.

The question of "What is the most negative thing you can say about the Christian right?" was coded with the following attributes in mind.

1. *Everything is negative*—Respondent indicated that everything about the Christian Right is negative or bad.
2. *Evil*—The respondent brought up evil as an important negative of the Christian right. See above for definition of evil.
3. *Bad character is negative*—The respondent brought up bad characteristics (racists, arrogant, etc.) not directly noted in other attributes as an important negative of the Christian right.
4. *Intolerant/bigoted is negative*—The respondent brought up intolerance and/or bigotry as an important negative of the Christian right. See above for definition of intolerance and/or bigotry.
5. *Religion is bad*—Respondent indicated that the fact that the Christian right is a religious group is negative as religion in and of itself is bad.
6. *Bad religion*—The respondent brought up the misuse or misapplication of a religious faith is an important negative of the Christian right.
7. *Bad politics*—The respondent brought up the misuse or misapplication of the Christian right's bad political solutions is an important negative of the Christian right.
8. *Ignorance is negative*—The respondent brought up ignorance as an important negative of the Christian right. See above for definition of ignorance.
9. *Antiscience is negative*—The respondent brought up antiscience as an important negative of the Christian right. See above for definition of antiscience.
10. *Stupidity is negative*—The respondent brought up stupidity as an important negative of the Christian right. See above for definition of stupidity.

11. *Crazy is negative*—The respondent brought up crazy as an important negative of the Christian right. See above for definition of crazy.
12. *Backward is negative*—The respondent brought up Christian right being backward as an important negative. See above for definition of backward.
13. *Sexuality concerns as negative*—The respondent brought up sexuality as an important negative of the Christian right. See above for definition of sexuality.
14. *Claiming victimhood as negative*—The respondent brought up claiming victimhood as an important negative of the Christian right. See above for definition of claiming victimhood.
15. *Takeover as negative*—The respondent brought up the threat of the Christian right taking over society as an important negative. See above for definition of takeover.
16. *Violence as negative*—The respondent brought up violence as an important negative. See above for definition of takeover.
17. *Judgmental as negative*—The respondent brought up judgmental attitudes in the Christian right as an important negative of the Christian right.
18. *Hypocrisy as negative*—The respondent brought up hypocrisy as an important negative of the Christian right. See above for definition of hypocrisy.
19. *Proselytizing as negative*—The respondent brought up proselytizing as an important negative of the Christian right. See above for definition of proselytizing.
20. *Hateful as negative*—The respondent brought up hateful attitudes within the Christian right as an important negative of the Christian right.

The question of "What is your most memorable personal encounter with a member of the Christian right? What happened in that encounter, and how did you feel about that experience? Please list more than one such encounter if you so desire." was coded with the following attributes in mind.

1. *None*—Respondent indicated no personal encounter that could be remembered with a person of the Christian right.
2. *General encounter*—The encounter was not defined well enough to fit into the following parameters, or the respondent merely discussed general encounters without putting them in a situational context.

3. *Family*—The encounter involved the respondent's own family members or in-laws as members of the Christian right.
4. *Friends*—The encounter involved the respondent's own friends as members of the Christian right.
5. *Work*—The encounter involved the respondent's own coworkers or clients/customers/students met at work as members of the Christian right.
6. *Church*—The encounter involved the respondent's experience in a church or religious setting.
7. *Member*—Respondent indicated that he or she was once a member of the Christian right or grew up in a Christian right church.
8. *Target of proselytizing*—The encounter involved attempts to proselytize the respondent.
9. *Date/marry*—The encounter involved a romantic engagement between the respondent and a member of the Christian right.
10. *Political protest*—The encounter involved the respondent's engagement in political protests or at public events where there was generalized intergroup conflict.

The question of "Did that encounter alter how you perceived members of the Christian right? If so then how did it do that?" was coded with the following attributes in mind.

1. *Negative*—The respondent indicated that the encounter produced a more negative perception of the Christian right.
2. *No effect*—The respondent indicated that the encounter had no effect on perceptions of the Christian right.
3. *Reaffirmation of previous beliefs*—The respondent indicated that the encounter reaffirmed previous perceptions of the Christian right.
4. *Human*—The respondent indicated that the encounter helped to humanize a perception of the Christian right and/or produced a more positive perception of the Christian right.

The question of "Which of the two hypothetical neighbors do you desire less and why do you have a lower desire for the neighbor you ranked lower?" was coded with the following attributes in mind.

1. *Christians proselytize*—Respondent indicated that the proselytizing of Christians is why the apolitical Christian is less desired.
2. *Christians are hypocrites*—Respondent indicated that the hypocrisy of Christians is why the apolitical Christian is less desired.

3. *Christians are bad people*—Respondent indicated that the low character or negative personal characteristics of Christians is why the apolitical Christian is less desired.
4. *Christians are intolerant/bigoted*—Respondent indicated that the intolerance or bigotry of Christians is why the apolitical Christian is less desired.
5. *Christians are stupid or ignorant*—Respondent indicated that the stupidity or ignorance of Christians is why the apolitical Christian is less desired.
6. *Christians are alright*—Respondent indicated a direct preference for apolitical Christians over non-Christian Republicans. Generally the respondent stated some degree of appreciation of Christians relative to Republicans.
7. *Republicans support bad policies*—Respondent indicated that the support of political policies that are seen as detrimental is why non-Christian Republicans are less desired.
8. *Republicans are bad people*—Respondent indicated that the low character or negative personal characteristics of Christians is why the non-Christian Republicans are less desired.
9. *No Republicans*—Respondent indicated more of a desire to avoid non-Christian Republicans but did not indicate why.
10. *Republicans are alright*—Respondent indicated a direct preference for non-Christian Republicans over apolitical Christians. Generally the respondent stated some degree of appreciation of Republicans relative to Christians.
11. *Both are bad*—Respondent indicated an inability to choose which is worse as both are undesirable.
12. *Both are alright*—Respondent indicated an inability to choose which is worse as both are desirable.

The question of "Would it bother you if most of your neighbors were members of the Christian right and if so then why?" was coded with the following attributes in mind.

1. *Already live near Christian right*—Respondent indicated already living in a neighborhood with many members of the Christian right.
2. *Used to live near Christian right in the past*—Respondent indicated having used to live in a neighborhood with many members of the Christian right.
3. *No problem*—Respondent indicated that there is not any problem living in a neighborhood with members of the Christian right.

4. *Just ignore them*—Respondent indicated that there is not a problem living in a neighborhood with members of the Christian right since they can be ignored.
5. *No problem if keep away*—Respondent indicated that as long as members of the Christian right do not infringe on others' rights and/or home then there is no problem living in a neighborhood with members of the Christian right.
6. *Rejection*—Respondent indicated that living in a neighborhood with members of the Christian right is undesirable because of the possibility of rejection from those neighbors.
7. *Would move*—Respondent indicated a willingness to move or refusing to locate in a neighborhood with members of the Christian right.
8. *Do not want to be near stupidity or ignorance*—Respondent indicated that living in a neighborhood with members of the Christian right is undesirable because the neighbors would tend to be stupid or ignorant.
9. *Fear violence*—Respondent indicated a fear that of suffering from physical violence or property damage if living near members of the Christian right.
10. *Neighbors would be unpleasant*—Respondent indicated that living in a neighborhood with members of Christian right is undesirable because the neighbors would be unpleasant to be around. A variety of reasons (e.g., loudness, arrogance) were given for this potential unpleasantness.
11. *Slightly unpleasant*—Respondent indicated that it is unpleasant to live near the Christian right but only slightly unpleasant.
12. *Political activism*—Respondent indicated that political activism of Christian right members is why he or she does not want to be in a neighborhood with them. Respondent fears that the schools and political structure of area will be negatively affected by voting patterns of Christian right members.
13. *Attempts at proselytizing*—Respondent indicated that living in a neighborhood with members of the Christian right is undesirable because the neighbors would try to proselytize.
14. *Intolerant neighbors*—Respondent indicated that living in a neighborhood with members of the Christian right is undesirable because the neighbors would be intolerant or bigoted.
15. *Protect children*—Respondent indicated that living in a neighborhood with members of the Christian right is undesirable because of fears of how it would affect the respondent's children.

The question of "Do you think that we should pass laws that would affect members of the Christian right? If you do want to pass such law(s), what would they be and why?" was coded with the following attributes in mind.

1. *No laws*—Respondent indicated that laws protect everybody and that no laws should be changed to deal with the Christian right.
2. *Enforce existing laws*—Respondent indicated that the existing laws are sufficient. Respondent sometimes argued that the laws were not enforced strictly enough, such as in matters of separation of church and state, but that new laws were not needed.
3. *Laws out of religion*—Respondent indicated that laws had to be kept out of religious concerns.
4. *Freedom of speech*—Respondent indicated that freedom of speech dictated that such laws cannot and/or should not be passed.
5. *Not like Christian right*—Respondent indicated not wanting to do so because that would make the respondent like the Christian right, whom the respondent saw as trying to use laws to enforce their will. Also those who feared that laws used against the Christian right may one day be used against them were coded with this attribute.
6. *Need laws for separation of church and state*—Respondent indicated a desire to create laws that strengthen the separation of church and state. Such laws may deal with aspects such as religious symbols, religious groups getting financial support to do good works, or use of religion in governmental decisions.
7. *Tax exemption for religious institutions*—Respondent indicated a desire to create laws about the tax exemption on religious institutions, wanting the tax exemption taken from all religious institution or those that engaged too heavily in politics.
8. *Protection of abortion clinics*—Respondent indicated a desire to create laws that strengthen the protection of abortion clinics.
9. *Homeschooling*—Respondent indicated a desire to create laws that limit the rights of homeschoolers or get rid of homeschooling altogether.
10. *Other laws*—Respondent indicated a desire to create laws not mentioned in the other attributes.

The question of "Are there any comments about the Christian right you would like to add that you did not get a chance to in any of the other questions?" was coded with the following attributes in mind.

1. *No comment*—The respondent did not make a comment or indicated that there was no other comment forthcoming.
2. *Christian right is dangerous/frightening*—Respondent indicated some degree of fear of the Christian right and further noted how dangerous they are.
3. *Not like them*—Respondent once again indicated some aspect of the Christian right that is not liked or respected.
4. *Just leave me alone*—Respondent indicated wanting to be left alone by members of the Christian right.
6. *Christian right are just humans*—Respondent indicated some humanizing aspect of the Christian right or pointed out some good aspect of them.
7. *Christian right promotes ignorance and nonreason*—Respondent once again noted that ignorance and stupidity characterize members of the Christian right and their movement.
8. *Need for better teaching*—Respondent indicated that there is a need for teaching either members of the Christian right so that they can have the proper perspective and/or larger society about them.
9. *Mentally unbalanced*—Respondent argued that members of the Christian right are mentally unbalanced or crazy.
10. *Stop them*—Respondent indicated a need for urgency in finding ways to stop the Christian right.

TABLE A.3
Factor Loadings of Variables That Explain Animosity toward Christian Right

	Political activist	Cultural warrior	Feminist	Religion is poison	Religion has been corrupted	Christianity is unevolved	Christians as political oppressors
Master bad politics	.553	.157	.169			.342	.176
Master bad religion					.170	.365	.229
Master religion is bad				.212	.326		
Master no science	.120		.180				
Master stupid				.305			
Some good	.115						
Gender issues			.561				
Homophobia		.593	.277				
Abortion rights		.715					
Attitude of fear				.191			
Negative encounter					.184		
Used to live near Christian right							
Master backward						.229	
Republicans bad people							.174
No problem						.113	
Freedom of speech							.221
Anti-fundamentalist							.193

Notes

Chapter 1

1. While the influence of Christianity has waned in Europe, there is clearly a growing influence of Islam. It remains to be seen whether the secular society of Europe can withstand the emerging Islamic culture. One reason it may not is that the birth rate among white Europeans is not a replacement rate and is much lower than that of the Muslim immigrants coming into the European countries. The culture war does continue in Europe, but the traditional religious combatants have changed.
2. The acceptance of Muslims as potential allies of this new traditional coalition was clearly a possibility in the 1980s and 1990s. However, with 9/11 so fresh in our minds, it is unclear how much they remain a significant part of that coalition. Recent work has indicated that traditional Muslims show a preference for the Democratic Party (Barreto & Bozonelos, 2009; Gallaher, 1997; Wald & Calhoun-Brown, 2007), the party of the cultural progressives. This preference likely emerged as these Muslims perceived less acceptance from the "war on terrorism" dialog emerging among political conservatives.

3   Information about the history of these organizations was obtained by visiting the home pages of each organization and reading about their history in their own words. Those homepages are http://ffrf.org for Freedom From Religion Foundation, http://atheists.org for American Atheists, and http://www.jewsonfirst.org for Jews On First.

4   For example, it is hard to imagine that a popular and successful television producer such as Norman Lear would have difficulty finding wealthy individuals to contribute to his organization. While this is merely one example of a wealthy benefactor for cultural progressive movements, the demographical information in our research indicates that many other individuals with significant financial means are active within cultural progressive movements.

5   We realize that this statement will offend prolifers, who do not see the fetus as part of a woman's body, and prochoicers, who do not see the fetus as a baby. Our reaction to such offense is, so be it. We are not taking sides in the abortion debate but merely pointing out the different claims made by both groups in this debate. Representing the perspectives of either side in a way in which the members of that side will recognize their own arguments is likely to make the adherents on the other side angry, and there is nothing that can be done about that.

6   There are obvious conceptual differences between the idea of a Christian right and the idea of a religious right. The term *Christian right* implies that a group may have hostility directed specifically at Christians, while the term *religious right* brings in conservatives of other religious faiths. But while there are conservative Jews and Mormons active in the religious right, Christianity is still the dominant religion in the United States and thus has the overwhelming influence in conservative religious politics. Even Jewish religious conservatives such as Michael Medved and Dennis Prager are quick to defend Christianity against secular opponents. Thus, in many ways the Christian right is synonymous with the religious right.

7   Our question assessing social networks used the term *born-again Christians*, while our thermometer questions ask about *fundamentalists*. We used *fundamentalist* in the latter questions since that is the standard term used in most of the thermometer studies we have found. But we did decide to use *born-again* in our other question since we were unsure if the respondents conceptualized what a fundamentalist was at the age of 15, whereas *born-again* is a more common term.

8   Our basic style is to use several quotes to back up most of our points. We do this first because the sheer number of our respondents provided us with many examples but also produced the possible charge that we are cherry-picking our data for some preconceived result. Using several quotes indicates the accuracy of our statements about the data. This is especially true given that many of the quotes could be used to

illustrate several of the points made throughout this book, reinforcing the patterns that we claim are present in the data. Second, we do this to provide a reader with the tone that many of the respondents set for their answers. It is one thing to tell the reader about the perspectives of the respondents, but quite another to demonstrate that perspective again and again. Finally, presenting multiple quotes allows several individuals to comment on a given issue. This assures us the we have provided ample opportunity for the respondents in the survey to give their voice to these issues.

Chapter 3

1. There is an exception to this tendency. We found that some individuals connected to the Christian right joined these oppositional organizations in an effort to monitor them. Indeed, we eliminated several of our surveys when it was clear that the individuals who filled out the survey were quite sympathetic to the Christian right. It is possible that a couple of these "plants" got through our screens; however, the power of the results we report is so strong that one or two individuals would probably not have skewed our results.
2. "Overview of Race and Hispanic Origin: 2010" (March 2011) United States Census Bureau. Washington, D.C.
3. "Age and Sex Composition: 2010" (May 2011) United States Census Bureau. Washington, D.C.
4. This is based on the 2005–2009 American Community Survey (2010) (U.S. Census Bureau. Washington, D.C.) five-year estimate.
5. 2010 American Community Survey (2010). U. S. Census Bureau: Washington, D.C.
6. Calculated by the 2000 Census 5% PUMS data set.
7. It is possible that some individuals who are Mormon may have indicated themselves as "Other" in the survey. Since we did not create a category for them in the survey, this remains a possibility. However, it seems just as likely that such individuals utilized one of the Christian categories as well. While we may have missed a few Mormons, it is unlikely that locating and including the Mormons in the sample would greatly alter the basic findings about the non-monotheistic nature of the sample.
8. Of course the term *fundamentalist* is imprecise, and individuals in society have many different ways to conceptualize fundamentalism. There was a reason to define this term for our respondents—so that we could be sure that their comparisons were with similar groups. But we did not define fundamentalist for our respondents due to the fact that they already had their own definitions that they brought to these questions. Furthermore, how the respondents defined

fundamentalists was part of what we hoped to capture in our research, especially through their responses to our short-answer questions. An expansive or restrictive definition of fundamentalist was relevant for the size of the out-group that a respondent perceived. Thus, we did not want to give the respondents a definition of fundamentalism early in the research instrument that the respondent would then use through the rest of the survey.

9 We asked the respondents to rate their warmness toward eight different religious belief groups. Those who rated fundamentalists at least one standard deviation lower than other groups were seen as having significantly more animosity toward fundamentalists than toward other religious groups.

Chapter 4

1 For those who want a more statistical treatment of that topic, a more complete explanation is provided in the appendix.
2 This technique determines which characteristics tend to occur within the same respondent. We reasoned that if similar variables were occurring among the respondents, then there are certain social forces generating these types of relationships. Each set of loaded factors was seen as a different subgroup that provides a unique explanation for why individuals are cultural progressives and oppose the Christian right. The actual names we gave the different sets of variables that were coded are subjective, but the fact that certain variables tend to occur together is not. The factor analysis provided a coefficient for each variable that is included in the loaded factor. We used the value of that coefficient to weigh each positive response to a given variable. The factor loading that scored the highest was used to determine which subgroup a respondent belonged to. This accounts for the information seen in the table 3.3.
3 We chose not to ask about sexual preference to make the survey less threatening. In hindsight, that was likely a mistake. Since 56 of the respondents voluntarily indicated their homosexuality, probably very few would have objected to the question. Since we did not include this question, and thus we have no real estimate of the percentage of respondents who are homosexual as many of our respondents may have chosen not to indicate their sexual preference. However, correlation analysis indicates that those who openly admitted to being homosexuals were more likely to be *sexual progressives* than other cultural progressive activists ($r = .081, p < .01$).
4 In fact, Schiebinger (2000) comments on how feminism and gender studies have influenced science for the better. In this sense one

can argue that scientific inquiry has become an important tool for feminists.

5   Roeder was convicted of murdering George Tiller.
6   Of course this is not unlike the Marxian critique of religion being a drug that creates a false consciousness among the proletariat. We are unsure of how many of the respondents were aware of this critique, but given the educational level of our sample, there is a decent chance that many of them are familiar with this Marxian argument. But to avoid making unsubstantiated presuppositions, we argue that many of these individuals likely have come to such a conclusion without direct knowledge of Marx's work.

Chapter 5

1   We are not claiming that these assertions are absolutely without merit. Indeed, there is plenty of research suggesting that atheists suffer from lower levels of social status than many other groups in the United States (Bishop, 2007; Gey, 2006). However, our point is that regardless of the degree of oppression atheists may face, given that atheists have higher SES and more education than other Americans, we do not place their degree of marginalization on par with that of minority groups such as African Americans or the poor. There is a powerful sociopsychological need for cultural progressives to rationalize this victim image. It is likely that at least some of the reason why this image is so powerful in this subculture is the need to generate unity within this social movement as well as real grievances that such individuals may have.
2   It should be noted that forgiveness is a concept much more aligned with Western religions than Eastern religions. In critiquing this concept, these arguments deal only with certain types of religions.

Chapter 6

1   In fact, while Dobson and other conservative Christians were often used by cultural progressive activists as examples of what they do not like about Christian activism, not a single respondent used King, Jessie Jackson, Jim Wallis, or some other more progressive Christian figure as a negative reference group. This reinforces the argument that it is the mixing of conservative politics and religion that motivates cultural progressive activists as opposed to religiously based political activism in general.
2   Indeed, we found that Christians in our sample had higher levels of education and were older than other respondents. Given the already highly educated and older nature of the general sample, these Christians had exceptionally high levels of education compared to the rest of

the general population, and this education may drive their attitudes. We also found that the Christians in the sample were more likely than the other respondents to be female. Many of them may be attracted to feminist ideology. The strong correlations between the feminist group and the two critics of Christianity groups (.436 with *Christianity as unevolved* and .367 with *Christians as political oppressors*; see table 4.1) suggest that this type of relationship is likely. It is quite possible that these female Christians are reacting to Christian patriarchy, but the factor analysis captures their concerns about the corruption of their chosen religion more powerfully than their overall feminist concerns.

3   This is not merely speculation on our part. Factor loadings for this group did indicate that concern for bad politics was marginally important (.176), but loadings on bad religion (.229) and ranking fundamentalism below all other religious groups (.193) were more powerful.

4   This letter is famous because Jefferson used the phrase "separation of church and state." Since the phrase is not directly in the Constitution, Jefferson's letter allows advocates of this concept to argue that it was the intention of the early writers of the Constitution to support church/state separation, even if that concept cannot directly be found in the Constitution.

Chapter 7

1   Many of the respondents labeled themselves as "freethinker." The overt image of a freethinker is that individuals have become open to all possibilities and thus have rationally deducted the most logical possibility concerning issues of ultimate meaning. This allows the respondent to conceptualize himself or herself as open to all possibilities in comparison to the religious other, who has closed off secular options. Such a conceptualization can be used to indicate the higher degree of rationality the respondent possesses. Thus, use of the term *freethinker* contains its own cognitive attractions for cultural progressive activists.

2   For example, the highly educated may take on politically progressive ideas instead of politically conservative ideas because progressive ideas support the notion of innovation that is valued in education. A highly educated individual is more likely to be connected, either occupationally and/or philosophically, to the education sector of a society. The norm of innovation, rather than the worthiness of a particular progressive political idea, may convince highly educated individuals to support that idea so that they can protect their own right to academically and socially innovate within the educational community. As such, many of their policy positions are related to a desire to support the education community. In protecting the education community,

the highly educated are protecting a community that is more beneficial to them than it is to those without a high level of education. If this is true, then the tendency of cultural progressive activists, who are more likely to be highly educated, to take on political progressiveness may be linked to a desire to promote innovation as much as to the soundness of politically progressive ideas.
3. In a few of the smaller groups located in the Southwest whites did make up less than 90 percent of the group. But these groups were small, and these findings are likely an anomaly of certain friendship patterns and being located in the Southwest, where Hispanics make up a high percentage of the general population. In the three larger groups where friendship patterns are unlikely to create such an anomaly, the percentages of whites were not less than 93.9. This was the case even for the larger group located in the South, and where most of the sample lives in a state that is quite racially diverse.
4. Just as there is a common stereotype of Christians being proselytizers, sexually repressed, and backward, there seems to be a common stereotype among cultural progressive activists that cultural conservatives are racist. The idea that politically conservative groups are seen as employing racism is quite common among politically progressive groups. One needs to note only the recent flap between the Tea Party movement and the NAACP to see such a phenomenon in action.
5. For an alternative scholarly viewpoint of who conservative Protestants are, we recommend checking out C. Smith's (2002) work.

Chapter 8

1. For the balance of the book we use *irreligiosity* to illustrate not just the rejection of religion itself but also the rejection of traditional expressions of Western religion such as Christianity, Mormonism, Judaism, and Islam. Even though some cultural progressive activists are adherents to these faiths, if they practice a more inclusive and less traditional version of that faith, then they still are adhering to the value of irreligiosity in that they reject the more traditional applications of their faith.
2. It may be argued that we are being too hard on the respondents. After all, they do not have the benefit of having conducted a survey to understand that cultural progressives are not marginalized in this society by race, sex, income, and/or education. However, many of the respondents openly acknowledged their relatively high educational status as they critiqued the lack of education of their ideological opponents. Concerning the other characteristics, we believe that members who are sufficiently involved in these organizations have had many opportunities to observe the relative racial, gender, and SES aspects

of other members of their group. For example, when one of the coauthors attended a training session for one of the groups, he found that it was in a city that is less than half white and noted that the only nonwhites in the room were the two trainers sent to the city. If members of this group meet on a regular basis, it would be impossible for them not to notice the racially homogenous nature of the organization. Likewise, we believe that many of the respondents have been in such organizations for some time and have had an opportunity to learn about the racial, gender, and economic standing of other members. Nevertheless, the argument of marginalization better promotes the ability of cultural progressive activists to make claims on society, and so respondents are unlikely to engage in the level of self-examination to observe the racial, gender, and economic dynamics of their peers. A rational self-assessment of the demographic makeup of those who support organizations run by cultural progressives does not serve the social movement well, and the value of rationality is not sufficiently strong to compel these organizations to engage in such an assessment.
3   In fact, a common theme within the writings of the primary literature of cultural progressive activists is the touting of the recent victories they have won. At the time of this writing, a judge had recently outlawed the National Day of Prayer, and almost all of the literature of cultural progressive activists indicated a sense of joy at this great legal victory.
4   We did make inquires about these dimensions, but the locations of the organizations we used do not provide us with much confidence about our ability to make assertions about possible regional and city size effects.

Appendix

1   We also set the program so that it did not record the IP addresses of the respondents. This provided an extra level of privacy.
2   On this variable we only included *political definition*, *political aspects*, *political difference*, and *bad politics*. We did not include any variables that focused on a specific political issue such as abortion rights.

Works Cited

Abramowitz, A., & Saunders, K. (2005). Why Can't We All Just Get Along? The Reality of a Polarized America. *The Forum*, 3(2), Article 1. http://www.dartmouth.edu/~govt/docs/Abramowitz.pdf.

Almond, G. A., Appleby, R. S., & Sivan, E. (2003). *Strong Religion: The Rise of Fundamentalism around the World*. Chicago: University of Chicago Press.

Balibar, E. (2007). Is There a "Neo-Racism"? In T. D. Gupta (Ed.), *Race and Racialization: Essential Readings* (pp. 83–88). Toronto: Canadian Scholars' Press.

Barbour, I. G. (1997). *Religion and Science: Historical and Contemporary Issues*. San Francisco: HarperCollins.

Barker, D. (2008). *Godless: How an Evangelical Preacher Became One of America's Leading Atheists*. Berkeley, Calif.: Ulysses Press.

Barreto, M. A., & Bozonelos, D. N. (2009). Democrat, Republican, or None of the Above? The Role of Religiosity in Muslim American Party Identification. *Politics and Religion*, 2, 200–229.

Battle, M. (2006). *The Black Church in America: African American Christian Spirituality*. Malden, Mass.: Blackwell.

Benford, R., & Hunt, S. (1992). Dramaturgy and Social Movements: The Social Construction and Communication of Power. *Sociological Inquiry*, 62, 35–55.

Berg, J. A. (2010). Race, Class, Gender, and Social Space: Using an Intersectional Approach to Study Immigration Attitudes. *Sociological Quarterly*, 51(2), 278–302.

Berger, P., David, G., & Fokas, E. (2008). *Religious America? Secular Europe: A Theme and Variations*. Hampshire, UK: Ashgate.

Berger, P., & Luckmann, T. (1967). *The Social Construction of Reality: A Treatise in the Sociology of Knowledge*. Garden City, N.Y.: Anchor Books.

Bimber, B. (1998). The Internet and Political Transformation: Populism, Community, and Accelerated Pluralism. *Polity*, 31(1), 133–60.

Bishop, R. (2007). *Taking on the Pledge of Allegiance: The Media and Michael Newdow's Constitutional Challenge*. Albany: State University of New York Press.

Black, B., Oles, T., & Moore, L. (1998). The Relationship between Attitudes: Homophobia and Sexism among Social Work Students. *Affilia*, 13(2), 166–89.

Bloor, D. (2001). *Knowledge and Social Imagery* (A. Yan, Trans.). Beijing: Orient Press.

Boas, M. (1958). *History of Science*. New York: Macmillan.

Bolce, L., & De Maio, G. (1999). The Anti-Christian Fundamentalist Factor in Contemporary Politics. *Public Opinion Quarterly*, 63(4), 508–42.

———. (2008). A Prejudice for the Thinking Classes. *American Politics Research*, 36(2), 155–85.

Boles, J. K. (2001). Women Networking with Their Neighbors: The Universal Thread of Civic Activism. In D. L. Hoeveler & J. K. Boles (Eds.), *Women of Color: Defining the Issues, Hearing the Voices* (pp. 45–56). Santa Barbara, Calif.: Greenwood Press.

Bolks, S. M., Evans, D., Polinard, J. L., & Wrinkle, R. D. (2000). Core Beliefs and Abortion Attitudes: A Look at Latinos. *Social Science Quarterly*, 81(1), 253–60.

Bolzendahl, C. I., & Myers, D. J. (2004). Feminist Attitudes and Support for Gender Equality: Opinion Change in Women and Men, 1974–1998. *Social Forces*, 83(2), 759–90.

Bonanno, G. A., & Jost, J. T. (2006). Conservative Shift among High-Exposure Survivors of the September 11th Terrorist Attacks. *Basic and Applied Social Psychology*, 28(4), 311–23.

Bonilla, L., & Porter, J. (1990). A Comparison of Latino, Black and Non-Hispanic White Attitudes towards Homosexuality. *Hispanic Journal of Behavioral Sciences* 12, 437–52.

Bonilla-Silva, E. (2003). *Racism without Racists: Color-Blind Racism and the Persistence of Racial Inequality in the United States*. New York: Rowman & Littlefield.

Brooks, A. C. (2006). *Who Really Cares: The Surprising Truth about Compassionate Conservatism*. New York: Basic Books.

Burack, C. (2003). Getting What "We" Deserve: Terrorism, Tolerance, Sexuality, and the Christian Right. *New Political Science,* 25(3), 329–49.

———. (2008). *Sin, Sex, and Democracy: Antigay Rhetoric and the Christian Right.* Albany: State University of New York.

Bureau of Labor Statistics. (2010). *Volunteering in the United States—2009.* Washington, D.C.: U.S. Department of Labor.

Carlton, C. L., Nelson, E. S., & Coleman, P. K. (2000). College Students' Attitudes toward Abortion and Commitment to the Issue. *Social Science Journal,* 37(4), 619–25.

Carr, L. G. (1997). *Color-Blind Racism.* Thousand Oaks, Calif.: Sage.

Carroll, J. W., & Marler, P. L. (1995). Culture War? Insights from Ethnographies of Two Protestant Seminaries. *Sociology of Religion,* 56(1), 1–20.

Carter, J. S., & Borch, C. A. (2005). Assessing the Effects of Urbanism and Regionalism on Gender-Role Attitudes, 1974–1998. *Sociological Inquiry,* 75(4), 548–63.

Carter, J. S., Carter, S., & Dodge, J. (2009). Trends in Abortion Attitudes by Race and Gender: A Reassessment over a Four-Decade Period. *Journal of Sociological Research,* 1(1), 1–17.

Caspi, A. (1984). Contact Hypothesis and Interage Attitudes: A Field Study of Cross-Age Contact. *Social Psychology Quarterly,* 47, 74–80.

Chatters, L. M., Taylor, R. J., & Lincoln, K. D. (1999). African American Religious Participation: A Multi-Sample Comparison. *Journal for the Scientific Study of Religion,* 38(1), 132–45.

Cho, F., & Squier, R. K. (2008). "He Blinded Me with Science": Science Chauvinism in the Study of Religion. *Journal of the American Academy of Religion,* 76(2), 420–48.

Christiano, K. J. (2000). Religion and the Family in Modern American Culture. In S. K. Houseknecht & J. G. Pankhurst (Eds.), *Family, Religion, and Social Change in Diverse Societies* (pp. 43–78). Oxford: Oxford University Press.

Cohen, A. B. (2002). The Importance of Spirituality in Well-Being for Jews and Christians. *Journal of Happiness Studies,* 3(3), 287–310.

Cohen, A. B., Malka, A., Hill, E. D., Hill, P. C., & Sundie, J. M. (2009). Race as a Moderator of the Relationship between Religiosity and Political Alignment. *Personality and Social Psychology Bulletin,* 35(3), 271–82.

Cohen, E. (2001, February 12). Bush the Bold? *The Weekly Standard,* 20.

Collins, P. H. (2000). *Black Feminist Thought: Knowledge, Consciousness, and the Politics of Empowerment.* New York: Routledge.

Comte, A. (1896). *The Positive Philosophy of Auguste Comte.* London: G. Bell & Sons.

Conger, K. H. (2009). *The Christian Right in Republican State Politics*. New York: Palgrave Macmillan.

Crawford, A. (1980). *Thunder on the Right: The "New Right" and the Politics of Resentment*. New York: Pantheon Books.

Davis, K. (2008). Intersectionality as Buzzword: A Sociology of Science Perspective on What Makes a Feminist Theory Successful. *Feminist Theory*, 9(1), 67–85.

Dawkins, R. (2006). *The God Delusion*. Boston: Houghton Mifflin.

De la Garza, R. O., DeSipio, L. F., Garcia, C., Garcia, J., & Falcon, A. (1992). *Latino Voices: Mexican, Puerto Rican and Cuban Perspectives*. Boulder, Colo.: Westview.

Demerath, N. J., III. (2005). The Battle over a U.S. Culture War: A Note on Inflated Rhetoric versus Inflamed Politics. *The Forum*, 3(2). Article 6. http://www.bepress.com/forum/vol3/iss2/art6/.

Dew, R. E., Daniel, S. S., Goldston, D. B., McCall, W. V., Kuchibhatla, M., Schleifer, C., Triplett, M.F., & Koenig, H.G. (2010). A Prospective Study of Religion/Spirituality and Depressive Symptoms among Adolescent Psychiatric Patients. *Journal of Affective Disorders*, 120(1), 149–57.

Dey, E. L. (1997). Working with Low Survey Response Rates: The Efficacy of Weighting Adjustments. *Research in Higher Education*, 38(2), 215–27.

di Mauro, D., & Joffe, C. (2009). The Religious Right and the Reshaping of Sexual Policy: Reproductive Rights and Sexuality Education during the Bush Years. In G. H. Herdt (Ed.), *Moral Panics, Sex Panics: Fear and the Fight over Sexual Rights* (pp. 47–103). New York: New York University Press.

Diani, M., & McAdam, D. (Eds.). (2003). *Social Movements and Networks: Relational Approaches to Collective Action*. New York: Oxford University Press.

Dillon, M. (1996). The American Abortion Debate: Culture War or Normal Discourse? In J. L. Nolan (Ed.), *The American Culture Wars: Current Contests and Future Prospects*. Charlottesville: University of Virginia Press, 115–32.

Dixon, J. C., & Rosenbaum, M. S. (2004). Nice to Know You? Testing Contact, Cultural, and Group Threat Theories of Anti-Black and Anti-Hispanic Stereotypes. *Social Science Quarterly*, 85, 257–80.

Dowbiggin, I. (2008). *The Sterilization Movement and Global Fertility in the Twentieth Century*. New York: Oxford University Press.

Durham, M. (2000). *The Christian Right: The Far Right and the Boundaries of American Conservatism*. Manchester, UK: Manchester University Press.

Ellison, C. G., Echevarria, S., & Smith, B. (2005). Religion and Abortion

Attitudes among U.S. Hispanics: Findings from the 1990 Latino National Political Survey. *Social Science Quarterly, 86*(1), 192–208.

Ellison, C. G., & Levin, J. S. (1998). The Religion-Health Connection: Evidence, Theory, and Future Directions. *Health Education & Behavior, 25*(6), 700–720.

Emerson, M. O., & Smith, C. (2000). *Divided by Faith: Evangelical Religion and the Problem of Race in America*. Oxford: Oxford University Press.

Erickson, D. (2007, February 25). The Atheist Calling. *Wisconsin State Journal*, A1.

Feltey, K. M., & Poloma, M. M. (1991). From Sex Differences to Gender Role Beliefs: Exploring Effects on Six Dimensions of Religiosity. *Sex Roles, 25*(3/4), 181–93.

Ferree, M. M., & Miller, F. D. (2007). Mobilization and Meaning: Toward an Integration of Psychological and Resource Perspectives on Social Movements. *Sociological Inquiry, 55*(1), 38–61.

Ferriss, A. L. (2002). Religion and the Quality of Life. *Journal of Happiness Studies, 3*(3), 199–215.

Fetto, J. (2000). Interracial Friendships Slip? *American Demographics, 22*(1), 23.

Ficarrotto, T. J. (1990). Racism, Sexism, and Erotophobia: Attitudes of Heterosexuals toward Homosexuals. *Journal of Homosexuality, 19*(1), 111–16.

Fiorina, M. (2005). *Culture War? The Myth of a Polarized America*. New York: Pearson Longman.

Frank, T. (2004). *What's the Matter with Kansas? How Conservatives Won the Heart of America*. New York: Henry Holt.

Freeman, P. K., & Houston, D. J. (2009). The Biology Battle: Public Opinion and the Origins of Life. *Politics and Religion, 2*, 54–75.

Gallaher, C. (1997). Identity Politics and the Religious Right: Hiding Hate in the Landscape. *Antipode, 29*(3), 256–77.

Gallup, G., & Lindsay, D. M. (2000). *Surveying the Religious Landscape*. Harrisburg, Pa.: Morehouse.

Gamson, W. A. (1992). The Social Psychology of Collective Action. In A. D. Morris & C. M. Mueller (Eds.), *Frontiers in Social Movement Theory* (pp. 53–76). New Haven, Conn.: Yale University Press.

Gartner, J. D. (1986). Antireligious Prejudice in Admission to Doctoral Programs in Clinical Psychology. *Professional Psychology: Research and Practice, 17*(5), 473–75.

Gey, S. G. (2006). Atheism and the Freedom of Religion. In M. Martin (Ed.), *The Cambridge Companion to Atheism* (pp. 250–66). New York: Cambridge University Press.

Gilgoff, D. (2008). *How James Dobson, Focus on the Family, and Evangelical America Are Winning the Culture War.* New York: St. Martin's.

Glaeser, E. L., & Sacerdote, B. I. (2008). Education and Religion. *Journal of Human Capital, 2*(2), 188–215.

Glick, P., Lamerias, M., & Castro, Y. R. (2002). Education and Catholic Religiosity as Predictors of Hostile and Benevolent Sexism toward Women and Men. *Sex Roles, 47*(9–10), 433–41.

Gould, S. J. (1999). *Rocks of Ages: Science and Religion in the Fullness of Life.* New York: Ballantine Books.

Green, J. C. (1995). The Christian Right and the 1994 Elections: An Overview. In M. J. Rozell & C. Wilcox (Eds.), *God at the Grass Roots* (pp. 1–18). Lanham, Md.: Rowman & Littlefield.

Green, J. C., & Guth, J. L. (1988). The Christian Right in the Republican Party: The Case of Pat Robertson's Supporters. *Journal of Politics, 50,* 150–65.

Green, J. C., Guth, J. L., Smidt, C. E., & Kellstedt, L. A. (1996). *Religion and the Culture Wars: Dispatches from the Front.* Lanham, Md.: Rowman & Littlefield.

Gross, M., & Landers, S. (2008). Sexual Bigotry: Unhealthy, Unremitting, Ubiquitous. *Sex Roles, 59,* 605–8.

Gross, R. M. (1996). *Feminism and Religion: An Introduction.* Boston: Beacon.

Gullett, G. (1995). Women Progressives and the Politics of Americanization in California, 1915–1920. *Pacific Historical Review, 64*(1), 71–94.

Gunnoe, M. L., & Moore, K. A. (2002). Predictors of Religiosity among Youth Aged 17–22: A Longitudinal Study of the National Survey of Children. *Journal for the Scientific Study of Religion, 41*(4), 613–22.

Guth, J. L. (2007, January 3–7). *Religious Leadership and Support for Israel: A Study of Clergy in Nineteen Denominations.* Paper presented at the annual meeting of the Southern Political Science Association, New Orleans, La.

Guth, J. L., & Green, J. C. (1990). Politics in a New Key: Religiosity and Participation among Political Activists. *Political Research Quarterly, 43,* 153–79.

Guveli, A., Need, A., & De Graaf, N. D. (2006). Socio-political, Cultural and Economic Preferences and Behaviour of the Social and Cultural Specialists and the Technocrats. Social Class or Education? *Social Indicators Research, 81,* 597–631.

Hallinan, M. T., & Williams, R. A. (1989). The Stability of Students' Interracial Friendships. *American Sociological Review, 52,* 653–64.

Halman, L., & Draulans, V. (2006). How Secular Is Europe? *British Journal of Sociology, 57*(2), 263–88.

Hampton, K., & Wellman, B. (2003). Neighboring in Netville: How the Internet Supports Community and Social Capital in a Wired Suburb. *City and Community*, 2(3): 277–311.

Haraway, D. (1991). *Simians, Cyborgs, and Women: The Reinvention of Nature*. New York: Routledge.

Harding, S. (2005). From the Woman Question in Science to the Science Question in Feminism. In Harding, S. (Ed.), *The Science Question in Feminism* (pp. 15–29). Ithaca, N.Y.: Cornell University Press.

Harris, S. (2005). *The End of Faith: Religion, Terror, and the Future of Reason*. New York: Norton.

Hartmann, B. (2009). Rethinking the Role of Population in Human Security. In R. A. Matthew, J. Barnett, B. McDonald, & K. O'Brien (Eds.), *Global Environmental Change and Human Security* (pp. 193–214). Cambridge, Mass.: MIT Press.

Hatfield, E., & Rapson, R. L. (1992). Similarity and Attraction in Close Relationships. *Communication Monographs*, 59, 209–12.

Hayes, B. C. (1995). The Impact of Religious Identification of Political Attitudes. *Sociology of Religion*, Summer, 56(2), 177–94.

Hedges, C. (2007). *American Fascists: The Christian Right and the War on America*. New York: Free Press.

Hempel, L. M., & Bartkowski, J. P. (2008). Scripture, Sin and Salvation: Theological Conservatism Reconsidered. *Social Forces*, 86(4), 1647–74.

Herek, G. M., & Capitanio, J. P. (1996). "Some of My Best Friends": Intergroup Contact, Concealable Stigma, and Heterosexuals' Attitudes toward Gay Men and Lesbians. *Personality and Social Psychology Bulletin*, 22(4), 412–24.

Hertel, B. R., & Russell, M. C. (2007). Examining the Absence of a Gender Effect on Abortion Attitudes: Is There Really No Difference? *Sociological Inquiry*, 69(3), 364–81.

Hicks, G. R., & Lee, T.-T. (2006). Public Attitudes toward Gays and Lesbians: Trends and Predictors. *Journal of Homosexuality*, 51(2), 57–77.

Hitchens, C. (2007). *God Is Not Great: How Religion Poisons Everything*. New York: Twelve.

Hobsbawm, E. J. (1959). *Primitive Rebels*. New York: Norton.

Hodge, D. R. (2002). Does Social Work Oppress Evangelical Christians? A "New Class" Analysis of Society and Social Work. *Social Work*, 47(4), 401–14.

Hubbard, R. (1989). Science, Facts, and Feminism. In N. Tuana (Ed.), *Feminism and Science* (Vol. 2, pp. 119–31). Bloomington: Indiana University Press.

Huberman, J. (2006). *The Quotable Atheist: Ammunition for Non-Believers, Political Junkies, Gadflies, and Those Generally Hell-Bound*. New York: Nation Books.

Hunt, L. L., & Hunt, M. O. (2001). Race, Region, and Religious Involvement: A Comparative Study of Whites and African Americans. *Social Forces*, 80(2), 605–31.

Hunt, S., & Benford, R. (2004). Collective Identity, Solidarity, and Commitment. In D. A. Snow, S. A. Soule, & H. Kriesi (Eds.), *The Blackwell Companion to Social Movements* (pp. 433–57). Malden, Mass.: Blackwell.

Hunter, J. (1991). *Culture Wars: The Struggle to Define America*. New York: Basic Books.

Hunter, M. (2002). Rethinking Epistemology, Methodology, and Racism: Or, Is White Sociology Really Dead? *Race and Society*, 5(2), 119–38.

Inglehart, R., & Welzel, C. (2005). *Modernization, Cultural Change and Democracy: The Human Development Sequence*. New York: Cambridge University Press.

Jeansonne, G. (1996). *Women of the Far Right*. Chicago: University of Chicago Press.

Jensen, L. A. (2006). Culture Wars: American Moral Divisions across the Adult Lifespan. *Journal of Adult Development*, 4(2), 107–21.

Johnson, D. C. (1997). Formal Education vs. Religious Belief: Soliciting New Evidence with Multinomial Logit Modeling. *Journal for the Scientific Study of Religion*, 36(2), 231–46.

Jones, S. G. (1998). Information, Internet, and Community in the Information Age: Notes towards an Understanding of Community. In S. G. Jones (Ed.), *Cybersociety 2.0* (pp. 1–34). Thousand Oaks, Calif.: Sage.

Joyce, K. (2009). *Quiverfull: Inside the Christian Patriarchy Movement*. Boston: Beacon.

Kandel, D. B. (1978). Homophily, Selection, and Socialization in Adolescent Friendships. *American Journal of Sociology*, 84(2), 427–36.

Keller, E. F. (1982). Feminism and Science. *Signs*, 7(3), 589–602.

Kimmel, M. S. (1994). Masculinity as Homophobia: Fear, Shame, and Silence in the Construction of Gender Identity. In H. Brod & M. Kaufman (Eds.), *Theorizing Masculinities* (pp. 119–41). Thousand Oaks, Calif.: Sage.

Kinsley, M. (1994, May 23). No, Quayle Was Wrong. *Time*, 143, 78.

Kite, M. E., & Whitley, B. E. J. (2003). Do Heterosexual Women and Men Differ in Their Attitudes toward Homosexuality? A Conceptual and Methodological Analysis. In L. Garnets & D. C. Kimmel (Eds.), *Psychological Perspectives on Lesbian, Gay and Bisexual Experiences* (2nd ed., pp. 165–87). New York: Columbia University Press.

Klemp, N. J. (2009). The Christian Right: Engaged Citizens or Theocratic Crusaders? *Politics and Religion*, 3, 1–27.

Knuckey, J. (2005). A New Front in the Culture War? Moral Traditionalism and Voting Behavior in U.S. House Elections. *American Politics Research*, 33(5), 645–71.

———. (2006). Explaining Recent Changes in the Partisan Identifications of Southern Whites. *Political Research Quarterly*, 59(1), 57–70.

Kosmin, B. A., & Keysar, A. (2008). *American Religious Identification Survey*. Hartford, Conn.: Trinity College.

Kuhn, T. (1962). *The Structure of Scientific Revolutions*. Chicago: University of Chicago Press.

Larson, D. B., Sherrill, K. A., Lyons, J. S., Craigie, F. C., Thielman, S. B., Greenwold, M. A., & Larson, S. S. (1992). Associations between Dimensions of Religious Commitment and Mental Health Reported in the *American Journal of Psychiatry* and *Archives of General Psychiatry*. *American Journal of Psychiatry*, 149, 557–59.

Larson, D. B., Sweyers, J. P., & McCullough, M. E. (1998). *Scientific Research on Spirituality and Health: A Consensus Report*. Rockville, Md.: National Institute for Healthcare Research.

Layman, G. C., & Green, J. C. (2005). Wars and Rumours of Wars: The Contexts of Cultural Conflict in American Political Behaviour. *British Journal of Political Science*, 36, 61–89.

Legge, J. S. (1983). The Determinants of Attitudes toward Abortion in the American Electorate. *Western Political Quarterly*, 36(3), 479–90.

Levin, J. S., & Vanderpool, H. Y. (1992). Religious Factors in Physical Health and the Prevention of Illness. In K. I. Pargament, K. I. Maton, & R. E. Hess (Eds.), *Religion and Prevention in Mental Health: Research, Vision, and Action*, 83–103. New York: Haworth Press.

Lewis, G. B., & Gossett, C. W. (2008). Changing Public Opinion on Same-Sex Marriage: The Case of California. *Politics & Policy*, 36(1), 4–30.

Lichter, S., Rothman, S., & Lichter, L. (1986). *The Media Elite*. Bethesda, Md.: Adler & Alder.

Lienesch, M. (1993). *Redeeming America: Piety and Politics in the New Christian Right*. Chapel Hill: University of North Carolina Press.

———. (2007). *In the Beginning: Fundamentalism, the Scopes Trial, and the Making of the Antievolution Movement*. Chapel Hill: University of North Carolina Press.

Lind, A. (2009). Governing Intimacy, Struggling for Sexual Rights: Challenging Heteronormativity in the Global Development Industry. *Development*, 52(1), 34–42.

Ling, R., & Stald, G. (2010). Mobile Communities: Are We Talking about a Village, a Clan, or a Small Group? *American Behavioral Scientist, 53*(8), 1133–47.

Loftus, J. (2001). America's Liberalization in Attitudes toward Homosexuality 1973 to 1998. *American Sociological Review, 66*(5), 762–82.

Lugg, C. A. (1998). The Religious Right and Public Education: The Paranoid Politics of Homophobia. *Educational Policy, 12*(3), 267–83.

Mannheim, K. (1954). *Ideology and Utopia: An Introduction to the Sociology of Knowledge*. New York: Harcourt Brace.

Marsden, G. M. (1996). *The Soul of the American University: From Protestant Establishment to Established Nonbelief*. New York: Oxford University Press.

Martos, J., & Hegy, P. (1998). Gender Roles in Family and Culture: The Basis of Sexism in Religion. In J. Martos & P. Hegy (Eds.), *Equal at the Creation: Sexism, Society, and Christian Thought* (pp. 3–24). Toronto: University of Toronto Press.

Marx, S. (2006). *Revealing the Invisible: Confronting the Passive Racism in Teacher Education*. New York: Routledge.

Mattingly, C. (2006). Uncovering Forgotten Habits: Anti-Catholic Rhetoric and Nineteenth-Century American Women's Literacy. *College Composition and Communication, 58*(2), 160–81.

Mazur, P. (1997). Religion in American Politics and the Religious Right. In W. Swan (Ed.), *Gay/Lesbian/Bisexual/Transgender Public Policy Issues: A Citizen's and Administrator's Guide to the New Cultural Struggle* (pp. 3–14). Binghamton, N.Y.: Haworth Press.

McCall, L. (2005). The Complexity of Intersectionality. *Signs, 30*(3), 1771–1800.

McConkey, D. (2001). Whither Hunter's Culture War? Shifts in Evangelical Morality, 1988–1998. *Sociology of Religion, 62*(2), 149–74.

McCroskey, L. L., McCroskey, J. C., & Richmond, V. P. (2005). Analysis and Improvement of the Measurement of Interpersonal Attraction and Homophily. *Communication Quarterly, 54*(1), 1–31.

McPherson, M., Smith-Lovin, L., & Cook, J. (2001). Birds of a Feather: Homophily in Social Networks. *Annual Review of Sociology, 27*, 415–44.

Medved, M. (1992). *Hollywood vs. America*. New York: HarperCollins.

Melucci, A. (1989). *Nomads of the Present: Social Movements and Individual Needs in Contemporary Society*. Philadelphia: Temple University Press.

———. (1995). The Process of Collective Identity. In H. Johnston & B. Klandermans (Eds.), *Social Movements and Culture* (pp. 41–63). Minneapolis: University of Minnesota Press.

Miller, A. H., & Wattenberg, M. P. (1984). Politics from the Pulpit: Religiosity and the 1980 Elections. *Public Opinion Quarterly, 48*(18), 301–17.

Moen, M. C. (1992). *The Transformation of the Christian Right*. Tuscaloosa: University of Alabama Press.

Morone, J. A. (2004). *Hellfire Nation: The Politics of Sin in American History*. New Haven, Conn.: Yale University Press.

Moody, J. (2001). Race, School Integration, and Friendship Segregation in America. *American Journal of Sociology, 107*(3), 679–716.

Morris, A. D., & Mueller, C. M. (Eds.). (1992). *Frontiers in Social Movement Theory*. New Haven, Conn.: Yale University Press.

Mulligan, K. (2008). The "Myth" of Moral Values Voting in the 2004 Presidential Election. *Political Science & Politics, 41*, 109–14.

Nash, J. C. (2008). Re-thinking Intersectionality. *Feminist Review, 89*(1), 1–15.

Nisbet, M. C. (2005). The Competition for Worldviews: Values, Information, and Public Support for Stem Cell Research. *International Journal of Public Opinion Research, 17*(1), 90–112.

Noll, M. (1994). *The Scandal of the Evangelical Mind*. Grand Rapids: Eerdmans.

———. (2001). *American Evangelical Christianity: An Introduction*. Oxford: Blackwell.

Ohlander, J., Batalove, J., & Treas, J. (2004). Explaining Educational Influences on Attitudes towards Homosexual Relations. *Social Science Research, 34*(4), 781–99.

Patel, C. J., & Johns, L. (2009). Gender Role Attitudes and Attitudes to Abortion: Are There Gender Differences? *Social Science Journal, 46*(3), 493–505.

Peek, C. W., Lowe, G. D., & Williams, S. L. (1991). Gender and God's Word: Another Look at Religious Fundamentalism. *Social Forces, 69*, 1205–21.

Pettigrew, T. F. (1998). Intergroup Contact Theory. *Annual Review of Psychology, 49*, 65–85.

Pharr, S. (2000). Homophobia: A Weapon of Sexism. In L. Umansky & M. Plott (Eds.), *Making Sense of Women's Lives: An Introduction to Women Studies* (pp. 424–37). Lanham, Md.: Rowman & Littlefield.

Polanyi, M. (1958). *Personal Knowledge: Towards a Post-critical Philosophy*. Chicago: University of Chicago Press.

Popper, K. (1959). *The Logic of Scientific Discovery*. New York: Routledge.

Prager, D. (2004). What Does "Judeo-Christian" Mean? Retrieved from http://www.jewishworldreview.com/0304/prager_2004_03_30_04.php3

Preston, S. H., & Sten, C. R. (2010). The Future of American Fertility. In J. Shoven (Ed.), *Demography and the Economy*, 11–36. Chicago: University of Chicago Press.

Principe, L. M. (2003). *History of Science: Antiquity to 1700* [Audiobook]. Chantilly, Va.: Teaching Company.

Pyke, K. (2010). An Intersectional Approach to Resistance and Complicity: The Case of Racialised Desire among Asian American Women. *Journal of Intercultural Studies*, 31(1), 81–94.

Rackleff, R. B. (1972). Anti-Catholicism and the Florida Legislature, 1911–1919. *Florida Historical Quarterly*, 50(4), 352–65.

Ressler, L. E., & Hodge, D. R. (2003). Silenced Voices: Social Work and the Oppression of Conservative Narratives. *Social Thought*, 22(1), 125–42.

Revenson, T. A. (1989). Compassionate Stereotyping of Elderly Patients by Physicians: Revising the Social Contact Hypothesis. *Psychology and Aging*, 4(2), 230–34.

Rheingold, H. (1993). *The Virtual Community: Homesteading on the Electronic Frontier*. Reading, Mass.: Addison-Wesley.

Ringenberg, W. C. (1984). *The Christian College: A History of Protestant Higher Education in America*. Grand Rapids: Eerdmans.

Rose, H. (1994). *Love, Power, and Knowledge: Towards a Feminist Transformation of the Sciences*. Bloomington, Ind.: Polity Press.

Rose, S. D. (1987). Women Warriors: The Negotiation of Gender in a Charismatic Community. *Sociological Analysis*, 48, 245–58.

Rosser, S. V. (1990). *Female-Friendly Science*. New York: Pergamon.

Roth, L. M. (2004). The Social Psychology of Tokenism: Status and Homophily Processes on Wall Street. *Sociological Perspectives*, 47(2), 189–214.

Rozell, M. J., & Wilcox, C. (1995). The Past as Prologue: The Christian Right in the 1996 Election. In M. J. Rozell & C. Wilcox (Eds.), *God at the Grass Roots* (pp. 253–63). Lanham, Md.: Rowman & Littlefield.

Ruether, R. R. (1974). *Religion and Sexism: Images of Women in the Jewish and Christian Traditions*. New York: Simon & Schuster.

Ryckman, R. M., Kaczor, L. M., & Thornton, B. (1992). Traditional and Nontraditional Women's Attributions of Responsibility to Physically Resistive and Nonresistive Rape Victims. *Journal of Applied Social Psychology*, 22, 1453–63.

Sax, L., Gilmartin, S., & Bryant, A. N. (2003). Assessing Response Rates and Nonresponse Bias in Web and Paper Surveys. *Research in Higher Education*, 44(4), 409–32.

Sax, L., Gilmartin, S., Lee, J. J., & Hagedorn, L. S. (2008). Using Web Survey to Reach Community College Students: An Analysis of Response

Rates and Response Bias. *Community College Journal of Research and Practice*, 32(8), 712–29.

Schalatter, E. A. (2006). *Aryan Cowboys: White Supremacists and the Search for a New Frontier 1970–2000*. Austin: University of Texas Press.

Schiebinger, L. (2000). Has Feminism Changed Science? *Signs*, 25(4), 1171–75.

Sharlet, J. (2008). *The Family: The Secret Fundamentalism at the Heart of American Power*. New York: HarperCollins.

Sherkat, D. E., de Vries, K. M., & Creek, S. (2010). Race, Religion and Opposition to Same-Sex Marriage. *Social Science Quarterly*, 91(1), 80–98.

Shields, S. A. (2008). Gender: An Intersectionality Perspective. *Sex Roles*, 59(5–6), 301–11.

Smedes, T. A. (2008). Beyond Barbour or Back to Basics? The Future of Science-and-Religion and the Quest for Unity. *Zygon*, 43(1), 235–58.

Smith, A. (2006). Dismantling the Master's Tools with the Master's House: Native Feminist Liberation Theologies. *Journal of Feminist Studies in Religion*, 22(2), 85–97.

Smith, B. G. (2010). Attitudes towards Religious Pluralism: Measurements and Consequences. *Social Compass*, 57(1), 127–42.

Smith, C. (2002). *Christian America? What Evangelicals Really Want*. Berkeley: University of California Press.

Smith, C., Emerson, M., Gallagher, S., Kennedy, P., & Sikkink, D. (1998). *American Evangelicalism: Embattled and Thriving*. Chicago: University of Chicago Press.

Smith, D. E. (1972). Women's Perspective as a Radical Critique of Sociology. In S. Harding (Ed.), *Feminism and Methodology: Social Science Issues* (pp. 84–96). Bloomington: Indiana University Press.

Smith, T. (1994). Attitudes toward Sexual Permissiveness: Trends, Correlates, and Behavioral Connections. In A. S. Rossi (Ed.), *Sexuality across the Life Course* (pp. 63–98). Chicago: University of Chicago Press.

———. (1998). Public Opinion on Abortion. Retrieved from http://www.norc.uchicago.edu/library/abortion.htm. [url no longer available]]

Snow, D. A., & Benford, R. (1988). Ideology, Frame Resonance, and Participant Mobilization. In B. Klandermans, H. Kriesi, & S. Tarrow (Eds.), *From Structure to Action: Comparing Social Movements across Cultures* (Vol. 1, pp. 197–217). Greenwich, Conn.: JAI.

———. (1992). Master Frames and Cycles of Protests. In A. D. Morris & C. McClurg (Eds.), *Frontiers in Social Movement Theory* (pp. 133–55). New Haven, Conn.: Yale University Press.

Snyder, R. C. (2007). The Allure of Authoritarianism: Bush Administration

Ideology and the Reconsolidation of Patriarchy. In M. L. Ferguson & L. J. Marso (Eds.), *W Stands for Women: How the George W. Bush Presidency Shaped a New Politics of Gender* (pp. 17–40). Durham, N.C.: Duke University Press.

Stark, R. (2004). *For the Glory of God: How Monotheism Led to Reformations, Science, Witch-Hunts, and the End of Slavery*. Princeton, N.J.: Princeton University Press.

Staver, J. R. (2010). Skepticism, Truth as Coherence, and Constructivist Epistemology: Grounds for Resolving the Discord between Science and Religion? *Cultural Studies of Science Education, 5*(1), 19–39.

Stein, A. (2001). Revenge of the Shamed: The Christian Right's Emotional Culture War. In J. Goodwin, J. M. Jasper, & F. Polletta (Eds.), *Passionate Politics: Emotions and Social Movements*. Chicago: University of Chicago Press.

Sutter, D. (2001). Can the Media Be So Liberal? The Economics of Media Bias. *Cato Journal, 20*(3), 431–51.

Swidler, A. (1995). Cultural Power and Social Movements. In H. Johnston & B. Klandermans (Eds.), *Social Movements and Culture* (pp. 25–40). Minneapolis: University of Minnesota Press.

Swidler, A., & Arditi, J. (1994). The New Sociology of Knowledge. *Annual Review of Sociology, 20*, 305–29.

Swim, J. K., & Hyers, L. L. (2009). Sexism. In T. D. Nelson (Ed.), *Handbook of Prejudice, Stereotyping, and Discrimination* (pp. 407–30). New York: Psychology Press.

Taylor, V., & Whittier, N. (1992). Collective Identity in Social Movement Communities: Lesbian Feminist Mobilization. In A. D. Morris & C. McClurg (Eds.), *Frontiers in Social Movement Theory* (pp. 104–29). New Haven, Conn.: Yale University Press.

———. (1995). Analytical Approaches to Social Movement Culture. In H. Johnston & B. Klandermans (Eds.), *Social Movements and Culture* (pp. 163–87). Minneapolis: University of Minnesota Press.

Turner, R. H., & Killian, L. M. (1987). *Collective Behavior* (3rd ed.). Englewood Cliffs, N.J.: Prentice Hall.

Unnever, J. D., & Cullen, F. T. (2007). Reassessing the Racial Divide in Support for Capital Punishment: The Continuing Significance of Race. *Journal of Research in Crime and Delinquency, 44*(1), 124–58.

Vennochi, J. (2003, November 20). A "Culture War" on Gay Marriage Could Hurt GOP. *Boston Globe*, p. A23.

Viki, G. T., & Abrams, D. (2002). But She Was Unfaithful: Benevolent Sexism and Reactions to Rape Victims Who Violate Gender Role Expectations. *Sex Roles, 47*(5–6), 289–93.

Wald, K. D., & Calhoun-Brown, A. (2007). *Religion and Politics in the United States*. Lanham, Md.: Rowman & Littlefield.

Ward, J., Bruce, T., Holt, P., D'Este, K., & Sladden, M. (1998). Labour-Saving Strategies to Maintain Survey Response Rates: A Randomised Trial. *Australian and New Zealand Journal of Public Health, 22*(3), 394–96.

Wellman, B., Hasse, A. Q., Witte, J., & Hampton, K. (2001). Does the Internet Increase, Decrease, or Supplement Social Capital? Social Networks, Participation, and Community Commitment. *American Behavioral Scientist, 45*(3), 436–55.

White, M. J., Muhidin, S., Andrzejewski, C., Tagoe, E., Knight, R., & Reed, H. (2008). Urbanization and Fertility. *Demography, 45*(4), 803–16.

Wilcox, C. (1992). *God's Warriors: The Christian Right in Twentieth-Century America*. Baltimore: Johns Hopkins University Press.

Wilcox, C., & Larson, C. (2006). *Onward Christian Soldiers? The Religious Right in American Politics*. Boulder, Colo.: Westview.

Wuthnow, R. (1988). *The Restructuring of American Religion*. Princeton, N.J.: Princeton University Press.

Yancey, G. (1998). Differential Attitudes of American Sociologists in Assessment of NOW: A Test of the Gender Gap in a Progressive Subculture. *Sociological Imagination, 35*(2/3), 119–36.

———. (2002, October). *A Comparison of Religiosity between European-Americans, African-Americans, Hispanic-Americans and Asian-Americans*. Paper presented at the Society for the Scientific Study of Religion, Salt Lake City.

———. (2007). *Interracial Contact and Social Change*. Boulder, Colo.: Lynne Rienner.

———. (2010). Who Has Religious Prejudice? Differing Sources of Antireligious Animosity in the United States. *Review of Religious Research, 52*(2), 159–71.

———. (2011). *Compromising Scholarship: Religious and Political Bias in American Higher Education*. Waco, Tex.: Baylor University Press.

Yorgason, E., & Chen, C. H. (2008). "Kingdom Come": Representing Mormonism through a Geopolitical Frame. *Political Geography, 27,* 478–500.

Zimmerman, J. (2002). *Whose America? Culture Wars in the Public Schools*. Cambridge, Mass.: Harvard University Press.

Index

abortion, 9–10, 12, 13, 16, 23, 49, 54, 61, 64, 87–90, 92, 96–99, 106–7, 167, 216–17; clinics, 92–94, 96
ACLU, 12
African Americans, 32, 36–37, 48
Alliance Defense Fund, 14
American Atheists, 13
American Center for Law and Justice, 14
Americans United for the Separation of Church and State, 12
atheists, 13, 16, 50, 60, 64, 67, 71–73, 111–12, 128, 165, 182, 187; books, 111

backwardness of Christianity, 69, 140; of Christian Right, 141, 189
brainwashed, 116–17, 166, 211
Bush, George W., 10, 74

Carter, Jimmy, 137
Catholics, 9, 12
"Christian Nation," 142, 159
Christian takeover, 12, 92, 161–64, 188, 195, 197

Christianity as unevolved, 24, 58, 69, 72–73, 78–80, 140, 143–44, 148, 152, 225
Christians as political oppressors, 24, 58, 70–73, 79, 147, 149–50, 152
Clinton, William, 10
collective action frames, 25, 30–31, 35, 37, 171, 202; diagnostic, 25, 35, 110, 185, 188; motivational, 25, 36, 195; prognostic; 25, 36, 189, 212; used by cultural progressives, 184–99
collective behavior, 29
collective identity, 22, 25, 31, 38–42, 45, 57–58, 110, 137, 164, 171–72, 177, 184, 199–202, 206–9, 212, 216
critical thinking, 24, 61, 67, 113–15, 117–19, 121, 209–10
culture war, 1–3, 6, 19, 26, 44, 105–6, 108, 211–15, 216

education, 14–15, 47–48, 55, 61, 74, 83, 134, 143; as a solution for cultural progressives, 67, 85, 116, 201; influenced by Christian right, 85–86, 133, 144, 208; of

cultural progressives, 26, 54–56, 72, 86, 150, 187, 214
education institutions, 7, 201
emergent norms, 22, 25, 30–35, 37, 57, 74, 105, 172, 184–85, 199, 202
Enlightenment Movement, 4–6
Europe, 5–6, 207, 216
evolution, 9, 65, 143, 174; societal, 143–44, 165

feminist, 23, 57–58, 63–65, 73, 78, 98, 100, 102–3, 225–26
framing, 35–37
Freedom from Religion Foundation, 13
fundamentalist, 6–7, 72, 108, 137, 150–53; animosity toward, 55, 71–72, 127, 155

Galileo, 4–5

Hispanics, 48
Hitchens, Christopher, 66–67, 112–13, 122
homophobia, 96, 101–2
homosexuality, 9, 16, 23, 49, 54, 61–62, 64, 87–90, 92, 94, 98, 106, 125, 217; same-sex marriage, 10, 12–13, 97, 167, 192, 215
hypocrisy, 131

ignorant, 84, 131, 137, 141–42, 160
immorality, 135; of Christian Right, 122
income, 49, 72, 150; as independent variable, 54; of cultural progressives, 51, 54, 74, 214
intolerant, 68, 131, 137, 141, 149, 210; Christians as, 24, 153; Christian Right as, 92, 106, 148, 154–55, 211; Republicans as, 1
irreligiosity, 25, 53, 109, 200–1, 206–10, 212, 218

Jews, 9, 157
Jews on First, 13

judgmental, 24, 68, 126–27, 135–36, 148, 153, 155

living in neighborhood of Christian Right, 60, 68–70, 81–82, 125, 127–28, 147, 149, 152–53, 211

Mormons, 9
Muslims, 9, 152

new left movements, 8–9, 11
nonconformity, 48, 56

Obama, Barack, 10

People for the American Way, 13
political activist, group, 23, 57–61, 65, 78–80, 84, 86, 102, 225; Christians, 19
political conservatives, 86, 90, 108, 165, 172, 177, 182–83, 210, 212
progressive political action, 25, 199, 219
proselytizing, 6–7, 97, 149–50, 153, 179, 194, 211
Protestants, 9; conservative, 96; mainline, 151–52

racism, 36, 96, 188–89
rationality, 3–4, 6, 11, 16, 24–25, 27, 30, 43–45, 110, 116, 165–66, 172, 174–77, 184, 188, 197, 199–202, 206–10, 212–13, 219
religion has been corrupted, 24, 57–58, 68, 79, 112, 124, 126–130, 137, 148, 224
religion is poison, 24, 57, 65–66, 68, 79–80, 112–14, 117, 119–22, 124, 127–28, 137, 218, 224–25
resource mobilization theory, 30–32

science, 7; disregarded by Christian Right, 61, 65, 84–85, 102, 188, 208; in conflict with religion, 4–5, 26, 209; seen as solution by

cultural progressives, 65, 85, 102, 201
secularization, 4
separation of church and state, 5, 12–13, 138, 160, 165, 173–74
sex education, 174
sexism, 65, 98–103
sexual progressive, 23, 57, 61–63, 65, 73, 78–79, 86–88, 90–98, 218, 225
sociology of knowledge, 177
stem cell research, 10, 13, 217

"The Family," 108
theocracy, 8, 14, 25, 181, 196–98, 213, 216
Tiller, Dr. George, 106–7

victim perception, 16, 45, 55–56, 74, 100–1, 133–35, 178, 188, 194, 207–8, 214–15

women, 15, 48, 52–53, 61, 63–64, 98, 100–3, 106–7